Guide
to
CHINESE RELIGION

*The
Asian
Philosophies
and
Religions
Resource
Guides*

Guide
to
CHINESE RELIGION

DAVID C. YU

with contributions by
Laurence G. Thompson

G.K.HALL &CO.

70 LINCOLN STREET, BOSTON, MASS.

Library of Congress Cataloging in Publication Data

Yu, David C.
  Guide to Chinese religion.

  (Asian philosophies and religions resource guide)

  Includes indexes.
  1. China—Religion—Bibliography. I. Thompson,
Laurence G. II. Title. III. Series.
Z7757.C6Y8 1985   016.299'51 85-932
[BL1802]
ISBN 0-8161-7902-6

This publication is printed on permanent/durable acid-free paper
MANUFACTURED IN THE UNITED STATES OF AMERICA

Project on Asian Philosophies and Religions

Sponsoring Organizations
Center for International Programs and Comparative Studies of the New York
State Education Department/University of the State of New York
Council for Intercultural Studies and Programs, Inc.

Steering Committee

Kenneth Morgan	Emeritus, Colgate University
	Chairman
Wing-tsit Chan	Chatham College
	Emeritus, Dartmouth College
David J. Dell	Foreign Area Materials Center
	Columbia University
	Project Manager, 1975-77
Edith Ehrman	Foreign Area Materials Center
	Project Manager, 1971-74
Robert McDermott	Baruch College, City University of New York
Bardwell Smith	Carleton College
H. Daniel Smith	Syracuse University
Frederick J. Streng	Southern Methodist University

Editorial Coordinators
David J. Dell
Edward S. Haynes

Preparation of this series of guides to resources for the study of Asian philosophies and religions was made possible by a grant from the National Endowment for the Humanities, supplemented through the Endowment's matching funds scheme, with additional financial support from the Ada Howe Kent Foundation, C. T. Shen, and the Council on International and Public Affairs, Inc. None of the above bodies is responsible for the content of these guides, which is the responsibility of those listed on the title page.

This project has been undertaken by the Foreign Area Materials Center, State Education Department, University of the State of New York, under the auspices of the Council for Intercultural Studies and Program, 60 East 42nd Street, New York, NY 10017.

Straightway I was 'ware
So weeping, how a mystic shape did move
Behind me, and drew me backward by the hair
And a voice said in mastery while I strove, . . .
'Guess now who holds thee? — 'Death', I said, but there
The silver answer rang . . . 'Not Death, but Love.'

Elizabeth Barrett Browning

Contents

Contents

Contents

Contents

Contents

Contents

Contents

Contents

Series Preface

Asian Philosophies and Religions and the Humanities in America

This guide is one of a series of books on resources for the study of Asian philosophies and religions. The series includes volumes on Chinese, Indian, Islamic, and Buddhist philosophies and religions. Since the preparation of the series has been undertaken as a contribution to advancing humanistic learning in America, it is important to place the study of these traditions in that larger context.

Humanistic scholarship and teaching in America has understandably concentrated on Western civilization of which we are a part. Yet Western civilization has historically drawn significantly upon the humanistic accomplishments of other traditions and has interacted with these traditions. Given the increasing mobility of scholars and students in the second half of the twentieth century and the rapidly advancing technological capacity of communicating ideas in the modern world, this interaction is accelerating as we approach the twenty-first century.

Liberal education for American students in the 1970's and 1980's must reflect not only our human heritage in all of its diversity as it has accumulated through past centuries, but also the nature of the future in its intellectual and cultural as well as economic, social and political dimensions. By the year 2000, a logical future reference point for today's college students who will spend most of their adult lives in the next century, four out of five human beings will live in the "Third World" of Asia, Africa, and Latin America about which we study least in our colleges and universities today.

Numerical distribution of humanity is certainly not the only criterion which should determine the content of humanistic learning in our institutions of higher education. But when orders of magnitude achieve the proportions which, according to most demographic projections, will exist in the year 2000, geographical location of humanity is certainly one criterion which will be applied by today's students in assessing the "relevance" of their undergraduate education to the real world of the future.

The argument becomes all the more compelling when the qualitative aspects of civilizations other than our own are considered. Western man can claim no corner on creative accomplishment, as Herbert Muller has rightly recognized in this passage from The Uses of the Past.

> Stick to Asia, and we get another elementary lesson in
> humility. Objectively its history looks more important
> than the history of Europe. . .It has produced more civi-
> lizations, involving a much greater proportion of man-
> kind, over a longer period of time, on a higher level
> of continuity. As for cultural achievement, we have
> no universal yardstick; but by one standard on which
> Western Christendom has prided itself, Asia has been
> far more creative. It has bred all the higher re-
> ligions, including Christianity.*

There is little doubt that the rapid growth of student interest in the study of these traditions is the result in part of their search for new value systems in contemporary society. But this interest is also a recognition of other civilizations as being intrinsically worthy of our attention.

Origins of the Project on Asian Philosophies and Religions

The project was initiated in response to this growth of student interest, which began in the 1960's and has persisted in the 1970's, notwithstanding a current general decline in the growth rates in American colleges and universities. Faculty members with specialized training in Asian philosophical and religious traditions, however, are still limited in number and most courses in these subjects are being taught by non-specialists. While the proportion of those with specialized training has certainly increased in recent years, the situation is unlikely to improve greatly due to the ceilings on facul-ty size which many institutions have imposed because of financial stringency.

The need for a series of authoritative guides to literature in these fields for use in both undergraduate and beginning graduate study of Asian philosophies and religions, which first prompted us to seek support from the National Endowment for the Humanities for the project in 1971, remains just as compelling as the project draws to a close.

Organization of the Project

The project on Asian philosophies and religions was conceived from the beginning as a cooperative venture involving scholars and teachers of these subjects. The key element in the organization of the project

---

*The Uses of the Past, New York: New American Library, 1954, p. 314.

has been the project team or working group, a deliberately informal structure with its own leader, working autonomously but within a general conceptual framework developed early in the project by all of those who were involved in the project at that time.

The individual working groups have been linked together by a project steering committee, which has been concerned with the overall organization and implementation of the project. The members of the project steering committee, working group leaders, and other key project personnel are as follows:

Kenneth Morgan, Emeritus, Colgate University (Chairman of the Project Steering Committee)

Wing-tsit Chan, Chatham College and Emeritus, Dartmouth College (Member, Project Steering Committee; Leader of Working Group on Chinese Philosophy and Religion)

Bardwell Smith, Carleton College (Member, Project Steering Committee and Working Group on Buddhist Religion)

H. Daniel Smith, Syracuse University (Member, Project Steering Committee and Working Group on Hinduism)

Robert McDermott, Baruch College, City University of New York (Member, Project Steering Committee and the Working Group on Hinduism)

Thomas Hopkins, Franklin and Marshall College (Leader of the Working Group on Hinduism)

David Ede, Western Michigan University and McGill University (Leader of the Working Group on Islamic Religion)

Karl Potter, University of Washington (Leader of the Working Group on Indian Philosophy)

Frank Reynolds, University of Chicago (Leader of the Working Group on Buddhist Religion)

Kenneth Inada, State University of New York at Buffalo (Leader of the Working Group on Buddhist Philosophy)

Frederick J. Streng, Southern Methodist University (Member, Project Steering Committee and Working Groups on Buddhist Religion and Philosophy)

David Dell (Project Manager, 1957-77 and a Member of the Working Group on Hinduism)

Series Preface

Two characteristics of the project's organization merit mention. One has been the widespread use of other scholars and teachers, in addition to the members of the project steering committee and working groups, in the critical review of preliminary versions of the guides. Reviewers were asked to comment on both commissions and omissions, and their comments were used by the compilers in making revisions. A far more extensive exercise than the customary scholarly review of manuscripts, this process involved well over 200 individuals who contributed immeasurably to improving the quality of the end product.

A similar effort to enlarge participation in the project has been made through discussions at professional meetings about the project among interested scholars and teachers while it was in progress. Over the past four years a dozen such sessions, involving over 300 participants, have been held at both national and regional meetings of the American Academy of Religion and the Association for Asian Studies.

The Classification Scheme and Criteria of Selection for the Guide

Early in the project a conference of most of the key project personnel mentioned above, as well as other members of the project working groups, was held in New York City in June 1972 to develop a common classification scheme and criteria for inclusion of materials in the resource guides.

This task generated lively and intense debate because underlying any classification scheme are the most fundamental issues of conceptualization and periodization in the study of religious and philosophical traditions. The classification schemes for guides in religion and in philosophy have generally been followed by each working group, although there have been inevitable variations. Each of the traditions included in the project has distinctive qualities and characteristics which make it difficult to fit all aspects of all traditions into the same set of categories.

The objective of developing a common set of categories was to facilitate examination of parallel phenomena across traditions. We believe this objective has been at least partially achieved through this series, although we recognize the need for continued refinement before a common set of categories compatible with all the traditions being covered can be evolved.

If developing categories to span diverse religious and philosphical traditions has been difficult, definition and reasonably uniform application of criteria for inclusion of material in the guides has been no easier. The project's basic objective, as originally elaborated at the June 1972 working conference, has been to provide an authoritative guide to the literature, both texts in translation and commentary and analysis, for teachers and advanced undergraduate and beginning graduate students who are not specialized scholars with access to primary texts in their original languages. Because of the limited number of teachers in American colleges and universities who have the necessary language skills, particularly outside their own primary field of scholarly interest, it was expected that the guides would be useful to those teaching in the field who, even though they might have a high level of scholarly specialization on one tradition, would often find it necessary to deal with other traditions in their teaching.

We also sought to achieve some consistency in annotations of entries in the guides. The objective has been to provide short, crisp, critical annotations which would help the user of the guide in identifying material pertinent to his or her interest or most authoritative in its coverage of a particular topic. We recognize, of course, that we have not achieved this objective throughout the entire series of guides encompassing more than 12,000 individual entries.

Because of the difficulties in applying a common set of categories and subcategories to the diverse traditions being covered by the guides, not all categories have been covered in each guide, and in some cases, they have been grouped together as seemed appropriate to the characteristics of a particular tradition. Extensive cross-referencing has been provided to guide the user to related entries in other categories.

The Problem of Availability of Resources in the Guide and the Microform Resource Bank

We realized from the beginning that a series of guides of this character would have little value if the users could not acquire materials listed in the guides. We therefore sought the cooperation of the Institute for the Advanced Studies of World Religions, which is engaged in a major effort to develop a collection of resources for the study of world religions in microform, and through the Institute, have established a microform resource bank of material in the guides not readily available from other sources.

Subject to the availability of the material for microfilming and depending upon its copyright status, the Institute is prepared to provide in microform any item included in any of the guides out-of-print or otherwise not readily available, in accordance with its usual schedule of charges. Where an item is already included in the Institute's microform collection, those charges are quite modest, and an effort is being made by the Institute to increase its holding of materials in the guides. Material can also be provided in hard xerographic copy suitable for reproduction for multiple classroom use at an additional charge.

Under the terms of a project agreement with the Institute, the Institute is undertaking the microfilming of some 30,000 pages of material included in these guides. In addition, the Institute already has in its microform collection a substantial number of titles in the fields of Buddhist and Chinese philosophy and religion.

The Institute will from time to time issue lists of material in microform from the guides available in its collections, but as its microform collections are continually being expanded, users are urged to contact the Institute directly to see if a particular title in which they are interested is available:

> Institute for Advanced Studies of World Religions
> Melville Memorial Library
> State University of New York
> Stony Brook, New York 11794

Acknowledgments

An undertaking of this scope and magnitude, involving such wide-spread participation, is bound to accumulate a long list of those who have contributed in one way or another to the project. It would be impossible to identify by name all of those who have contributed, and it is hoped that those who are not so identified will nonetheless recognize themselves in the categories which follow and understand that their help, interest, and support are also appreciated.

To begin with, primary thanks must be extended to the members of the project steering committee, the leaders of the various project working groups, and the members of each of the groups. Those responsible for each guide in the series are separately listed on the title page of that volume.

Thanks should also be expressed to the large number of scholars and teachers who served as critical reviewers of preliminary versions of the guides and the many who participated in sessions at regional and national meetings where the guides were subject to further scrutiny and where many constructive suggestions for their improvement were made.

We wish to acknowledge with grateful thanks the generous financial support of the National Endowment for the Humanities, and through its matching fund scheme, additional support from the Ada Howe Kent Foundation, C.T. Shen, and Council for International and Public Affairs, Inc. The patience and understanding of the Endowment's Education Division during the long and protracted period of completion of this project has been particularly noteworthy.

Many institutions have provided support to the project indirectly by making possible participation of their faculty in the various project working groups. In addition, both the South Asia Center at Columbia University and the Institute for Advanced Studies of World Religions have provided special assistance.

The project has been undertaken under the auspices of the Council for Intercultural Studies and Programs by the Foreign Area Materials Center, a project office of the Center for International Programs and Comparative Studies, State Education Department, University of the State of New York. The last-named institution, acting as the agent of the Council for Intercultural Studies and Programs, has been responsible for administering the National Endowment for Humanities grant and other financial support received for the project and has contributed extensively out of its own resources throughout the project, particularly in the concluding months, to assure its proper completion. Without the interest and support of key officials in the Center for International Programs and the New York State Education Department, the project could not have been completed.

A particular word of appreciation is in order for Norman Abramowitz of the Center, who succeeded me as Project Director after my resignation from the directorship of the Center in October, 1976 and to whom fell the unenviable task of overcoming administrative and financial obstacles in the final three years of the project. Appreciation should also be expressed to G.K. Hall and Company, the publishers of this series, and to its editorial staff. Their forebearance, as the manuscripts have been completed over a far longer time than we anticipated, has been exemplary.

Last but certainly not least are the project managers who have carried responsibility from day to day for implementing the project. Perhaps the most difficult and demanding role has been played by David J. Dell who came into the project at mid-stream and who struggled to assure its orderly completion. He and Edward Haynes have shared responsibility for final preparation of manuscripts for publication as editorial coordinators for the series, with the former handling two (Chinese Philosophy and Hindu Religion) and the latter, the remaining five titles in the series.

Different, but in many ways no less difficult, was the task confronting the interim project director, Josephine Case, whose services were kindly made available to the project by the New York Public Library in 1974 and 1975. She responded with dignity and sensitivity to the demands of this task.

But in many ways the most important figure in the project is one who is no longer with us. Edith Ehrman was the Manager of the Foreign Area Materials Center from its inception in 1963, a key figure in the conceptualization of this project, and its manager from the beginning until her untimely death in November, 1974. She was the moving spirit behind the project during its first three years. It is to her memory that this series of guides is dedicated by all those involved in the project who witnessed the extraordinary display of courage borne of her love of life during her last difficult illness.

Ward Morehouse, Chairman
Editorial and Publications Committee

Preface

Guide to Chinese Religion, begun in 1972, is one of a series of books on resources for the study of Asian philosophies and religions planned by the Project Steering Committee and undertaken by the working group chaired by Wing-tsit Chan.

The Guide is concerned primarily with the religious elements indigenous to China; hence Chinese Buddhism is excluded. However, we have not succeeded in omitting it entirely for the obvious reason that many Chinese religious features are inextricably related to Buddhism. Due to the fact that there is a companion book, Guide to Chinese Philosophy, in this series, our concern here is to concentrate on the religious entities. But this objective has not been fully realized because the distinction between "religion" and "philosophy" did not exist in the Chinese intellectual tradition. This is specially so for Neo-Confucianism, which can be designated either as "philosophy" or "religion," depending entirely upon the personal opinion of the writer. Those who desire a broader perspective of Chinese Religion should consult the Guide to Chinese Philosophy, Guide to Buddhist Philosophy, and Guide to Buddhist Religion in this series.

The eleven categories, as the organizing scheme of the Guide, were adopted uniformally by the different working groups on Asian Religions. However, as can be expected, we were compelled to modify them considerably in order to suit the unique character of Chinese religion and to conform to the availability of the resources. One of the obvious results is that these eleven categories were treated unevenly both in the quantitative and qualitative sense. In the following, we shall report briefly how each category was applied for the recruitment of the entries and what problems we faced in the process:

1. General Introduction and Historical Development

For the General Introduction, we have selected some appropriate and up-to-date introductory works on Chinese religion; under Historical Development, entries are listed chronologically in relation to the development of the religious history of China. In order to show the complexity and diversity of the subject matter, we have avoided the traditional threefold division of Chinese religion--Confucianism, Taoism, Buddhism; our emphasis is on the diversity of trends, movements, sects, and schools in which these three religions were intertwined. There is also the nebulous but persisting folk religion of China, whose origins predate these three religions but whose development is indebted to them. We hope that the use of the subcategories will enable the readers to have a "feel" for the complexity of the subject matter. In spite of our effort to avoid the traditional threefold division of Chinese Religion, we have in many instances continued to use it as a nomenclature for the three modes of religious apprehension in China and as a convenient means for identifying the religious texts.

2. Religious Thought

The number of entries under this category is far larger than that under the other categories, reflecting the amount of scholarship devoted to it. Again, we find that it is almost impossible to distinguish "religion" from "philosophy" or the "sacred" from the "profane," mainly because the ultimate authority in China is "secular" or "civil" rather than "religious" in the Western sense. In China, one cannot find a religious authority that exists independently of the civil authority. In this respect, the Chinese state in some sense can be regarded as a "church" in the Western sense.

3. Authoritative Texts

We have distinguished the Confucian texts from the Taoist texts in this category, although we recognized the fact that there is a great deal of mutual borrowing between them. We regret to say that there has been a paucity of English translations of the Taoist texts, largely because the study of the Taoist canon has been woefully neglected by Chinese scholars in the past. However, since World War II, Western and Japanese scholars have begun to investigate the Taoist canon more intensively. As a result, there is now a flood of Japanese and French works on Taoism awaiting translation into English. In the meanwhile, we are compelled to use some of the semi-Taoist or folk religion texts in English as part of the Taoist texts.

4. Popular Literature

The entries under this category contain myths and tales that cannot be attributed to a particular Chinese religion. Whether this popular literature is "secular" or "religious," once again, is an intriguing issue. In many instances, most of the short stories and novels listed here can be considered as both: "secular" because they deal with mundane affairs and worldly success; "religious" because they involve themes such as divine retribution and reward, rebirth, transformation, paradise.

5. Arts, Architecture, and Music

Here we are primarily concerned with the art motifs or symbols that are indigenous to the Chinese tradition, such as totemism, the yin-yang polarity, the five elements, and the magical numbers that appear in ceramics, jades, paintings, or engravings. It should be noted that this category does not include Buddhist art or architecture. Readers interested in this topic should consult Guide to Buddhist Religion. The very limited number of entries in music is partly due to the paucity of sources in English and partly to the fact that the members of this working group are not experts in music. We hope that a separate bibliography on Chinese music will be forthcoming.

6. Social, Economic, and Political Developments

Here we have in mind how socioeconomic factors and religion have affected each other in Chinese history. Due to the fact that the "religious" and the "secular" are so inseparable in Chinese society, this category especially conveys a sense of the spirit of religion in China. It also overlaps with category 1 (Historical Development).

7. Practices

We are mainly interested here in the performance of rituals, festivals, and magic. Because such practices usually involve myths and beliefs, this section overlaps with category 2 (Religious Thought).

8. Ideal Beings, Biography, and Hagiography

Entries under this category concern either the mythologization of historical beings or the historicization of mythological beings, the latter being characteristic of Chinese religion. Since religion in China is highly syncretistic, the "biography" of a folk divinity often embodies some elements of all three religions. In addition, because the Chinese pantheon strongly reflects the bureaucracy of its secular state, the celestial world of China also reflects the moral valuation of its terrestrial world.

9. Mythology, Cosmology, and Basic Symbols

These terms actually refer to the origins, crises, and destiny of the Chinese people, although they ostensibly refer to the creation of the world and the lives of the deities. The "basic symbols" are close in meaning to the "ideal beings" mentioned in the preceding category. "Cosmology" refers to speculations about how the world came into being. "Mythology" has to do with archetypes or the paradigmatic models. Due to the fact that many archaic myths of the Chinese people were either lost or underwent rationalistic transformations or redactionary changes by Confucian editors, they have become fragmentary and, in many instances, unintelligible in their present forms. How these mythological fragments and interpretations can be reconstructed or restored to their

original forms is indeed a formidable task. It should be noted that
the Taoist canon contains many different accounts of the cosmogonic
myths. But until careful research is made to determine the origins
and dates of these myths, we are in no position to know how important
they are in the history of Chinese religion.

10. Sacred Places

Here we are mainly interested in the sacred mountains associated
with the Taoist and Confucian temples, although most of the sacred
mountains in China are the abodes of Buddhist monasteries.

11. Soteriological Experience and Processes

This refers to the phenomenon of enlightenment and personal transformation in the Confucian and Taoist traditions. Maoism is also included here because it emphasizes the need for personal transformation.

The Guide is a selected bibliography that includes publications up
to 1977. A much more inclusive bibliography on Chinese religion, though
without annotations and including works up to 1970, is Laurence G.
Thompson's Studies of Chinese Religion, which should complement this
one.

Throughout the preparation of this book Wing-tsit Chan, my mentor
and overseer, gave me continuous guidance and suggestions without which
it would never have been completed. Laurence G. Thompson contributed
more than two hundred entries, particularly on arts and architecture,
popular literature, and ancient religion. Moreover, he has been a continuous critic and reviewer of the manuscripts, and his contributions
have made an indelible mark in this book.

I must acknowledge my gratitude to the following scholars who have
read the manuscript and have offered valuable suggestions: William
Doub, Norman Girardot, Jan Yün-hua, Joseph M. Kitagawa, Daniel Overmyer,
Michael Saso, Frederick Streng, Tu Wei-ming, Frederick Wakeman, Jr.,
and Holmes Welch.

My special gratitude goes to Ellen Frances Bolser who, over the
years, has provided me with a conducive environment in which to work.

My deep appreciation goes to David J. Dell for the difficult task
of determining the final structure of the Guide and for incorporating
the successive groups of entries into the appropriate categories. To
Edward S. Haynes goes my wholehearted appreciation for checking the
final manuscript and for compiling the index. To Pamela Grath goes
my gratitude for retyping the manuscript. And, lastly, I must express
my indebtedness to Janice Meagher, Karin Kiewra, Mary Allen, and other
staff members of G.K. Hall & Co. for their invaluable editorial and
technical support in bringing this book to print.

1. General Introduction and Historical Development

GENERAL INTRODUCTION

(1) BLOOM, ALFRED. "Far Eastern Religious Tradition." In Religion and Man: An Introduction. Edited by Richard Comstock. New York: Harper & Row, 1971, pp. 254-394.
   Of these pages, 254-333 deal with the religions of the Shang-Chou period: Confucianism, Taoism, and Buddhism. The emphasis is on the elucidation of ideas and different schools of thought and the concept of ultimate harmony which serves as a guiding principle for the interpretation of Chinese religion.

(2) CHAN, WING-TSIT; AL FARUQI, ISMA'EL RAGI; KITAGAWA, JOSEPH M.; and RAJU, P.T., comps. "Religions of China." In The Great Asian Religions: An Anthology. New York and London: Macmillan, 1969, pp. 99-227.
   Contains ten groups of excerpts of readings translated by Chan on Confucianism, Taoism, and Buddhism. These materials are preceded by a section on the "harmony of religions." Most of the selections, determined by the Confucian principle of rationalism, should complement Thompson's The Chinese Way in Religion (15).

(3) CHAN, WING-TSIT. Religious Trends in Modern China. New York: Octagon, 1969, 327 pp. (Orig. pub. New York: Columbia University Press, 1953.)
   A scholarly work on the religious situation of twentieth-century China up to the eve of Communist victory. Based upon personal observations in 1948-49, it deals with the following issues: a) the destiny of Confucianism as an ethical and religious philosophy, b) Buddhist movements and Buddhist philosophy, c) the syncretistic phenomenon of Chinese religion (religion of the masses), d) Chinese Islam, and e) modern debate by the intellectual leaders on the pros and cons of religion. It concludes with the author's own view on the Chinese intellectuals' definition of religion based on: sanction of ethics, fulfillment of human nature, and realization of principle (li).

1. *General Introduction and Historical Development*

(4) COHEN, ALVIN P. "A Bibliography of Writings Contributing to
the Study of Chinese Folk Religion." Journal of the American
Academy of Religion 43 (1975):238-63.
    A useful bibliography of books and articles on Chinese folk
religion in English, French, and German, prior to 1974. Some
works on Taoist religion are also included.

(5) EBERHARD, WOLFRAM. "Studies in Chinese Religion: 1920-1932."
In Moral and Social Values of the Chinese. Taipei: Chinese
Materials and Research Aids Service Center, 1971, pp. 335-99.
    This is a review concerning the state of research in Chinese
religion. Although it was written in 1932, it is still valuable,
both in terms of methodological insights and information concerning research publications on Chinese religion in Chinese. Eberhard
classifies Chinese religion under four headings: a) state cult,
b) scholarly world-view, c) folk religion, and d) Buddhism. According to this classification, much of what is generally called
Confucianism and philosophical Taoism is placed under b), and what
is termed religious Taoism is placed under c). The author's
classification was strongly influenced by Marcel Granet. The
most valuable part of this essay is the section on folk religion,
in which the author reviews the works of Chinese historians,
chiefly of Ku Chieh-kang. Some complex myths on early China are
discussed in relation to Chinese society and history.

(6) FREEDMAN, MAURICE. "On the Sociological Study of Chinese
Religion." In Religion and Ritual in Chinese Society. Edited by
Arthur P. Wolf. Stanford: Stanford University Press, 1974, pp.
19-41.
    A critique of the sociological studies of Chinese religion by
such writers as de Groot, Granet, and C.K. Yang. According to
Freedman, a general view of Chinese religion can be deduced on
the basis of the elite religion of Confucianism and the religion
of the Chinese masses: they enhance each other. He proposes the
"transformation theory," that is, a folk belief can be transformed
into an elite belief and vice versa. This position is diametrically opposite to the one held by Arthur Wolf. Freedman is in basic
agreement with de Groot, Granet, and C.K. Yang, who believe that
one must have a general view of the Chinese religion before pro-
ceeding to investigate the religious cult of a particular Chinese
community. Freedman also believes that Chinese religion was in
a sense a civil religion, "based upon a conception of authority
that in the last analysis would not allow the religious to separate off from the secular."

(7) GIRARDOT, NORMAN J. "Part of the Way: Four Studies on
Taoism." History of Religions 11 (Feb. 1972):319-37.
    A critical review of the following four books: What is

1.   General Introduction and Historical Development

Taoism? by H.G. Creel; Lao Tzu and Taoism by M. Kaltenmark;
L'Empereur Wou des Han dans la légende taoiste ("Han Wou-Ti Nei-
Tchouan") by K.M. Schipper; The Key Philosophical Concepts in
Sufism and Taoism (vol. 2, pts. 2 and 3) by Izutsu Toshihiko.
Besides delineating the diverse methodologies toward Taoist studies adopted by these four writers, Girardot's main concern is to
point out the two divergent views regarding Taoism held by contemporary scholars: one is the position that there should be a
clear separation between philosophical Taoism and religious Taoism,
and the other view is that philosophical and religious Taoism are
in fact two substrata of a common tradition. The reviewer's own
position is that both forms of Taoism are rooted in the same so-
teriology of the sacred cosmology--the union of matter and spirit.

(8) KITAGAWA, JOSEPH M. "Chinese Religions and the Family System."
In Religions of the East. Philadelphia: Westminster, 1960, pp.
40-98.
     The author uses the concept of the "holy community" as the in-
terpretative principle. The "holy community" refers to the Chinese
nation viewed as a "family." In discussing Communist China, the
author is fearful that it might destroy the religion of "family-
ism." His thesis is valid for Communist China only if certain
attitudes formerly associated with the family are now being culti-
vated solely to boost the state.

(9) LAI, WHALEN W. "Toward a Polarization of the Taoist Religion."
History of Religions 16 (1976):75-83.
     A review of Japanese Taoist scholar Yoshioka Yoshitoyo's Eisei
e no negai: Dokyō [Taoism: The quest for physical immortality
and its origin] (1970). According to the reviewer, this book is
perhaps the only popular introduction to the history of religious
Taoism from its inception to the twentieth century. For those who
do not know Japanese, this review offers a microscopic view of the
important aspects of Taoism in historical development: sects,
leaders, scriptures, its relation to the state, its relation to
Confucianism, Buddhism, and folk religion. A significant section
of the book not covered in the review is the author's impressions
and ideas on Taoism after 1949, based on his visit to China.

(10) McCASLAND, S. VERNON; CAIRNS, GRACE E; and YU, DAVID C.
"Religions of East Asia." In Religions of the World. New York:
Random House, 1969, pp. 523-730.
     A historical and philosophical interpretation of Chinese,
Tibetan, and Japanese Buddhism, of Confucianism, Taoism, Shinto,
and of the schools and sects that emanated from these religions.
Emphasis is upon the dynamics of religion in the historical con-
text and the interaction between religion and the political, so-
cial, and intellectual forces of China and Japan.

(11) NOSS, JOHN B. "The Religion of East Asia." In <u>Man's</u>
<u>Religions</u>. 5th ed. New York: Macmillan, 1974, pp. 238-331.
   This section covers archaic religion, Taoism, Confucianism,
and Shinto of Japan. The treatment is basically historical and
philosophical. In Confucianism, attention is given to the similarity between Confucianism and Maoist puritanism in present-day
China, but no consideration is given to the relationship between
Confucianism and the state cult, i.e., the relation between Heaven
and the emperor. In religious Taoism, the designation of the
"Three Purities," or the three divinities, is misleading: instead
of listing the Jade Emperor, Lao Tzu, and Ling Pao in this order
as the Three Purities, the order and names should be: Primordial
Heavenly Worthy (Lord of Heaven), Ling Pao Heavenly Worthy (Lord
of Earth), Tao Tê Heavenly Worthy (Lord of Lao or Lord of Man).

(12) SMITH, D. HOWARD. <u>Chinese Religions</u>. London: Wiedenfeld
& Nicolson, 1968, 222 pp.
   This is primarily a historical and textual study of religion
with philosophical emphasis: its strength lies in the studies of
the Shang and Chou periods, the religion of Confucius, and the
traditions of Han and pre-Han periods. The following points should
be corrected: Shang-ti (Ruler Above), the ancestor god of the Shang
and Chou rulers, is viewed as the "supreme god," which seems to
imply that the Chinese universally believed in a monotheistic god
in early China. The chapter on pre-Han religion is largely a
discussion of religion as disclosed in the Han literature (e.g.,
<u>Book of Rites</u>, <u>Book of Changes</u>). Folk religion in the pre-Han
period is not presented. The author says that <u>T'ai-p'ing ching</u>
<u>ling-shu</u> is lost; it is in fact present in the Taoist canon and
is the same as the <u>T'ai-p'ing ching</u> [The scripture of supreme
peace].

(13) SOYMIE, M., and LITSCH, F. "Bibliographie du taoisme:
Études dans les langues occidentales." <u>Études taoistes</u> 3 (1968):
1-72.
   A comprehensive bibliography of writings on religious Taoism
in Western languages.

(14) THOMPSON, LAURENCE G. <u>Chinese Religion: An Introduction</u>.
Belmont, Calif.: Dickenson, 1969, 119 pp. (3d ed., rev. and
enl., Belmont: Wadsworth, 1979, 163 pp.)
   A compact and balanced book on the nature of Chinese folk religion, which the author views as "animistic." This religion is
discussed in terms of family, community, and state. The author
does not wish to call the state religion of China "Confucianism,"
because its many ingredients had existed before the time of
Confucius. The strength of this book lies in exposing the dynamics of Chinese religion by following a different method from the

4

1. *General Introduction and Historical Development*

traditional one of considering Chinese religion primarily in terms of Confucianism. But by doing so, the true nature of Confucianism as a religion is adumbrated. In referring to Taoism in relation to the adept's desire to become an immortal, it is said that the goal of religious Taoism is the triumph of the yang over the yin. It should be noted that in the practice of inner alchemy, the adept makes use of both his yin and yang forces.

(15) THOMPSON, LAURENCE G., ed. The Chinese Way in Religion. Encino and Belmont, Calif.: Wadsworth, 1972, 241 pp.
    Following the same emphasis upon the popular level of Chinese religion as the author's Chinese Religion (14), the present volume is a masterful anthology of selected readings exposing the particular characteristics of Chinese religion. The edited materials are grouped according to the following scheme: a) ancient native religious tradition, b) Taoism, c) Buddhism, d) religion of the state, e) family religion, f) popular religion, and g) religion under Communism. These seven divisions reflect both historical developments and phenomenological types. The methodological efforts to eliminate the term "Confucianism" as a religion are evidenced in the above divisions where this term is absent, although the readings under d) all deal with Confucianism. The readings are diverse and cogent insofar as they exhibit the reality of popular religion. Caution should be taken in approaching the selections under a) ancient native tradition, which is meant to be the archaic religion prior to the establishment of Confucianism. Some of the selections, however, completed during the Han period (206 B.C.–A.D. 220), contain strong Confucian interpretation of the "archaic tradition." The Chung Yung [The conduct of life] as a Confucian philosophical treatise should not belong to the "ancient native tradition."

(16) THOMPSON, LAURENCE G. Studies of Chinese Religion: A Comprehensive and Classified Bibliography of Publications in English, French, and German through 1970. Encino and Belmont, Calif.: Dickenson, 1976, 109 pp. (2d ed., retitled Chinese Religion in Western Languages [Phoenix: University of Arizona Press, 1985].)
    This is the first work of its kind. It is divided into three main parts: Bibliography and General Studies; Chinese Religion Exclusive of Buddhism; and Chinese Buddhism. Within each part there are numerous sections: two under part one, forty-one under part two, and twenty-two (with a number of subsections) under part three. The front matter includes a lengthy section giving details concerning serial sources. There is an exhaustive index of authors, editors, compilers, translators, photographers, and illustrators. This is a basic reference tool for the field.

1. *General Introduction and Historical Development*

(17) WEBER, MAX. The Religion of China: Confucianism and Taoism. Translated by Hans H. Gerth. Introduction by C.K. Yang. New York: Macmillan, 1964, 308 pp.

This is not a study of Chinese religion in the narrow sense, but an exploration of the social structure and values of Chinese tradition, with religion as an inseparable component. Indeed, the religious ideas are not discussed until the second half of the volume. Following the same methodology in evaluating Communist China today, one may say that it was the union between certain traditional institutional-cultural forces and Western Marxism that brought forth Maoist Communism today. For example, Weber considers the Chinese State primarily as a "welfare state" and says that the redistribution of properties in terms of needs has been a pre-occupation of the Chinese reformer-statesmen in the past. This work contains many insights concerning the nature of Confucianism and its comparison with Protestant ethics. As is well known, Weber says that there are cultural-institutional reasons why capitalism could not have arisen in Confucian China, though it had similarities to Confucianism. C.K. Yang, in introducing this book, says, "We find this book more richly endowed with vital ideas and hypotheses on the structure and value system of traditional Chinese society than any other volumes today."

(18) WEI, FRANCIS C.M. The Spirit of Chinese Culture. New York: Scribner, 1947, 186 pp.

Four of the six chapters deal with Confucianism, Buddhism, and Taoism, with emphasis upon the overriding influences of Confucianism in Chinese culture. The author considers the Neo-Confucianism of Chu Hsi as representing the moral and spiritual core of Confucianism. His approach to Chinese religion is philosophical. The chapter on Taoism is paradoxically both informative and derogatory.

(19) WOLF, ARTHUR P., ed. Introduction to Religion and Ritual in Chinese Society. Stanford: Stanford University Press, 1974, pp. 1-18.

An introductory essay on the papers included in the book. Wolf lays down two positions concerning the sociological study of Chinese religion: 1) The study of Chinese religion must begin with the social and economic history of the particular communities. 2) There is no such thing as a general view of Chinese religion. The author is taking issue with such writers as de Groot, Granet, C.K. Yang, and Maurice Freedman, who believe that there can be a general view of Chinese religion as shared by both the elite and the masses.

(20) YANG, C.K. Religion in Chinese Society. Berkeley and Los Angeles: University of California Press, 1961, 473 pp.

A ground-breaking book by a sociologist. The traditional approach to Chinese religion in terms of the three religions (Confucianism, Taoism, Buddhism) is consciously discarded. Instead, the author stresses the function of religion in Chinese society and particularly its relation to politics. Using local gazettes as a major written source, the author made a study of the conditions of the temples in eight counties in the present century. He defines religion primarily in terms of theism (polytheism), though he does not rule out the non-theistic religions such as Chinese Communism. The book also distinguishes Chinese religion in terms of institutional religion and diffused religion. Institutional religion is independent from society, whereas diffused religion is entirely dependent upon society for its expression. Whereas these two religions influenced each other, the diffused religion was dominant. For the most part, Yang's theoretical debt is to Max Weber.

(21) YU, DAVID C. "Present-Day Taoist Studies: A Bibliographical Essay." Religious Studies Review 3, no. 4:(1977):220-39.
   A review of selected books and articles on Taoist religion in Chinese, Japanese, French, and English since 1950. It discusses works under the following headings: 1) philosophical and religious Taoism, 2) Taoism and Chinese folk religion, 3) Taoist religion in Chinese history, 4) Taoist sects and priesthood, 5) alchemy, 6) Taoist rituals and theology, 7) Taoist Canon, 8) Taoist studies in the People's Republic of China. The reviewer concludes that the study of Taoist religion has made considerable strides since the day of Chavannes, Granet, and Maspero.

1.2 ARCHAIC RELIGION PRIOR TO THE RISE OF CONFUCIANISM AND RELIGIOUS TAOISM, FROM PRE-HSIA TO MIDDLE CHOU (THE THIRD MILLENIUM TO 551 B.C.)

1.2.1 Shamanism

(1) EBERHARD, WOLFRAM. "Dance of Yü." In The Local Cultures of South and East China. Translated by A. Eberhard. Leiden: E.J. Brill, 1968, pp. 72ff.
   The major part of this volume deals with religion and myth but includes a description of an ancient shamanic rite performed by Yü (the mythical founder of the Hsia dynasty) and related to the fertility cult.

(2) ELIADE, MIRCEA. "Shamanic Symbolisms and Techniques in Tibet, China, and the Far East." In Shamanism. Translated by W.R. Trask. London: Routledge & Kegan Paul, 1964, pp. 423-65.
   A discussion of shamans and shamanesses, magic flight,

possession, exorcism, and the relations between shamanism and
traditional religions of China.

(3) GROOT, J.J.M. de. The Religious System of China: Its
Ancient Forms, Evolution, History and Present Aspect, Manners,
Customs and Social Institutions Connected Therewith. 6 vols.
Vols. 1-3, Disposal of the Dead; Vols. 4-6, On the Soul and
Ancestral Worship. New York: Paragon; Taipei: Literature
House, 1964, 6:975-81. (Orig. pub. Leiden: E.J. Brill, 1910.)
   De Groot translated passages from Chinese sources showing
the state rite of na, a community exorcism taking place prior
to the arrival of the spring, when totemic symbols were used.
There is information concerning both male and female shamans,
the latter being predominant.

(4) HAWKES, DAVID. "Quest of the Goddess." Asia Major, n.s.
13 (1967):71-94.
   Concerns the poem "Hsiang chün" in Ch'u Tz'u [Songs of Ch'u],
a late Chou collection from the southern state of Ch'u. Hawkes
gives a new translation (he had translated it earlier in his
complete version of Ch'u Tz'u) and modifies his earlier theories
about the nature of the poem: "the whole of it is sung by the
guesting shaman, who, for the benefit of an audience of wor-
shippers, describes the extraordinary difficulties of his journey in pursuit of the goddess." The poem "embodies a religious
rite whose pattern has been evolved and hallowed by long tradition." This article discusses cosmology, magic, and religious
ideas revealed in this literature.

(5) WALEY, ARTHUR, trans. Nine Songs: A Study of Shamanism in
Ancient China. London: Allen & Unwin, 1955, 69 pp.
   These are nine shamanic songs dedicated to various natural
and astronomic gods. Waley's introduction gives a historical
background of Chinese shamanism in relation to shamanism of
other religions. His comments following the songs offer valuable information on ancient divinities and shamanic practices.

1.2.2 Fertility Cults

(1) GRANET, MARCEL. "Agricultural Rites." In Chinese
Civilization. Translated by Kathleen E. Innes and Mabel R.
Brailsford. New York: Meridian, 1958, pp. 160-79.
   A description and interpretation of the prewinter and post-
winter agricultural rites from anthropological and sociological
viewpoints. Describes the relationship between the holy place
and the power of the chieftans.

(2) GRANET, MARCEL. "Peasant Religion." In The Religion of
the Chinese People. Translated by Maurice Freedman. New York:
Harper & Row, 1977, pp. 37-56. (French ed. La religion des
chinois. Presses universitaires de France, 1922, 200 pp.)
   A description of the prehistorical fertility cults of the
Shang period. The central idea discussed is the "Holy Place,"
the locus of the fertility cults, where the "sacred" resides.
All public rites were conducted around the holy place. According to Granet, the beliefs in the Mother Earth, in the sacred-
ness of the soil, and in the ancestor-deity were all originated
from the worship of the holy place.

(3) _____. "Rite of Pa-cha." In Festivals and Songs of Ancient
China. Translated by E.D. Edwards. London: Routledge, 1932,
pp. 166-80. (Orig. pub. Paris, 1919.) Reprint. Ann Arbor:
University Microfilms, 1969, 281 pp.
   A description of the autumn thanksgiving rite of pa-cha as a
prototype of seasonal festival. The first part of the book is
a translation of sixty-eight love songs drawn from the Shih-
ching [Book of songs], and the second is the author's interpretation of these songs. Granet demonstrated that festivals were
the substance of pre-Chou religion: they serve as a basis for
an understanding of ancient Chinese social institutions. Taken
as a whole, this volume is concerned with presenting a recon-
struction of ancient Chinese folk religion.

(4) KARLGREN, BERNARD. "Fecundity Symbols in Ancient China."
Bulletin of the Museum of Far Eastern Antiquities 2 (1930):1-54.
   Attempts to prove, through examination primarily of paleo-
graphic evidence, that the ancestral cult in ancient China "was
at the same time and above all a fecundity cult." Many other
challenging theories about ancient symbolism emerge in the course
of the argumentation. (See complementary notes in the same
journal: Arthur Waley, "Magical use of phallic survival in
China and Japan," 3 (1931):61ff, and Eduard Erkes, "Some Remarks
on Karlgren's Fecundity Symbols . . . ," 3:63-68.) Rather technical.

(5) _____. "Some Ritual Objects of Pre-Historical China."
Bulletin of the Museum of Far Eastern Antiquities 14 (1942):
65-69. Illus.
   Attributes phallic significance to certain artifacts and
bronze vessel ornaments of the archaic period. A complementary
note to author's earlier article on fecundity symbols.

(6) LING SHUN-SHENG. "Ancestral Tablet and Genital Symbolism
in Ancient China." Academia Sinica, Bulletin of the Institute
of Ethnology 8 (1959):39-46 (English summary). Illus.

1. *General Introduction and Historical Development*

1.2.2 1.2 Archaic Religion

In this article, the author asserts that "the ancient
Chinese ancestral tablet was derived from dolmen and menhir. . . .
Furthermore, the worship of genital organs helps to explain the
Yin-yang philosophy of ancient China. . . . This Yin-yang philosophy was in fact the basis of the religious belief and social
life of the Chinese. . . ." Unfortunately, only an English
summary is available.

(7) _____. "Comparative Study of the Ancient Chinese Feng-shan
and the Ziggurat of Mesopotamia." Academia Sinica, Bulletin of
the Institute of Ethnology 19 (1965):39-51 (English summary).
An elaborate proof of the author's main thesis: that the
sacrificial places of ancient China derived from the ziggurat
of Mesopotamia. Utilizes both literary and archaeological
sources. Quite technical although presenting only a summary
in English.

(8) _____. "Origin of the Shê in Ancient China." Academia
Sinica, Bulletin of the Institute of Ethnology 17 (1964):36-44.
The author offers some new opinions on the subject, differing from the traditionally received opinion that "shê was in
sacrifice to the Earth God and chi to the God of Grain." He
believes that "in fact, shê structures were just common tan and
shan establishments whereat sacrifices were made to gods, deities, and ghosts. Therefore, they could be named after a state,
a place, or by the event or even after individual persons."
Among the author's significant conclusions, two may be especially
interesting: "From the archaeological standpoint, it is assumed
that the shê culture in ancient China may have stemmed from the
Ziggurat of Mesopotamia" and "the shê culture originated during
the early stage of the Neolithic Age and ever since has continued
in existence. . . . It stemmed originally from the valleys of
the Tigris and Euphrates of West Asia and spread eastward to
East Asia through Central Asia, southward to Southeast Asia,
and reached South, Central, and North America across the Pacific
Ocean."

(9) _____. "Sacred Places in Ch'in and Han Periods." Academia
sinica, Bulletin of the Institute of Ethnology 18 (1964):136-42
(English summary).
A rather technical treatment of certain words for sacred
places in ancient Chinese documents. The conclusion is that
"the tai (pronounced as tzu in ancient times), chih, tsu (pronounced chieh), and shê had all emanated from one source--the
Ziggurat (translation of the first syllable of this word) of
ancient Mesopotamia. The Ziggurat culture had been introduced
into China during the prehistorical ages. . . ."

10

1.2 Archaic Religion   1.2.4

1.2.3 Culture Heroes

(1) GRANET, MARCEL. "Mythological heroes." In Chinese
Civilization (see 1.2.2[1]), pp. 185-204.
      Granet informs us that these mythological heroes represent
an archetype of two primordial forces: yin and yang. He also
says that the male divinities were transformations of earlier
female divinities.

(2) HIRTH, FRIEDRICH. "Mythological and Legendary Kings"; "The
Confucian Legends." In The Ancient History of China. New York:
Columbia University Press, 1908, pp. 1-26, 27-44. Reprint.
Taipei: Ch'eng-wen Publishing Co., 1968, 283 pp.
      Although written long before excavation of the last Shang
capital of Anyang, this is still the only English work to sum-
marize the traditionally received history of the most ancient
period. It is thus valuable for showing what most educated
Chinese would have learned in premodern times about mythological
matters.

(3) KARLGREN, BERNARD. "Legends and Cults in Ancient China."
Bulletin of the Museum of Far Eastern Antiquities 18 (1946):
199-365.
      A book-length monograph which painstakingly traces the legends
about the most important cult-figures of antiquity, using the
author's famous method of carefully distinguishing "free texts"
and "systematizing texts" of pre-Han times, and then documents
of Han and later times. Technical.

1.2.4 Totemism

(1) CHAU YICK-FU. "Religious Thought in Ancient China."
Translated by F.P. Erandauer. Ching Feng 10, no. 1 (1967):20-33;
2 (1967):20-33.
      The author finds totemism to be the earliest religion of the
Chinese. He then discusses ancestral worship, the magic of
shamans and diviners, the concept of Shang Ti, and the idea of
the Way of Heaven. In his Conclusion, the author states that
"it can be seen that the origin and evolution of religious
thinking in China is similar to that of other parts of the
world. In the beginning there was the worship of nature. This
was followed by the worship of ancestors. Finally there was a
kind of mental and spiritual worship." Based on the ancient
literature, but the use of the materials is uncritical, and the
article is thus a subjective, imaginative essay.

(2) FEHL, NOAH EDWARD. "Totemism." In Rites and Propriety in
Literature and Life. Hong Kong: Chinese University of Hong
Kong, 1971, pp. 12–24, 82–86.
These pages give a masterful summary of the recent findings
of ancient Chinese archaeology up to 1970. These findings show
that totemism and fertility cults existed in the earliest history of China. Following Granet, the author believes that the
ancestor cult was derived from totemism. According to him,
the highly refined Confucian principle of li, propriety, owes
its origin to the rites of totemism.

(3) GRANET, MARCEL. "Totemism." In Chinese Civilization (see
1.2.2[1]), pp. 180–84.
The author says that the ancestor cult was derived from
totemism. His concept of "reincarnated ancestor" is misleading.

(4) GROOT, J.J.M. de. "Descent of Men from Animals." In The
Religious System of China (see 1.2.1[3]), 4:253–71.
Although the author provides ample evidence that ancient
China believed in the descent of men from animals, he rejects
the view that totemism was present in early China.

(5) HUANG WEN-SHAN. "Artistic Representation of Totems in
Ancient Chinese Culture." Academia Sinica, Bulletin of the
Institute of Ethnology 21 (1966):1–13.
Theorizing about the significance of zoomorphic symbolism in
archaic bronzes, particularly the totemistic significance of
the much-discussed t'ao-t'ieh motif.

(6) _____. "Totemism and the Origin of Chinese Philosophy."
Academia Sinica, Bulletin of the Institute of Ethnology 9 (1960):
51–66.
A brief paper on progress by Chinese scholars in the study of
totemism in early Chinese society. "The ancient Chinese worldview is a peculiar socio-intellectual complex. Without an explanation from the anthropological aspect, it is almost impossible for us to see the common socio-cultural background out
of which Taoism, Confucianism, and the folk religion evolved.
Tao, as we see it, is a totemic principle which equates mana
and limits in a very general but definite way the thought and
action of every Chinese in the earliest period." A thought-
provoking article, which attempts to establish that "Laotze and
Confucius did not originate the philosophical concept of tao:
The totemistic principle was in existence long before these
philosophers."

(7) WEI HWEI-LIN. "Categories of Totemism in Ancient China."
Academia Sinica, Bulletin of the Institute of Ethnology 25
(1968):25–34.

Using evidences from traditional historical literature, Wei reduces ancient Chinese totemism to four types: horde, local clan, tribal, and national.

(8) WILHELM, RICHARD. "On the Sources of Chinese Taoism." Journal of the North China Branch, Royal Asiatic Society 45 (1914):1-12.
Discusses the way in which Taoist thought emerged from the common matrix of archaic Chinese thought as found in the Classics. The author believes in a "totemistic age" as "the common basis of Taoism and Confucianism." So far as modern Taoism is concerned, its "second source is undoubtedly the Buddhist church-organization. And a third source may be found in non-Buddhistic Indian influences during an earlier or later period of Taoist history." A stimulating, nontechnical essay.

1.2.5 Ancestor Cult and Divination

(1) BILSKY, LESTER J. The State Religion of Ancient China. 2 vols. Taipei: Oriental Cultural Service, 1975, 1:232 pp.; 2: 216 pp.
A study of the state sacrificial system for the worship of royal ancestors from Chou dynasty to the Western Han period (ca. 1111 B.C. to 8 A.D.). The author systematically shows that in ancient China, religion was predominantly an affair of the state. These two volumes present the development of the state cults as they were related to the political evolution of the Western Chou, Eastern Chou, Ch'in, and Western Han periods. In essence, im- perial ancestor worship was a principal means for the political expression of a unified dynasty. The author relies heavily on philological research on the sacrificial terms. A good contri- bution to the little-known field of imperial religion of the Chou period.

(2) CREEL, HERRLEE G. The Birth of China. London: P. Owen, 1958, pp. 174-216, 232-345. (Orig. pub. London: Reynolds & Hitchcock, 1937.)
Creel discusses the ancestor cult as the religious practice of the royal houses of Shang and Chou. He does not say that the ancestor cult was derived from totemism. Other than divin- ation (the use of oracle bones), Creel does not discuss ancestor rites and festivals. The ancestor cult for the author was pri- marily a cult of the state, a view apparently reflecting a later development of Chinese religion.

(3) GRANET, MARCEL. "Feudal Religion." In The Religion of the Chinese People (see 1.2.2[2]), pp. 57-96.

A description of the religion of the feudal families during
the Shang and Chou periods. The central idea is the hierarchy
of relations between the lord and his vassals. The lord, being
the chieftan of the clan, is the custodian of the sacred power
that permeates his domain. The cult of Heaven in this period
is essentially an ancestor cult involving the worship of the
deceased lords now joining Heaven or the Lord-above. Thus the
ancestor cult performs its political function by linking the
authority of the deceased lords with the sovereign power of the
living lord and his legitimate heirs. The practice of divination in terms of the sixty-four hexagrams was a part of the
ancestor cult then. The aim of the ancestor cult was to enhance
the feudal system by giving allegiance to the royal ancestors
on behalf of the reigning lord, his family, and his vassals.

(4) HO PING-TI. "Society, Religion, Thought." In The Cradle
of the East. Chicago and Hong Kong: University of Chicago
Press; Chinese University of Hong Kong, 1975, pp. 269-339.
    This chapter is primarily a study of the sinitic religion
from the Lungshan cultural period through the Shang and Chou
periods (the third millenium to 1,000 B.C.). The author identifies the ancestor cult as the genesis of the sinitic religion--
the worship of royal ancestors of the early kings. Thus the
sinitic religion emphasizes the patrilineal lines of kingship.
An important interpretation brought out by the author, based
upon the earlier works of Wang Kou-wei and Bernard Karlgren,
is that Shang-ti (God above), the ancestral god of the Shang
house, is identical to god-king Ti K'u or Ti Chün. Another
important view expounded by the author is that Shang-ti is no
different from T'ien (Heaven), a synonym of the Ancestral God
of the Shang House. Ho disagrees with the view held by Herrlee
Creel that T'ien was not known to the Shang House because it
was the Ancestral God of the Chou House which succeeded Shang.
The author derives most of his support from the early classical
texts instead of the oracle bones as is the case with Creel.
His rationale is that the Shang oracle bones are a "blind alley"
as a source of information regarding whether or not T'ien is
identical to Shang-ti. A stimulating and well-documented treatment of the inception of Chinese civilization.

(5) SHIH, C.C. "Study of Ancestor Worship in Ancient China."
In The Seed of Wisdom. Edited by W.S. McCullough. Toronto:
University of Toronto Press, 1964, pp. 179-90.
    A short summary of Shang ideas, with a few pages devoted to
Chou. Author claims to base his conclusions on archaeological
evidence, disregarding myths and legends in purely literary tra-
ditions unless they can be supported by artifacts. Be that as
it may, the article deals with the question of the concept of
Shang-ti as much as with ancestral cult. Semipopular style.

1. General Introduction and Historical Development

1.2.6 Mandate of Heaven

(1) CREEL, HERRLEE G. The Birth of China (see 1.2.5[2]),
pp. 367-75.
The doctrine of the Mandate of Heaven was introduced by the
Chou rulers for the purpose of initiating a moral and humanistic
religion of the state. This new concept was attributed to the
Duke of Chou (d. 1094 B.C.).

(2) DUBS, HOMER H. "The Archaic Royal Jou Religion." T'oung
Pao 46 (1958):217-59.
On the meaning of Shang-ti (synonym of T'ien), the full religious implications of the Mandate of Heaven, and the religious
views of Confucius.

1.2.7 Earliest Classics

(1) The Book of Songs (Shih-ching). Translated by Arthur Waley.
London: Allen & Unwin, 1937, 262 pp. Paperback reprint. New
York: Grove Press, Evergreen Books, 1960.
A translation of two hundred and ninety songs, accompanied
by the author's comments. Helpful for an understanding of the
rituals, folklore, and society of pre-Confucian China.

(2) CREEL, HERRLEE G. The Birth of China (see 1.2.5[2]), pp.
254-75.
The author discusses bronze inscriptions as the earliest
historical records of China. He also presents the literary
sources that were eventually embodied in the Shu-ching [Book
of history], Shih-ching [Book of songs], I-ching [Book of
changes], and I-li [Book of etiquette and ceremony]. Although
these works in the present form were set down in the late Chou
or early Han dynasty, they tell of the culture and history of
the Shang (ca. 1751-1112 B.C.) and Chou (ca. 1111-249 B.C.),
particularly the latter.

(3) I-ching [Book of changes]. Translated by Richard Wilhelm;
English translation by C.F. Baynes. Princeton: Princeton
University Press, 1967, 740 pp.
Supplies information concerning the sources that constitute
the basis of the book, the presentation of the sixty-four hexagrams. Each hexagram includes: a) a "judgment," a depiction
of a situation, b) an "image," an eternal ideal to which the
situation refers, and c) "lines," referring to the six alterna-
tive variations of the "image." The use of yarrowsticks or
coins as means of divination is explained toward the end of the
book. Includes important commentaries on the I-ching.

(4) "Shoo King [Shu-ching], or the "Book of History." In The
Chinese Classics. Translated by James Legge. Hong Kong: Hong
Kong University Press, 1960, 3:735 pp. (Orig. pub. 1865.)
   History covering the periods of Shun, Yü, Shang, and Chou,
with strong Confucian interpretation by the redactors. A rather
dated translation.

(5) "Tso Chuen" [Tso-chuan], or Tso's Commentary on the "Spring
and Autumn Annals." In The Chinese Classics (see 1.2.7[4]), 5:
933 pp.
   History of China from 721 B.C. to 463 B.C., presented from
the Confucian perspective.

1.2.8 The Hermit-Sages, the Yogins, the Alchemists Who Flourished
       between the Sixth and Second Centuries B.C.

(1) WALEY, ARTHUR. "Introduction"; "Taoist yoga." In The Way
and Its Power: A Study of the Tao Tê Ching. London: Allen &
Unwin, 1934, pp. 17-115; 116-20.
   A masterful survey of the quietist tradition in the pre-
Tao-tê ching period that subsequently influenced Taoism, Con-
fucianism, and even Legalism.

(2) WELCH, HOLMES H. "Beginning of Taoism"; "Period of Syn-
cretism." In The Parting of the Way: Lao-tzu and the Taoist
Movement. Boston: Beacon, 1957, pp. 88-97; 97-105.
   The author traces the four currents of Taoism: a) philosophical Taoism of Lao Tzu, Chuang Tzu, and Lieh Tzu, b) the
hygiene school, c) the school of alchemy, d) the magic island
of P'eng-lai.

1.3 TAOIST PHILOSOPHY OF LAO TZU, CHUANG TZU, AND LEIH TZU (SIXTH
     TO THIRD CENTURY B.C.)

(1) GIRARDOT, NORMAN J. "Part of the Way: Four Studies of Taoism"
(see 1.1[7]).

(2) IZUTSU, TOSHIHIKO. The Key Philosophical Concepts in Sufism and
Taoism. Vol. 2, Taoism; Vol. 10, Studies in the Humanities and Social
Relations. Tokyo: Keio Institute of Cultural and Linguistic Studies,
1967.
   The second volume of Izutsu's work deals with his argument that the
mysticism of Lao Tzu and Chuang Tzu reflects the metaphysics of ancient
Chinese shamanism. The author maintains that the works of Lao Tzu and
Chuang Tzu were composed in the region of Ch'u where Chinese shamanism
originated. This is a stimulating and learned work even if one may
disagree with his thesis.

(3) KALTENMARK, MAX. "Lao Tzu"; "Chuang Tzu." In <u>Lao Tzu and Taoism</u>.
Translated by Roger Graves. Stanford: Stanford University Press,
1969, pp. 5-18; 70-106.
  Concise discussions of Lao Tzu, Chuang Tzu, and Leih Tzu, with
emphasis on the philosophy of Chuang Tzu. The author does not attempt
to make a distinction between philosophical Taoism and religious Taoism
as diametrically different in nature.

1.4 <u>STATE RELIGION OF THE HAN PERIOD (202 B.C.-A.D. 220)</u>

  Our interest here is the religion of Confucianism, not Confucianism as a philosophical system. Readers interested in the life
of Confucius may consult category 6--Social, Economic, and Political Developments, and readers interested in the teaching of
Confucius may consult category 2--Religious Thought.

1.4.1 <u>Religious Nature of the Confucian Empire: Emperor as Son of</u>
      <u>Heaven (T'ien-tzu), Mandate of Heaven (T'ien-ming); Tung Chung-</u>
      <u>shu (176-104 B.C.), Architect of Religious Confucianism</u>

  (1) BISHOP, CARL W. "Worship of Earth in Ancient China."
<u>Journal of the North China Branch, Royal Asiatic Society</u> 64
(1933):24-43.
    Discusses Sky God, Shang-ti, T'ien, Earth Mother (Ti), Shê,
Hou T'u, and the worship of the latter down to reign of Han Wu
Ti (140-86 B.C.), using literary sources, especially the <u>Li Chi</u>
[Book of rites] and modern scholarly studies, including those
by B. Schindler, Chavannes, and Karlgren. Lacks critical philological methodology.

  (2) CREEL, H.G. "Sinism--A Clarification." <u>Journal of the</u>
<u>History of Ideas</u> 10 (1949):135-40.
    Should be read by students who consult Creel's <u>Sinism</u>. Ex-
plains that his book was written before Anyang excavations and
hence its picture of China is "in general, quite valid for the
Han period," but cannot now be considered as accurate for remote antiquity.

  (3) De BARY, W. THEODORE; CHAN, WING-TSIT; and WATSON, BURTON,
comps. <u>Sources of Chinese Tradition</u>. New York: Columbia
University Press, 1960, pp. 172-99. Paperback reprint. 1964,
1:156-83.
    These pages deal with source materials covering the political-
religious role of the emperor, the Mandate of Heaven, and the
theory of portents.

1. *General Introduction and Historical Development*

(4) DUBS, HOMER H. "The Victory of Han Confucianism." <u>Journal of the American Oriental Society</u> 58 (1938):435-49.
    Historical summary of the process by which Confucianism became the state doctrine between the beginning of the Han dynasty and the reign of Emperor Yüan (49-33 B.C.). Based on the <u>Han Shu</u> [History of former Han].

(5) GRANET, MARCEL. "The Official Religion." In <u>The Religion of the Chinese People</u> (see 1.2.2[2]), pp. 97-119.
    The systematization of Chinese religion by the literati class in the Han period. According to Granet, the religion of the officials (emphasizing the organic relation between the natural order and the human order based on a universal morality) evolved out of the feudal religion of the preceding period and represents the religion of the urban class. The ancestor cult, except in the case of the imperial ancestors, in this period became a private practice in contrast to the preceding period when it was a public rite for the solidarity of the feudal system.

(6) HUGHES, E.R., and HUGHES, K. "Religion in the Han Era." In <u>Religion in China</u>. London: Hutchinson's University Library, 1950, pp. 43-60.
    Brief summary of some salient characteristics of Han religion by an authority.

(7) KRAMERS, R.P., trans. <u>K'ung Tzu Chia Yü</u> [The school sayings of Confucius]. Leiden: E.J. Brill, 1950.
    A technical (philological) study (not a translation) of a work that the author describes as "a collection of all traditions about Confucius, with the exception of the <u>Lun-yü</u> [The Analects of Confucius] . . ." which was rediscovered (some think forged) by Wang Su in the first half of the third century A.D. For students with considerable background.

(8) LOEWE, MICHAEL. "Case of Witchcraft in 91 B.C." <u>Asia Major</u> 15 (1970):159-96.
    After detailed discussion of a historical incident of witchcraft reported in <u>Han Shu</u>, the author devotes his final section (pp. 190-96) to an examination of the meaning of <u>wu-ku</u> (witchcraft by shaman) and <u>chu-tsu shang</u> (cursing the emperor for magical purposes) in Han times.

(9) TJAN TJOE-SOM (Tseng Chu-sen). <u>Po Hu T'ung</u> [The comprehensive discussion in the White Tiger Hall]. 2 vols. Leiden: E.J. Brill, 1949-52.
    Rich repository of information about the views of Han scholars on ancient beliefs and rituals, reflecting their own

1.4   State Religion of the Han Period   1.4.2

thought-world and religious practices. Rather technical, but
the student can get much from the work without worrying about
the notes.

1.4.2   Texts that Support the State Religion

(1) Ch'un-ch'iu fan'lu [Luxuriant gems of the spring and autumn
annals], by Tung Chung-Shu. Translated by Wing-tsit Chan. In
A Source Book in Chinese Philosophy. Princeton: Princeton
University Press, 1963, pp. 273-88. Also in Sources of Chinese
Tradition (see 1.4.1[3]), pp. 174-75, 178-83, 187-88, 217-20.
   This work reflects what is generally referred to as Confucian
metaphysics, in which ethics, politics, religion, and cosmology
are fused.

(2) Hsiao-ching [Classic of filial piety]. Translated by Mary
L. Markra. New York: St. John's University Press, 1961, 67 pp.
   This book contains both the translation of the text and the
original text in Chinese. The translation is faithful and accurate. The footnotes are useful for an understanding of Han
Confucianism. The text explains why ancestor worship is necessary.

(3) I-ching [Book of changes] (see 1.2.7[3]).

(4) Li-chi [Book of rites]. Translated by James Legge. Edited
by Ch'u Chai and Winberg Chai. 2 vols. New York: University
Books. 1:479 pp.; 2:491 pp. With the exception of the editorial
introduction, this work is a reproduction of the translation,
The Sacred Books of the East, vols. 27-28 (London: Oxford
University Press, 1885).
   The introduction (pages ix-lxxx) explains the origin of the
I-li, Chou-li, and Li-chi as well as the four basic elements in
the book: a) interpretation of the rites, b) institution of
rites, including a discussion on the purpose of mourning and
of sacrificial rites, c) philosophical essays, which include
two famous treatises known as Ta-hsüeh [Great learning] and
Chung-yung [Doctrine of the mean], and d) anecdotes about
Confucius and his disciples, together with conversations between Confucius and his disciples.

(5) Lu-shih Ch'un-ch'iu [Spring and autumn annals of Mr. Lu].
In Sources of Chinese Tradition (see 1.4.1[3]), pp. 222-26.
(Paperback ed. 1:206-10.)
   This excerpt deals with the duties of the emperor during the
first month of the year regarding his personal conduct, law and
administration, sacrifice, music and dance, propitious acts, and

and taboos. The entire book is an "almanac," explaining the
"do's" and "don't's" that should be followed in each month.
It shows the interaction among religion, astronomy, politics,
and ethics.

1.4.3 State Control of Religions

(1) EDWARDS, E. "Some Aspects of the Conflicts of Religion in
China During the Six Dynasties and T'ang Periods." Bulletin of
the School of Oriental and African Studies 7 (1933-35):799-808.
   A general historical discussion of Confucian, Taoist, and
later Buddhist thought.

(2) YANG, C.K. "State Control of Religion." In Religion in
Chinese Society (see 1.1[20]), pp. 180-217.
   This chapter discusses the exclusive right of the state to
perform worship of Heaven in public and its control of religious
affairs in connection with the building of Buddhist and Taoist
temples, ordination, and conduct of the clergy.

1.5 THE CULT OF CONFUCIUS

(1) SHRYOCK, JOHN K. The Origin and Development of the State Cult
of Confucius. New York: Paragon, 1966, 298 pp. (Orig. pub. New York:
Century, 1932.)
   Describes the inception of the deification of Confucius in the Han
dynasty and the development of the Confucian cult under imperial spon-
sorship in the T'ang, Sung, Yüan, Ming, and Ch'ing periods, and traces
the rise and expansion of Buddhism and religious Taoism in the context
of the Confucius cult. The best available book on the history of the
cult.

1.6 ANCESTOR WORSHIP

(1) LIU-WANG HUI-CHEN. "An Analysis of Chinese Clan Rules." In
Confucianism in Action. Edited by David S. Nivison and Arthur F.
Wright. Stanford: Stanford University Press, 1959, pp. 63-96.
   An analysis of the social, political, and religious implications of
the clan rules in China in the Neo-Confucian period. The author applies
Redfield's concepts of the great tradition and little tradition to her
understanding of the relationship between the Confucian tradition and
the clan rules: they complement each other.

(2) YANG, C.K. "Religion in the Integration of Family." In Religion
in Chinese Society (see 1.1[20]), pp. 28-57.

1.7 Rise and Growth of Taoist Religion   1.7

   The author stresses the sociological significance of the ancestor
cult: it helped to integrate the family and stabilize the society.
Yang also emphasizes the rational and aesthetic characters of ancestor
by reference to Hsün-tzu and the Book of Rites. He thinks that the
Chinese ancestor cult involves the after-life of the ancestors without
requiring a doctrine of immortality of the soul. The author uses the
term "theistic" in the broadest sense to mean the personal nature of
the sacred: hence the ancestor cult is a theistic religion.

1.7 RISE AND GROWTH OF TAOIST RELIGION (SECOND TO SEVENTH CENTURY
     A.D.). T'AI-P'ING TAO (SUPREME PEACE SECT), AND THE YELLOW
     TURBANS REVOLT; T'IEN-SHIH TAO (CELESTIAL MASTER SECT); THE TAO
     OF THE FIVE BUSHELS OF RICE, ITS REVOLT AND ITS REFORM UNDER K'OU
     CH'IEN-CHIH (D. 432); MAO-SHAN TAO (SECT OF MAO MOUNTAIN), ITS
     REVIVAL UNDER T'AO HUNG-CHING (456-536); PRACTICE OF PLANCHETTE
     (FU-CHI); BEGINNING OF THE TAOIST CANON IN THE SIXTH CENTURY A.D.

     Aspects of Archaic Religion Inherited by Religious Taoism: See
     1.2.1 for Shamanism, 1.2.2 for Fertility Cults, 1.2.3 for Cultural
     Heroes, 1.2.4 for Totemism, 1.2.5 for Ancestor Cult and Divination.

(1) GRANET, MARCEL. "Religious Revivals." In The Religion of the
Chinese People (see 1.2.2[2]), pp. 120-43.
   A brief presentation of the two rival religions of the official
religion of Confucianism, regarded as complementing its deficiency.
Taoism continued to introduce "revelations" and sectarian practices
in contradistinction to Confucian conformism. Buddhist monks performed
the Ullambana ceremony for the delivery of the dead from suffering in
hell, thus fulfilling the Confucian concept of filial piety. Granet,
a forerunner of Taoist studies in the West, views philosophical Taoism
and Taoist religion as belonging to the same tradition.

(2) KALTENMARK, MAX. "The Taoist Religion." In Lao Tzu and Taoism
(see 1.3[3]), pp. 108-43.
   A summary/survey of the rise and development of religious Taoism
with reference to myths, sects, alchemy and hygiene, the Taoist Canon,
as well as the most basic Taoist texts. This book can be used as an
introductory reading.

(3) MIYAKAWA, HISAYUKI. "Legate Kao P'ien and a Taoist Magician Lü
Yung-chih in the Time of Huang Ch'ao's Rebellion." Acta Asiatica 27
(1974):75-99.
   A historical study of Kao P'ien, a prominant military official and
a Taoist practitioner in late T'ang dynasty. It involves Kao's relations with Lü Yung-chih, a Taoist priest-magician who was employed as
a member of Kao's staff. This study reflects the influence of Taoist
religion on some leading officials in the T'ang period and the political and worldly ambitions of some less noble Taoist priests.

(4) NGO VAN XUYET. Divination, magic et politique dans la Chine
ancienne: Essai suivi de la traduction des "Biographies des Magiciens"
tirées de l'"Histoire des Han postérieurs." Bibliothèque de l'École
pratique des hautes études sciences réligieuses, vol. 78. Paris:
Presses universitaires de France, 1976, 261 pp.
   A study of the tradition of the Taoist magicians (fang-shih) during
the later Han period (25-220). In the first part of the book the
Vietnamese author gives a historical explanation of the relationship
between politics and the Taoist magicians. The second part is an
annotated translation of forty-eight biographies of the Taoist magicians, entitled Pang-shu lieh-chuan [Biographies of the magicians who
possessed the esoteric arts] in the Hou Han Shu [History of later Han].
The book concludes with a discussion of the relationships between the
Taoist esoteric arts and their antecedents in earlier classics such
as the Book of Changes.

(5) SCHIPPER, KRISTOFER M. L'Empereur Wou des Han dans la légende
taoïste ("Han Wou-Ti Nei-Tchouan"). Publications de l'école française
d'Extrême-Orient, vol. 58. Paris: École Française d'Extrême-Orient,
1965, 132 pp. plus the Chinese text.
   A translation of the text Han Wu Ti Nei Chuan, dated between the
fourth and the sixth centuries A.D., a legendary romantic novel concerning the visit of goddess Hsi Wang-mu to Emperor Wu-ti, who receives
revelations and talismans from her. The volume includes Schipper's
monograph on the religious symbolism of the text, which in essence depicts the motif of hierogamy, or the union of yin and yang, through
the coming of the goddess.

(6) SEIDEL, ANNA K. "Taoism." In Encyclopaedia Britannica. 15th ed.
Chicago and London: Encyclopaedia Britannica, 1974. 17:1034-44.
   An excellent introduction to Taoism in both its philosophical and
religious subtraditions from ancient to modern times. It reflects the
most up-to-date research in Taoist studies today.

(7) STRICKMANN, MICHEL. "History of Taoism." In Encyclopaedia
Britannica. 15th ed. Chicago and London: Encyclopaedia Britannica,
1974. 17:1044-50.
   An outstanding survey of the history of the Taoist scriptures,
Taoist sects and rituals, as well as the major Taoist proponents, re-
formers, and priests in Chinese history. Buddhist influences upon
Taoist rituals and divinities are also noted.

(8) WELCH, HOLMES H. "The Taoist Church." In The Parting of the Way
(see 1.2.8[2]), pp. 113-23.
   A historical tracing of the Taoist Church, mainly the T'ien-shih
Tao and the T'ai-ping Tao, at their inception. The author believes
that there was a separation in the development between Taoist sects
and the Taoist alchemists and hygienists: the former participated in
a popular religion, and the latter in elitist practices.

1.8   TAOIST ALCHEMISTS BETWEEN THE SECOND AND SEVENTH CENTURIES A.D.

1.8.1   Wei P'o-yang (ca. A.D. 142-167):   Author of the "Ts'an-t'ung ch'i" [Three ways unified and harmonized], the Oldest Surviving Text on Alchemy

> (1) CHAN, WING-TSIT; AL FARUQI, ISMA'EL RAGI; KITAGAWA, JOSEPH M.; and RAJU, P.T., comps. "Excerpts on Ts'an-t'ung ch'i." In The Great Asian Religions (see 1.1[2]), pp. 162-66.
> The Ts'an-t'ung ch'i is a highly esoteric treatise which combines the philosophy of the Book of Changes with the external alchemy and internal alchemy.

> (2) WU LU-CH'IANG, and DAVIS, TENNEY L., trans. "An Ancient Chinese Treatise on Alchemy, Ts'an-t'ung ch'i." Isis 18 (1932): 210-89.
> Contains a complete translation of the work in sixty-seven chapters, with the Song of the Ting (tripod-cauldron) and the epilogue by Wu and an introduction and notes by Davis. According to Wu and Daivs, the title of the book refers to the conviction that the alchemic processes, the Book of Changes, and the Taoist doctrines are variations of the same thing under different names. The essence of the book is to show the alchemic meaning of the kua ("hexagrams") as discussed in the Book of Changes.

1.8.2   Ko Hung (A.D. 284-363):   Author of "Pao-p'u tzu" [The philosopher who embraces simplicity]

> (1) DUBS, HOMER H. "Beginnings of Alchemy." Isis 38 (1947): 62-86.
> Presents "the available historical material concerning alchemy in the pre-Christian era, in the period before any experimental alchemy appeared in the Mediterranean world." The essay includes translations from the Shih-chi, Huai Nan Tzu, and Pao-p'u Tzu. In the last section, the author gives his own theories as to the origin and earliest history of alchemy. A list of the Chinese characters is appended. The style is technical but not impossible for nonspecialists.

> (2) _____. "Origin of Alchemy." Ambix 9 (1961):23-36.
> This is a lucid historical survey of the subject, focusing especially upon the Chinese records and the background of the Chinese developments. A less technical article than the author's "Beginnings of Alchemy" (1).

(3) WARE, JAMES R., trans. "Ko Hung's Autobiography." In
Alchemy, Medicine, Religion in China of A.D. 320: The Nei
P'ien of Ko Hung (Pao-p'u tzu). Cambridge: MIT Press, 1966,
pp. 6-21.
    An autobiographical statement by a leading Taoist of the
fourth century, who followed his own quietist interest while
serving the state as an administrator and military leader.

(4) WELCH, HOLMES H. "Ko Hung." In The Parting of the Way
(see 1.2.8[2]), pp. 120-30.
    A resume of the contributions of Ko Hung to alchemy, hygiene,
physical immortality, and Confucian ethics.

1.9 TAOIST SECTS

(1) WELCH, HOLMES H. "Taoist Church Organization." In The Parting of
the Way (see 1.2.8[2]), pp. 141-57.
   Provides a brief account of the Taoist sects from the Six Dynasties
(A.D. 220-589) to 1912, with emphasis on the Ch'üan-chen sect and the
Cheng-i sect.

1.9.1 The Founding of Ch'üan-chen Chiao (Church of the Preservation
       of the True Nature) by Wang Chi(1112-1170) and its Growth in
       North China. Famous Ch'üan-chen Master Ch'iu Ch'ang-ch'un
       (1148-1227), Who Addressed Genghis Khan on Religious Taoism in
       Central Asia (1220-1224); Monasticism, Vegetarianism, Internal
       Alchemy; Controversies (1255-1256) between Taoism and Buddhism
       under Kublai Khan in Yüan China

(1) CH'EN, KENNETH K.S. "Buddhist-Taoist Controversy under the
Mongols." In Buddhism in China. Princeton: Princeton
University Press, 1964, pp. 421-25.
    Ch'en describes the controversy over some Taoist works show-
ing the superiority of Taoism to Buddhism and the eventual victory of Buddhism over Taoism in the Mongol empire of Yüan.

(2) WALEY, ARTHUR, trans. The Travels of an Alchemist. London:
Routledge & Kegan Paul, 1931, 165 pp.
    This is a description of the journey of Ch'iu Ch'ang-ch'un,
patriarch of the Ch'üan-chen sect in the thirteenth century,
to the Hindukush at the summons of Genghis Khan. It was recorded by his disciple, Li Chih-ch'ang. In addition to the
translation of the original text, Waley wrote an introduction
depicting the Mongol power in the Chinese continent and the
history of the sect. The travelog also throws light on the doctrines and practices of the sect. Waley's reference to Ch'iu as
an alchemist should be understood to mean only an interal alchemist.

1.9.2   The Cheng-i Chiao (Church of the Right Unity). Successor of
        the T'ien-shih Tao; Hereditary Priesthood within the Chang
        Family, its Headquarters at Dragon-Tiger Mountain; Magic,
        Talismans, Spells

        (1) WELCH, HOLMES H. "The Chang T'ien-shih and Taoism in China."
        Journal of Oriental Studies 4 (1957-1958):188-212.
           A report of the author's personal interviews with the sixty-
        third Celestial Master of the Cheng-i Sect in Taiwan in 1958
        and an account of religious Taoism in Taiwan since 1949. This
        article also presents valuable information on the institutional
        life of the sect as well as its history.

1.10   SECRET SOCIETIES

1.10.1   Secret Societies before the Twentieth Century. Rise of Secret
         Societies in Opposition to Foreign Rulers of the Yüan and
         Ch'ing Dynasties

        (1) DARDESS, JOHN W. "The Transformations of Messianic Revolt
        and the Founding of the Ming Dynasty." Journal of Asian Studies
        29 (1970):539-58.
           A historical study of the various military revolts against
        the Mongol Yüan dynasty toward the end of the period and the
        involvement of the White Lotus sects. It is a demonstration
        of the author's thesis that although these rebellious groups
        in their initial phases involved White Lotus sects' messianic
        ideology of the coming of the future Buddha (Maitreya), they
        soon discarded this Buddhist notion in order to gain support
        from the Confucian gentry class, who had no use for any mes-
        sianic notion.
           Among these rebellious leaders was the future founder of
        the Ming dynasty, Chu Yüan-chang, who was able to eliminate
        his rival groups by recruiting members of the gentry-scholar
        into his service. The author points out that it is important
        to have Buddho-Taoist or Buddho-Manichean ideology in order
        to gain support of the peasants, it is more important to gain
        the support of the gentry-scholar class if the leader wants
        to start a new dynasty in China.

        (2) GROOT, J.J.M. de. Sectarianism and Religious Persecution
        in China. Taipei: Ch'eng Wen, 1970, 2 vols. in one, 595 pp.
        (Orig. pub. Johanne Muller, 1903-4.)
           This work is a study of the persecution of the secret so-
        cieties by the Manchu (Ch'ing) government, based upon the
        official documents, written from the point of view of Confucian
        bureaucracy. Volume 1 contains sources describing the nature

of the Confucian state which cannot tolerate "heterodox" sectarian teaching contrary to the Confucian tradition. Volume
2 deals with official documents reporting the rebellious activities of the secret societies. Some of these groups are:
White Lotus Society, Eight Trigram Society, Society of Prior
Heaven, Lung-hua Hui, T'ien-ti Hui. Most of these groups were
Buddho-Taoist in belief and Confucian in outlook.

(3) NAQUIN, SUSAN. "Organization and Ideology of the White
Lotus Sects." In Millenarian Rebellion in China: The Eight
Trigrams Uprising of 1813. New Haven: Yale University Press,
1976, pp. 7-60.
    An excellent description of the beliefs, rituals, and obli-
gations of the members of the White Lotus Sects as well as
their organization. (See also 6.2[12].)

(4) OVERMYER, DANIEL L. "Sects of White Lotus and White Cloud
and Lo Sects." In Folk Buddhist Religion: Dissenting Sects
in Late Traditional China. Cambridge: Harvard University
Press, 1976, pp. 73-161.
    An interpretative analysis of the history, beliefs, and
organization of the White Lotus and related sects since the
sixteenth century A.D. (See also 6.2[13].)

(5) THOMPSON, LAURENCE G. "The Lung-hua Sect." In The Chinese
Way in Religion (see 1.1[5]), pp. 202-9.
    A condensation of Chapter 7 of de Groot's Sectarianism and
Religious Persecution in China (1.10.1[2]), which describes
the subversive activities of the Lung-hua Sect in the nineteenth century.

(6) YANG, C.K. "Religion and Political Rebellion." In
Religion in Chinese Society (see 1.1[20]), pp. 218-43.
    This chapter deals primarily with sectarian societies in the
Ch'ing dynasty (1644-1912). The sectarian rebellions against
the state were not confined to the Taoist groups; Buddhist
groups also took part. The author entertains the view that
political rebellion is a characteristic of Chinese folk religion which religious Taoism shared.

1.10.2 Secret Societies in the Twentieth Century: Common Beliefs and
        Practices. Revealed Scriptures; Prophecy; Messianism; Politi-
        cal Rebellions against the State under Foreign Rule

(1) CHESNEAUX, JEAN. Secret Societies in China in the Nineteenth
and Twentieth Centuries. Translated by Gillian Nettle. Ann
Arbor: University of Michigan Press, 1972, 210 pp.

A description of the beliefs, rituals, and activities of
seventeen secret societies in modern China prior to 1949.
These societies, whose members came from the rural districts
and lower urban class, were anti-Manchu (the Ch'ing government)
and against foreign domination in China. They were highly
syncretistic, accepting Confucian ethics, Buddhist theology,
and Taoist cosmology. The author's thesis is that these groups
were incapable of making history on their own, although they
did represent the sentiments of the masses.

(2) De BARY, W. THEODORE; CHAN, WING-TSIT; and WATSON, BURTON,
comps. "Popular Religion and Secret Societies." In Sources
of Chinese Tradition (see 1.4.1[3]), pp. 630-59 (omitted in
paperback reprint).
    The second half of the chapter describes the secret societies
particularly the Hung Society and its varieties, and provides
four documents of the Hung Society. It should be emphasized
that the demarcation between the lay societies and secret societies is difficult to draw: generally speaking, the lay
societies did not engage in political rebellion, whereas the
secret societies did.

(3) DUNSTHEIMER, GUILLAUME. "Some Religious Aspects of Secret
Societies." In Popular Movements and Secret Societies in China,
1840-1950. Edited by Jean Chesneaux. Stanford: Stanford
University Press, 1972, pp. 23-28.
    A brief explication of several common doctrines of secret
societies: the supremacy of Heaven, the cult of Maitreya, the
concept of the Three Kalpas, the belief in the Eternal Mother.
Dunstheimer emphasizes that religious elements are found in
all secret societies, whatever other character they may have.

(4) HUTSON, JAMES, trans. "History of Chinese Secret Societies."
China Journal 9 (1928):164-70, 215-21, 276-82; 10 (1929):12-16.
    Abridged translation of a Japanese work by Hirayama Amane
that had already appeared in Chinese. This is a straightforward historical survey in a very brief, noncritical form.
Useful as an outline of events rather than as an analysis of
causes or meanings.

(5) SCHRAM, STUART R. "Mao Tse-tung and Secret Societies."
China Quarterly 27 (1966):1-13.
    Somewhat disappointing, as the author admits that "explicit
evidence is extremely limited" for the subject. There is nothing specifically on religion, and there are only tentative suggestions as to the influence of secret societies in Mao's life
and the Communist movement. An appendix translates the "Appeal
of the Central Soviet Government to the Ko-lao-hui," signed by
Mao on 15 July 1936.

1.11 TAOIST LAY ASSOCIATIONS IN THE TWENTIETH CENTURY: COMMON BELIEFS
AND PRACTICES. CONFESSION OF SINS, REPENTENCE, FAITH-HEALING;
MEDITATION AND YOGA; EDUCATION AND PUBLIC WELFARE; DIVINATION,
ASTROLOGY, OCCULTISM; CONFUCIAN ETHICS; AFFILIATION WITH LABOR
ASSOCIATIONS AND EMIGRANT SOCIETIES

(1) CHAN, WING-TSIT. "Religion of the Masses." In Religious Trends
in Modern China (see 1.1[3]), pp. 136-85.
    The latter half of the chapter deals with the Taoist lay societies.
The author stresses the view that these lay groups are syncretic: they
embrace Confucian ethics, Buddhist divinities, and Taoist rituals, with
the predominance of the last. This is the phenomenon of Chinese folk
religion which transcends Taoist religion in its pure sense.

1.12 RELIGION DURING AND AFTER THE REPUBLIC PERIOD (1912-1949)

(1) CRESSY, EARL. "Study in Indigenous Religions." In Laymen's
Foreign Missions Inquiry Fact-Finding Reports. Edited by D.A. Petty.
Supplementary series, pt. 2, vol. 5, China. New York and London:
Harper, 1933, pp. 655-716.
    A study of thirteen cities during the Nationalist period (ca. 1930),
utilizing government statistics, field investigations, plus a few documentary sources. Divided into sections which report on Taoism, Buddhism,
and "Special Aspects" (meditation, literature, Buddhist college at
Wuchang, etc.); includes summaries of interviews with ten families. A
practically unique attempt to get objective factual information on organized religion at this period, and hence of great value, despite certain reservations one may have concerning the methodology employed.

(2) RAWLINSON, FRANK. Revolution and Religion in Modern China: A
Brief Study of the Effects of Modern Revolutionary Movements in China
on Its Religious Life. Shanghai: Presbyterian Mission Press, 1929,
97 pp.
    Objective account of the situation in China between 1911 and 1927,
with chapters on revolution and religion, the revolt against religion,
new ways in old faiths, new religious quests (i.e., new religions or
sects), and an international religious society (called "World Union of
Six Religions Society" and several other names), with a conclusion on
problems and values. Personal observations during the period by an
author fluent in Chinese. He was for many years editor of the prominent
missionary periodical, The Chinese Recorder.

1.12.1 Religion of the Intellectuals: Confucianism

        (1) CHAN, WING-TSIT. "What is Living and What is Dead in
        Confucianism?" In Religious Trends in Modern China (see
        1.1[3]), pp. 3-53.

The author believes that Confucianism as an institutional
religion is dead or dying, but Confucianism as a religious
philosophy will not disappear. He includes an assessment of
the religious position of Confucius by prominent scholars and
an exposition of the idealistic philosophy of Hsiung Shih-li
(1885-1968) and the rationalistic philosophy of Fung Yu-lan
(1895-); both philosophers exemplify the modern trend to ex-
pound Confucianism as a religious philosophy.

(2) JOHNSTON, REGINALD F. Confucianism and Modern China.
London: V. Gollancz, 1934, New York: Appleton-Century, 1935,
272 pp.
   The author believes that "Confucianism is still a living
force among the Chinese people." He attempts to look at the
subject from within, first discussing several short passages
from the canon as explained by an eminent contemporary Confucian
scholar, and then continuing with eleven more chapters on such
subjects as filial piety, ancestral cult, political loyalty,
and the question of whether Confucianism is a religion. As
to the last, he says, "I should be inclined to set aside the
question of whether it is a religion or not and call it a life."
The author was a long-time resident of China, held positions
enabling him to study his subject thoroughly, and was distinguished by an empathetic and cosmopolitan outlook remarkable
in his time. Good photographs.

(3) LANCASHIRE, DOUGLAS, ed. "Confucianism in the Twentieth
Century." In China and Its Place in the World. Auckland:
University of Auckland, 1967, pp. 26-42.
   One of a series of public lectures delivered at the University
of Auckland. The subject is concisely yet lucidly presented. A
brief historical view of the main features of Cunfucius' thought
is included.

(4) ROY, A.T. [The Fate of Confucianism since the Republic],
in Chung-Chi Journal: "Liang Shu-ming (1893-) and Hu Shih
(1891-1962) on the Intuitional Interpretation of Confucianism"
1(1962):139-57; "Confucianism and Social Change" 3 (1963):88-
104; "Attacks upon Confucianism in the 1911-1927 Period from
the Left: Ch'en Tu-hsiu" 4 (1964):10-26; "Attacks upon Confucianism in the 1911-1927 Period from a Taoist Lawyer: Wu Yu"
4 (1965):149-63, 5 (1965):69-78; "Liberal Re-evaluation of
Confucianism in the 1911-1927 Period: The Attempt to Distinguish between the True Teaching of Confucius and Later Accre-
tions and Misinterpretations, and the Gradual Reduction of
Confucianism to One School among Many" 6 (1966):79-100; "Confucian Thought in China in the 1930s: Ch'en Li-fu, His Theory
of the Universe and of the Significance of Man" (Pt. 1) 7

(1967):72-89, and "Application of His Theory to Social, Cultural, and Political Questions" (Pt. 2) 8 (1968):63-92; "The Background of the Confucian Dilemma in the Period 1927-1947" 9 (1970):182-201.
    These articles are based on primary sources, which they frequently quote, as well as a broad background of social, philosophical, and sinological study.

1.12.2 Religious Taoism

(1) BLOFELD, JOHN. The Secret and the Sublime: Taoist Mysteries and Magic. London: Allen & Unwin, 1973, 216 pp.
    Memoirs of an English Buddhist who spent many years of his religious quest in China and who also took a great interest in Taoism. The book covers all facets of Taoist religion, based on the personal observations of the writer as well as his knowledge of the culture and literature. He is highly empathetic and inclined to believe in much of Taoist teaching and practice. Written in a most interesting style, with grace and humor. The best introduction to Taoism of the twentieth century.

(2) GOULLART, PETER. The Monastery of Jade Mountain. London: John Murray, 1961, 189 pp.
    An autobiographical account of the author's experience as a converted Taoist who lived during most of his adult life in China. It includes discussions on the Taoist sects (primarily Cheng-i and Ch'üan-chen), conversations with priests, Taoist rituals and ceremonies, and pilgrimages to temples and sacred mountains. Although this book gives a lively account of modern Taoism, its philosophical discussion is superficial and naive. Contains sixteen pictures of temples and priests.

(3) SASO, MICHAEL. "The Taoist Tradition in Taiwan." China Quarterly 41 (Jan.-Mar. 1970):83-102.
    An informing and scholarly report on the three principal sects of Taoist priests in Taiwan. They are popularly called the Black-heads, the Red-heads, and the Little Taoists. Whereas the first two are considered orthodox, the third is viewed as heterodox. Its members practice the rituals of mediumship and climbing the "sword-ladder." The author is concerned primarily with the Black-heads, who are the priests of the Cheng-i ("Celestial Master") sect. A delineation of the Taoist canonical texts is also provided.

1.12.3   Folk Religion

(1) BRIM, JOHN A.   "Village Alliance Temples in Hong Kong."
In Religion and Ritual in Chinese Society (see 1.1[19]), pp.
93-103.
A study of the function of the village alliance temples in
the New Territories of Hong Kong.   The author demonstrates that
these temples are fully supported by the village alliance organizations because of their ritualistic benefits to the allied
villages.   These temples have helped to solve the alliance
system's "latency problems," i.e., "the maintenance over time
of the system's motivational and cultural patterns."

(2) EBERHARD, WOLFRAM.   "Religious Activities and Religious
Books in Modern China."   In Moral and Social Values of the
Chinese (see 1.1[5]), pp. 161-75.
A survey concerning the religious activities of the Chinese,
conducted by the author in 1964 in Taipei, to which one hundred
and eighty-five persons responded.   Among other things, the
survey reveals that the most popular god in Taiwan is Kuan-yin,
or Avalokiteśvara.

(3) GRAHAM, DAVID CROCKETT.   "Changes in Religion in West China."
In Folk Religion in Southwest China.   Washington: Smithsonian
Press, 1961, pp. 189-214.
Mainly an account of the conditions of temples in Chengtu,
capital of Szechuen province, and its neighboring towns, based
upon the surveys by the author and his team between 1920 and
1948.   These surveys show the rapid decline of temple upkeeing.
For example, in Chengtu there were two hundred and ten temples
in 1948.   Of these numbers, eighty-nine temples had no worship,
ninety-three temples had little worship, and only eleven temples were used for worship.   The same pattern prevailed in
other West China towns.

(4) GRANET, MARCEL.   "Religious Sentiment in Modern China."
In The Religion of the Chinese People (see 1.2.2[2]), pp.
144-56.
Chinese religious life at the popular level as observed by
the author in 1911-13.   Granet is acutely aware that it is
difficult to distinguish between the "sacred" and the "profane"
among the Chinese.   The religion of the Chinese is not so much
the belief in certain doctrines or even the acceptance of a
particular religion but the practice of the traditionally accepted pattern of life that is deemed proper and correct.

(5) HARRELL, C. STEVEN.   "When a Ghost Becomes a God."   In
Religion and Ritual in Chinese Society (see 1.1[19]), pp. 193-
206.

        1.12 Religion during and after the Republic Period

A field study in the southern Taipei Basin in modern Taiwan concerning the ambiguous relationship between ghosts and gods, particularly the process of transformation from the status of a ghost to that of a god. An essential distinction between these two is that a ghost harms and a god blesses people. A ghost may become a god in time, due to the change of its character from malevolence to that of benevolence. The chief condition for this change depends upon the efficacy of the supernatural being upon the villagers who worship him. There are other factors related to the history of the person who becomes a ghost that make the transition equivocal.

(6) JORDAN, DAVID K. Gods, Ghosts and Ancestors in a Hokkien-Speaking Village of Southwestern Taiwan. Berkeley: University of California Press, 1972, 192 pp.

Anthropologist's report of field work. The author focuses "on the tight relation between religious beliefs and practices on the one hand and social structure, particularly family and village structure, on the other." Much useful information on the folk religion of this particular community, and especially on the centrally important practices of divination. Nontechnical style.

(7) OSGOOD, CORNELIUS. Village Life in Old China: A Community Study of Kao Yao, Yunnan. New York: Ronald Press, 1963, pp. 276-87.

Based upon the author's field study in 1938, although not published until well after China had come under Communist control, this is one of only a small number of community studies from which we can get some specific information concerning local variations in religious institutions and practices on the mainland. The author is a well-known anthropologist, who is also gifted with the ability to write in an interesting style. There are a number of good photographs.

(8) OVERMYER, DANIEL L. "A Preliminary Study of the Tz'u-hui t'ang, a Contemporary Religious Sect on Taiwan." Society for the Study of Chinese Religions Bulletin 4 (Oct. 1977):19-40.

A field study of popular religious sect, Tz'u-hui t'ang, founded on Taiwan in 1949, which claims the Yao-ch'ih Chin-mu (Golden Mother of the Jasper Pool) as its chief deity and which is centered on planchette revelations. The author traces its history, beliefs and mythology, ecclesiastical organization, and sacred texts. Membership and geographical distribution of the sect are also discussed. Questions concerning the historical relationship between this sect and the popular sects in the Ming and Ch'ing periods are also raised. There are close similarities between the scriptures of the earlier sects and

those of the Tz'u-hui t'ang, but the earlier sectarian scriptures are not ascribed to the planchette. Also, the earlier
sects' eschatology was more future-oriented, whereas the
eschatology of Tz'u-hui t'ang is more oriented toward the
present through the practice of the planchette.

(9) PLOPPER, CLIFFORD H. Chinese Religion Seen Through the
Proverbs. New York: Paragon, 1969, 381 pp. (Orig. pub.
Shanghai: Shanghai Modern Publishing House, 1935.)
     An elucidation of the syncreticism of Taoism, Buddhism,
and Confucianism seen through the proverbs. But a sizable
number of these "proverbs" are quotes from the Chinese classics
and the Buddhist sutras. In spite of this limitation, the book
contains colloquial proverbs which reveal the religious and
spiritual ethos of the ordinary Chinese. More familiar gods,
myths, and rituals are explained along with the proverbs.

(10) TOBIAS, STEPHEN F. "Buddhism, Belonging and Detachment:
Some Paradoxes of Chinese Ethnicity in Thailand." Journal of
Asian Studies 36 (1977):303-25.
     This is a recent anthropological field study about the
Chinese who live in the town of Ayutthaya near Bangkok,
Thailand. It concerns the problem of synthesis between Chinese
ethnicity and Thai Buddhism. The anthropological materials
used in this paper are illustrative of the mutual acceptance
between the Thais and the local Chinese. The locus of the
study involves an investigation of the local Buddhist temple,
Wat Phanan Choeng, which is strictly Buddhistic for Thais.
But for the local Chinese, this temple has special Chinese
meaning which reflects the history of their immigrant ancestors
in Thailand. From the Chinese perspective, the chief Buddha
at the timple, Sam Pao Kong, is no other than Cheng Ho (1370-
1433), an eminent eunuch-ambassador-admiral who visited the
countries in South and Southeast Asia, including a stay in
Ayutthaya. There is a separate shrine at the temple, dedicated
to a Chinese princess who married a Thai king. Yet for the
Chinese community, this princess is none other than Bodhisattva
Kuan Yin, or Tz'u-pei Niang-niang (Compassionate Lady). Although these identifications are unacceptable to Thai Buddhism,
yet the Thais in Ayutthaya do not feel offended by them. The
author's field experience was attested to by Chinese and Thai
literary sources.

(11) TOPLEY, MARJORIE. "Cosmic Antagonism: A Mother-Child
Syndrome." In Religion and Ritual in Chinese Society (see
1.1[19]), pp. 233-49.
     Based on interviews with twenty illiterate mothers in Hong
Kong in 1969, the author discusses the problem of mother-child

conflicts due to the Chinese belief system with respect to the horoscope. Many times there are conflicts between the horoscopes of the mother and that of the newly born infant. Such conflicts often cause tension between mother and child, thus creating psychological and sociological problems in the family. Among the many solutions to this problem is the ritual of "bonding" whereby the child is "bonded" to an auspicious woman outside of the family as the "ritual mother" of the child. A perceptive essay depicting the prevalence of ritualism among the "tradition-bound" Chinese woman.

(12) TWINEM, P. de W. "Modern Syncretic Religious Societies." Journal of Religion 5 (1925):463-82, 595-606.
     Describes five societies of the early twentieth century. Brief, but based on personal investigations. Popular style.

(13) WANG SHIH-CH'ING. "Religious Organization in the History of a Taiwanese Town." In Religion and Ritual in Chinese Society (see 1.1[19]), pp. 71-92.
     A study of the inception and development of temples in the town of Shu-lin, west of Taipei. All the divinities who reside in them have their origin in southern China whence the immigrants came. The purpose of the essay is to demonstrate that there is a parallel development between the ethnic groups of the immigrants and the inception and growth of temples whose gods are the protectors of these ethnic groups. But the author also points out that, as the town becomes more established and its population increased, one ethnical god becomes the chief protector of the town, and his temple becomes its major temple. By serving all the communities in the town, this god becomes the god of the entire region rather than of a particular ethnic group. In the town of Shu-lin, Pao-sheng Ta-ti is its chief divinity, and his temple is called Chi-an Kung.

1.12.4 Religion of the Ethnic Groups

(1) GRAHAM, DAVID CROCKETT. "Religions of the Non-Chinese." In Folk Religion in Southwest China (see 1.12.3[3]), pp. 68-102. Illus.
     Based upon the author's years of personal contacts with the different ethnic groups in southwest China, particularly Szechuen province, this is an interesting description of the customs, material culture, religious beliefs, and practices of the following peoples: Ch'uan Miao, Lolo, Ch'iang, Tibetans.

1.13 RELIGION UNDER COMMUNISM

(1) BUSH, RICHARD C. Religion in Communist China. Nashville and New
York: Abingdon Press, 1970, 432 pp.
    This book deals with the policy of the government of the People's
Republic of China toward the institutional religions of China. Half
of the book involves the relationship between the state and the
Christian church; the other half contains a chapter each on Confucianism, Buddhism, folk religion/Taoism, and Islam. Information ends with
the Cultural Revolution. In the chapter on Taoism and folk religion,
the author identifies the Taoist religion with the folk religion of
China. Since 1950 the Communist cadres have been trying to modify the
traditional festivals in terms of the Socialist and revolutionary ideology. The author is convinced that Maoism is the "new religion" of
China today.

(2) CH'EN, KENNETH K.S. "Religious Changes in Communist China."
Chinese Culture 11 (1970):56-62.
    A brief summary of the fate of institutional religions in Communist
China up to the Cultural Revolution of 1966-68. Although it is mainly
concerned with Buddhism, it is applicable to other religions as well.

(3) FAURE, EDGAR. The Serpent and the Tortoise. Translated by Lovett
F. Edwards. New York: St. Martin's Press, 1963, pp. 129-56.
    Author visited the People's Republic in 1955. Chapter 15 contains
his remarks on the Catholic church and chapter 16 those on Islam,
Buddhism, and Taoism. These are rather superficial impressions, based
on not much more than his hasty observations and a few conversations.
He seems optimistic about the ability of the "cults" to survive and
function under Communism.

(4) HUANG, LUCY JEN. "The Role of Religion in Communist Chinese
Society." Asian Survey 11 (July 1971):693-708.
    A strictly functional analysis of the religious elements of Maosim,
particularly the Cultural Revolution of 1966-68. These elements include the adoration of Mao, Mao's works as the sacred writings, dog-
matic doctrinism, asceticism. The author views Maoism as an integrating
and symbolic force which has unified Chinese youths who would otherwise
have been "confused, insecure, and alienated." Nevertheless, this article is unsympathetic to Maoism, which is considered a sort of religious fundamentalism. It does not touch on the structural character
of Maoism (i.e., its mythological, ritual, and magical elements).

(5) MacINNIS, DONALD E., comp. Religious Policy and Practice in
Communist China. New York: Macmillan, 1972, 392 pp.
    This book is a collection of primary sources derived from the
Chinese newspapers and Party periodicals concerning the governmental
policy toward religions and theories about religion, religious reforms

under Communism, and criticisms of traditional religions. The materials concerning the new liturgical forms (marriage, funeral, etc.),
on pages 330-43, show the possible emergence of new forms of rituals
with political and social coloration. These new forms bear some
affinity with China's traditional rites.

(6) NEEDHAM, JOSEPH. "Christian Hope and Social Evolution." China
Notes 23 (Spring 1974):13-20.
      This explanation of why Maoism is a religion is based upon the
author's two-month visit to China in 1972. He thinks that "China is
the only truly Christian country at the present day, in spite of its
absolute rejection of all religions." Needham uses the concept of
"Kingdom of God" to defend his thesis, while pointing out that the
core of Maoism is Confucianism without its feudalistic and elitist
elements.

(7) YANG, C.K. "Communism as a New Faith." In Religion in Chinese
Society (see 1.1[20]), pp. 378-404.
      The author discusses Chinese Communism as a nontheistic faith seek-
ing control over the theistic religions of traditional China. Although
this chapter discusses the fate of all theistic religions, its conclusions are applicable to religious Taoism.

(8) YU, DAVID C. "Religious Continuities: China Past and Present."
China Notes 23 (Autumn 1974):41-43.
      An analysis of the continuity of religious thought between tradi-
tional China and Communist China, with emphasis on the relationship
of Chinese Communism to Confucianism and to Christianity.

2. Religious Thought

2.1 FOLK BELIEFS

2.1.1 Heaven (T'ien). Moral and Cosmic Consciousness of Heaven; Emperor's Mandate of Heaven, Man, and Nature; Celestial and Terrestrial Divinities as Subordinate to Heaven

(1) CHAN, WING-TSIT. "The Growth of Humanism"; "On Strange Phenomena and Fate." In A Source Book in Chinese Philosophy (see 1.4.2[1]), pp. 3-13; 303-4.
Chapter 1 embodies the earliest sources on Shang-ti (Ruler-above), T'ien, Mandate of Heaven, spirits, soul and immortality. It should be mentioned that although these documents are claimed to be pre-Confucian, in their present forms they were redacted by Confucian scholars between 300 and 100 B.C. and hence reflect the Confucian outlook. Pages 303-4 on strange phenomena and fate by Wang Ch'ung (27-100) represent the classic Confucian attitude toward the impersonality of Heaven and the acceptance of fate by man.

(2) FINAZZO, GIANCARLO. The Principle of T'ien: Essay on Its Theoretical Relevancy in Early Confucian Philosophy. Taipei: Mei Ya Publication Co., 1967, 161 pp.
A technical study by a philosopher on "the question of the principle as the foundation and the reason of Being" as found in the classical usage of certain terms, particularly t'ien. Somewhat technical but a careful attempt to arrive at meanings through the usage of terms.

(3) FORKE, A. The World-Conception of the Chinese. London: Probsthain, 1925, 300 pp.
Although this book is not an ideal treatment, it is still the only work in English that gives something of the same general survey of the basic ideas of Chinese worldview that has been more completely done in French by M. Granet (La pensée chinoise). Hence it is useful for understanding the generally shared theoretical background in all forms of Chinese religion. Not difficult reading.

(4) GERNET, JACQUES. "The Seasons and the Universe." In <u>Daily
Life in China on the Eve of the Mongol Invasion, 1250-1276</u>.
Translated by H.M. Wright. London: Allen & Unwin, 1962, pp.
179-218.
    The first half deals with festivals (New Year, Memorial Day,
Fifth Day of the Fifth Moon, Seventh Day of the Seventh Moon,
Antipestilence Day, All Saints Day, Festival of the Moon, etc.).
The second half deals with a) the orientation of Chinese re-
ligion, b) the official cult, c) family cult, d) Buddhism and
Taoism. With the exception of the last mentioned, all items
refer to the basic elements of Confucian religion. Gernet's
discussion is perceptive and thoroughly authentic.

(5) HSIANG, PAUL S. "Humanism in the Religious Thought of
Ancient China." <u>Chinese Culture</u> 10 (1969):13-21.
    In contrast to the opinions of many earlier Western scholars
who saw ancient Chinese religion as either monotheism or animism,
this author proposes the thesis that it was primarily humanistic,
"for it originated in the human interest or, in other words, in
man's concern for his own well-being and prosperity. God was
conceived as the Emperor Above, ruling the universe and maintaining the natural order, like the emperor below, governing
the terrestrial empire and working for the peace of this
world. . . . The ancient Chinese considered God as benevolent
father rather than a fearful ruler. . . ." An interpretive
essay rather than a contribution to knowledge.

(6) LEGGE, JAMES. <u>Notions of the Chinese Concerning God and
Spirits</u>. Hong Kong: Hong Kong Register Office, 1852, 166 pp.
Reprint. Taipei: Ch'eng Wen Publishing Co., 1971.
    An important document in the long-debated "term question"--
the problem of translating the terms God and spirit into Chinese.
An elaborate treatise by the most eminent English translator of
the nineteenth century, which in the course of the argument goes
minutely into Chinese religious ideas. A technical study, but
not unintelligible to nonspecialists.

(7) SCHINDLER, BRUNO. "Development of Chinese Conceptions of
Supreme Beings." <u>Asia Major</u>, Hirth Anniversary Volume, 1923,
298-366.
    Detailed philological investigation of ancient classical texts
with special attention given to identity of Shang-ti. Many
other deities discussed in passing. Author discusses opinions
of other Western sinologues. Written before the oracle bones
were excavated at Anyang, his conclusions are often question-
able. Karlgren later took him severely to task on philological
grounds as well. Too technical for nonspecialists.

(8) SHIH, JOSEPH. "Notions of God in the Ancient Chinese
Religion." Numen 16 (1969):99-138.
   An elaborate discussion of the different possible meanings
of various terms used in ancient China, based on a philological
method that is not quite critical enough to satisfy the sinologist. In the course of the argument, many aspects of religion
and philosophical thought are considered. The scholar may not
be convinced, but the article does carry on in a somewhat modern
fashion discussion of matters that have been of central importance in the studies of generations of early Western writers.
May be too specialized for students without some background.

2.1.2 Doctrine of Spirits: Kuei (demonic) and Shen (benign)

(1) CHANG, WING-TSIT. "Treatise on Death." In A Source Book
in Chinese Philosophy (see 1.4.2[1]), pp. 299-302.
   A translation of Wang Ch'ung's view on death, in which he
attacked belief in the existence of spirits.

(2) CREEL, HERRLEE G. Sinism: A Study of the Evolution of the
Chinese World View. Chicago: Open Court, 1929, 127 pp.
   This is an attempt to delineate the Chinese worldview prior
to the rise of Confucianism and Taoism. It discusses archaic
terms such as shen (spirits), kuei (demons), tao, Shang-ti
(ruler-above), and particularly the Five Elements (wu-hsing)
and yin-yang. The author would have corrected some interpretations if he had revised the book. For example, his view that
T'ien (Heaven) was the celestial counterpart of the earthly
king, which could not have been the case prior to Confucianism.
(See 1.4.1[2] for Creel's own reexamination of this work.)

(3) FEUCHTWANG, STEPHEN. "Domestic and Communal Worship in
Taiwan." In Religion and Ritual in Chinese Society (see 1.1[9]),
pp. 105-29.
   Based upon the study of the religious rituals in a town near
Taipei, the author proposes to explain the metaphorical meanings
of gods, ghosts, and ancestors. Gods are the system of authority; ghosts are strangers, beggars, or supplicants; and ancestors
are natives or insiders.

(4) GROOT, J.J.M. de. "Kuei-shen." In The Religious System of
China (see 1.2.1[3]) 6:934-39.
   A discussion of the nature of spirits by Wang Ch'ung (27-100),
in which he repudiated their existence in the literal sense.
His arguments show that belief in spirits was prevalent in his
day.

(5) WOLF, ARTHUR P.   "Gods, Ghosts, and Ancestors."   In <u>Religion</u> <u>and Ritual in Chinese Society</u> (see 1.1[19]), pp. 131-82.
  A detailed field study of the district of San-hsia near Taipei concerning the three categories of supernatural beings: gods, ghosts, and ancestors.   The author's thesis is that these three kinds of beings are the projections or extensions of three categories of humans: gods are bureaucrats who uphold public morality and execute justice; ghosts are strangers, wanderers, or bandits who harm people and disturb peace; and anecstors are relatives who look after the welfare of their descendants. Within these broad distinctions, the author brings out a big range of similarities and differences.   For example, the difference between ancestors and ghosts is one that depends on perspectives: for family A's ancestors are actually family B's ghosts.   The author also points out that the three components of the soul of the deceased correspond to the three roles of a Chinese: 1) that which goes to the courts of the underworld to be judged reflects his role as a citizen, 2) that which resides in the spirit-tablet reflects his role as a member of the family, and 3) that which resides in the grave reflects his role as a stranger in the world.   The author also challenges some well-established views concerning the ancestor cult, e.g., the Chinese only offer sacrifices to ancestors who have produced descendants, or ancestors do not punish their offspring.   This is a stimulating anthropological paper on contemporary Taiwan.

2.1.3   <u>Doctrine of Soul</u>

(1) BODDE, DERK.   "The Chinese View of Immortality: Its Expression by Chu Hsi and Its Relationship to Buddhist Thought." <u>Review of Religion</u> 6 (1942):371-83.
  A critical survey of the conception of immortality in the history of Chinese philosophy, centered around the neo-Confucianist Chu Hsi (1130-1200).   The author points out that Chu Hsi, like other Chinese thinkers, rejects immortality as the survival of the personal soul.   Chu Hsi believes that Principle (<u>Li</u>), being nonmaterial and universal, is eternal.   When the Principle is embodied in man, it is called Nature (<u>hsing</u>).   But when man dies, the Nature he once possessed returns to its incorporeal status.   In the time of Chu Hsi, popular Buddhism included beliefs in the immortality of the soul (<u>shih-shen</u>), i.e., the perpetual transformation of the soul.   Chu Hsi repudiated this belief.   As the author points out, more sophisticated Buddhists did not believe in the immortality of the soul, and Chu Hsi's neglect to investigate Buddhism at a higher level has resulted in a rather superficial criticism.

(2) GROOT, J.J.M. de. The Religious System of China (see
1.2.1[3]). Vols. 4-6, On the Soul and Ancestral Worship.
    Although these volumes deal with the soul and ancestral wor-
ship, the title is misleading in so far as the contents are concerned; De Groot does not describe ancestor worship directly
and deals with the doctrine of the soul only in volume 4. The
reason the author refers to these volumes as a description of
the soul is because he identifies the meaning of soul with
"animism," i.e., the view that everything has a "soul." Hence
practically all Chinese religious phenomena are viewed as expressions of animism. Topics included are a) soul as yin-yang,
or hun-p'o (the spiritual and physical components of the soul),
b) transmigration of souls, c) demons and spiritual beings,
d) sorcery, and e) shamanism.

(3) HU SHIH. "The Concept of Immortality in Chinese Thought."
Harvard Divinity School Bulletin 43 (March 1946):23-42.
    A historical survey of the belief in life hereafter from the
Shang (c. 1751-1112 B.C.) and Chou (c. 1111-221 B.C.) dynasties
to the present. It shows that whereas the Chinese masses did
believe in the existence of the soul after death, scholars
tended to reject this belief. The scholar class believed in
the immortality of a) virtuous deeds, b) achievements, c) written words. Hu calls this the immortality of the "Three W's":
worth, work, words. This article ignores the importance of the
popular belief in life after death and its effects upon the
Chinese folk religion and society.

(4) LIEBENTHAL, WALTER. "Immortality of the Soul in Chinese
Thought." Monumenta Nipponica 8 (1952):80-122.
    Translation, with introduction, of materials found in Hung-
ming chi [Buddhist studies], ca. A.D. 515, and Kuang hung-ming
chi [Sequel to Buddhist studies], A.D. 664, which concern lengthy
debate on the immortality of the soul. The disputants, according to the author's opinion, were "members of the gentry of more
or less Buddhist or Taoist inclinations." The purpose of the
article is not only "to clarify the character of the debates"
but also "to clarify the position of Buddhism in the society of
the early centuries."

(5) SMITH, D. HOWARD. "Chinese Concepts of Soul." Numen 5
(1958):165-79.
    A study of the genesis and development of the notion of the
soul in early China. The earliest view of soul was understood
as kuei, the part of the corpse that lives on the earth after
man dies. This view was based on de Groot's statement: "In
the oldest works we have, the Kuei is represented to be that
part of the soul which returns with the corpse to the earth,

and that the belief that the soul resides there with the body
after death must have prevailed long before civilization could
possibly bring the people to the invention of profound theories
about a dualistic character of the soul." In short, the com-
posite view of soul (hun-p'o, the spiritual and physical components of soul) was a later development of the late Chou period.

(6) _____. "On Soul." In Chinese Religions (see 1.1[12]),
pp. 88-91.
    Explanations based upon the Book of Rites (Li-chi) on the
meaning of soul (hun-p'o).

2.1.4 Doctrine of Rite (Sacrifices)

(1) FEHL, NOAH EDWARD. "Li and Hsün Tzu." In Rites and
Propriety in Literature and Life (see 1.2.4[2]), pp. 151-222.
    A critical discussion of the meaning of li in the writings
of Hsün Tzu. Li is conceived of as the principle of learning,
of natural and moral law, and of affection and reason. Profuse
Western parallels with li are furnished by the author for the
purpose of comparison.

(2) FINGARETTE, HERBERT. Confucius: The Secular as Sacred.
New York: Harper Torchbook, 1972, 166 pp.
    A perceptive and stimulating interpretation of the meaning
of li to Confucius: "It is thus in the meaning of ceremony
that the peculiarly human part of our life is lived. The ceremonial act is the primary, irreducible event."

(3) _____. "Human Community as Holy Rite." Harvard Theological
Review 59 (1966):53-67.
    An article that later became one of the chapters in Confucius
(2).

(4) NEWELL, WILLIAM H. "Sociology of Ritual in Early China."
Sociological Bulletin 6 (1957):1-13.
    "From the earliest period of Chinese history, there has been
a clear distinction between ritual and religion. . . . Ritual
does not become so much a means of influencing the gods but of
so organizing society (of which the gods are a part) that the
dualistic universe will be rightly ordered. The discussion (of
the ancient thinkers) centers around the meaning of the phrase
'rightly ordered.'" The article then characterizes these discussions by what Newell calls the "sociological theorists,"
i.e., the major philosophers of the late Chou period. A nontechnical, if somewhat academic, type of writing.

(5) SMITH, D. HOWARD. "Further Religious Developments in pre-
Han China." In Chinese Religions (see 1.1[2]), pp. 78-93.
    The greater part of the chapter deals with a discussion of
li based upon the Book of Rites.

2.1.5 Ancestor Cult. See 1.2.5, Ancestor Cult and Divination

2.1.6 Geomancy (feng-shui): Its Relation to the Theories of Yin-Yang
and the Five Elements

Geomancy was universally practiced in traditional China, not
limited to Taoism.

(1) DORÉ, HENRI. "Feng-shui." In Researches into Chinese
Superstitions. Vol. 4, translated by M. Kennelly. Taipei:
Ch'eng-wen Publishing Co., 1966, pp. 402-14. (Orig. pub.
Shanghai: T'uswei Printing Press, 1914.)
    Contains information mostly derived from de Groot's work.
These pages also furnish arguments against geomancy by the
Confucian rationalists. However, much against his liking, Doré
found that by and large the leading Confucians supported the
feng-shui system. Doré is a highly opinionated author. The
reader should distinguish the sources Doré is describing from
his judgments upon these sources.

(2) EITEL, ERNEST J. Feng-shui, or the Rudiments of Natural
Science in China. London: Trubner & Co., 1873, 84 pp. Reprint. Bristol: Pentade Books, 1974.
    Still the only book-length treatment of the subject in
English. Eitel was a distinguished sinologist of the nineteenth
century who knew his subject well. His view of feng-shui as
"natural science" contrasts with that of Freedman (3), who views
it more as a ritualistic technique of divination. Easy-to-
understand style.

(3) FREEDMAN, MAURICE. "Geomancy." In Proceedings of the Royal
Anthropological Institute of Great Britain and Ireland for 1968.
London: Royal Anthropological Institute of Great Britain and
Ireland, 1968, pp. 5-15.
    A stimulating discussion of feng-shui by a leading British
anthropologist. He calls it "mystical ecology," and speaks of
"the ritual aspect of the interaction between men and their
physical environment. . . ." Includes a good bibliography.
Written in the best English style, literate and witty.

(4) GRAHAM, DAVID CROCKETT. "Yin-yang and Feng-shui." In Folk
Religion in Southwest China (see 1.12.3[3]), pp. 110-19.

Contains the author's observations on the influence of
geomancy in the cities where he lived in Szechuen. Graham
attributes geomancy to the concept of "mysterious potency,"
called <u>ling</u>, <u>shen</u>, or <u>ch'i</u> in Chinese. He believed that these
terms are equivalent to the concept of <u>mana</u> in primitive religion.

(5) GROOT, J.J.M. de. "Feng-shui." In <u>The Religious System
of China</u> (see 1.2.1[3]) 4:935–1056.
    A scholarly presentation of the "winds and waters" tradition,
showing that the root of <u>feng-shui</u> is in the concepts of yin-
yang and the Five Elements and that many of the <u>feng-shui</u> principles regarding construction, burial, topography, etc. are
derived from the <u>I-ching</u> [Book of changes].

(6) MARCH, ANDREW L. "An Appreciation of Chinese Geomancy."
<u>Journal of Asian Studies</u> 27 (Feb. 1968):253–67.
    A study of <u>feng-shui</u> (geomancy) from both the historical and
interpretative points of view, based on Chinese documents.
Geomancy as practice began in the Han period (206 B.C.–A.D. 220)
and flourished in the later Han (23–220). The author believes
that geomancy should not be understood in terms of causality
but in terms of "synchronicity," that improbable meaningful
coincidences can occur and that psychological and subjective
meanings are also a part of the natural world. In essence,
the demand for geomancy is due to human needs and its abstract
constructs are secondary.

(7) NEEDHAM, JOSEPH. "Geomancy." In <u>Science and Civilisation
in China</u>. Vol. 2, <u>History of Scientific Thought</u>. Cambridge:
Cambridge University Press, 1956, pp. 359–63.
    Needham points out that although much of geomancy involved
superstitions, it was coincident with an aesthetic concern for
the preservation of landscapes in their original setting. He
also reminds us that it was from the geomancer's board, used
for surveying land, that the magnetic compass was developed.

(8) POTTER, JACK. "Wind, Water, Bones, and Souls: The Religious
World of the Cantonese Peasant." In <u>The Chinese Way in Religion</u>
(see 1.1[15]), pp. 218–30.
    An anthropological study of geomancy as practiced by vil-
lagers of Ping Shan in the New Territories of Hong Kong. Although the article is informative, it has some cognitive flaws.
The author identifies the yang force as the <u>mana</u> of primitive
religion. On the other hand, he tells us that in the geomantic
situation, the yang and yin forces are inseparable. The article
implies that the yin force is bad and undesirable, which is certainly not the case in Chinese geomancy. He also views the

feng-shui (geomancy) as mana rather than as a body of knowledge
known to the geomantic expert.

2.1.7 Occultism: Divination, Exorcism, Planchette ("fu-chi"), Faith-healing

(1) ARLINGTON, L.C. "Chinese versus Western Chiromancy."
China Journal 7 (1927):228-35; 8 (1928):67-76.
  The author is apparently a sincere believer in the scientific
value of chiromancy (as well as physiognomy), but deplores the
fact that the Chinese "have departed from its purely scientific
aspects into a bewitching maze of crude humbug." The article
is based upon wide knowledge of Chinese documentary sources.
In the final section, the author attempts "to prove or disprove
certain signs as recorded by the Chinese chiromancers."

(2) BODDE, DERK. "The Chinese Cosmic Magic." In Studia Serica
Bernhard Karlgren Dedicata. Copenhagen: Ejnar Munksgaard, 1959,
pp. 14-35.
  The practice of "watching for the ethers" involved burying
twelve pitch pipes in a special room. The ends were left un-
covered, and the pipes were filled with fine ashes. At the
moment the yin or yang ch'i of each month arrived, this change
in the atmosphere was supposed to cause the ashes to be blown
out of the appropriate pitch pipe. The theory behind it was
developed in early Han times, and the author traces notices of
the practice through later periods. The rituals connected with
it were supposed to ensure continuing harmony between the natural and human worlds.

(3) _____. "Sexual Sympathetic Magic in Han China." History of
Religions 2 (Winter 1964):292-99.
  An explanation of why the "keng-tzu" day (the 37th day) of
the sixty-day cycle is a propitious day for sexual intercourse
between husbands and wives for the purpose of procreation. According to Tung Chung-shu (179-104 B.C.), the reason for this
is an appeal to "sympathetic magic" on the basis of word plays:
a homophone of keng (again), and a homophone of tzu (to engender).
Therefore, keng-tzu means "may we again engender."

(4) CHAO WEI-PANG. "Origin and Growth of the Fu-chi." Folklore
Studies 1 (1942):9-27.
  Analyzes the connection between definition by planchette (in
China originally using a sieve and later a forked stick) and
the goddess Tzu-ku, using literary documents. Some enthno-
graphical comparisons with other cultures. An interesting and
perceptive study.

(5) CH'EN HSIANG-CH'UN. "Examples of Charm against Epidemics, with Short Explanations." Folklore Studies 1 (1942):37-42.
  The author points out that the inscriptions on charms are even more difficult to read than those on the oracle bones and bronze; only professional magicians can give the true explanations. Fifteen charms are reproduced together with commentary about the literary sources and the purpose of the charm along with analysis of the writing and a full reading of the text. This will be most useful to students who have some background in the Chinese writing system.

(6) COMBER, LEON. Chinese Magic and Superstitions in Malaya. Singapore: Donald Moore, 1957, 80 pp.
  One of a series of small books by a former Chinese Affairs officer in Malaya, intended for the lay public. The variegated contents include brief chapters on such subjects as the creation myth, the Book of Changes (I-ching), the Chinese zodiac, symbols, charms, etc. Good illustrations. Shows persistence and modifications of Chinese tradition in overseas communications.

(7) DORÉ, HENRI. "Fortune-telling, Divination, Omens, Geomancy." In Researches into Chinese Superstitions (see 2.1.6[1]). Vol. 4, translated by M. Kennelly, pp. 231-462.
  A description of different kinds of divination: fortune-telling, physiognomy, "coin-method," "six-characters," lots-casting, casting-halves, dissecting characters.

(8) FENG HAN-YI, and SHRYOCK, JOHN K. "Black Magic in China Known as Ku." Journal of the American Oriental Society 55 (1935):1-30.
  "The method is to place poisonous snakes and insects together in a vessel until there is but one survivor, which is called the ku. The poison secured from this ku is administered to the victim, who becomes sick and dies. The ideas associated with ku vary, but the ku is generally regarded as a spirit, which secures the wealth of the victim for the sorcerer." The authors search ancient literature, gazetteers, and other literary sources for evidences of the practice, which "appears to be a connecting link between Chinese culture and the cultures of Southeastern Asia." The article is written in an interesting, nontechnical style.

(9) FRICK, J. "How Blood Is Used in Magic and Medicine." Anthropos 46 (1951):964-79.
  Based on the author's personal observations in a remote corner of the country. He discusses blood as a magic charm, blood as a medicinal cure, and blood in the Chinese pharmocopaeia. Important ethnographical data. Nontechnical style.

(10) _____ . "Magic Remedies Used on Sick Children." <u>Anthropos</u>
46 (1951):175-86.
   A detailed account of the author's personal observations.
Contents include brief sections on: encounter of a child with
a spirit, when the "Five-Way-Spirits" have molested a child,
when a ghost has defiled a child, healing a child by the burial
of an earthen vessel, etc. Important ethnographical data on
popular religion in a little-studied area of China. Nontechnical style.

(11) FUNG YU-LAN. "Philosophical Thought Prior to Confucius."
In <u>A History of Chinese Philosophy</u>. Translated by Derk Bodde.
2 vols. Princeton: Princeton University Press 1:22-42.
   A discussion of the six arts of divination before the time
of Confucius: a) astrology, b) almanacs, c) Five Elements,
d) stalks of plant and tortoise shell related to divination,
e) miscellaneous divinations, f) "system of forms," referring
to statements on constructions and the analysis of omens.

(12) GROOT, J.J.M. de. <u>The Religious System of China</u> (see
1.2.1[3]) 6:928-1341.
   The entire volume is about the use of charms for exorcism or
healing. Charms are mostly in the form of paper slips with
standard sacred inscriptions. The last section of the volume
deals with shamanistic Taoists, who were the professional exorcists (<u>wu</u>). Planchette or spirit-writing is also described in
Chapter 5.

(13) GULIK, R.H. van. "The Mango 'Trick' in China." <u>Transactions
of the Asiatic Society of Japan</u>, 3d ser. 3 (1954):117-75.
   In studying three examples of variations on the mango trick
(making a tree grow from a seed before the very eyes of the spec-
tators), the author traces many fascinating aspects of Taoist
magic in Chinese history. There is an especially lengthy treatment of the Eight Immortals, and of the connection of Han Yü, a
famous T'ang scholar, with one of them who was purported to be
his nephew (Han-hsiang tzu). Will be of interest especially to
students of Chinese history and culture.

(14) LESSA, WILLIAM. <u>Chinese Body Divination</u>. Los Angeles:
University of California Press, 1968, 220 pp.
   Only full-scale work on this subject in English, written by
an anthropologist. Has extended treatment of theory as well as
practice, relating these forms of divination to the general
principles of the Chinese worldview. Illustrations from
Chinese texts. Detailed and somewhat technical, but not for-
bidding.

2. Religious Thought

(15) POTTER, JACK M. "Cantonese Shamanism." In Religion and Ritual in Chinese Society (see 1.1[19]), pp. 207-31.
    A field study in the eight villages in Hong Kong's New Territories in the 1960s. It concerns the three female spirit mediums who are the professional shamanesses of the villages. The author proposes that these mediums control the dark side of the community through whom the personal tragedies of the villagers are disclosed and made public. The ghosts of tragic persons, often young women, speak of their grievances through these spirit mediums. In this way, the wrongs done to these unfortunate persons can be partially remedied through rituals and sacrifices on the part of the living.

(16) WARE, JAMES R. "Into Mountains: Over Streams." In Alchemy, Medicine, Religion in China of A.D. 320: The Nei P'ien of Ko Hung (Pao-p'u tzu) (see 1.8.2[3]), pp. 279-300.
    A description of a collection of charms in the form of scriptures, mirrors, prayers, and sacred objects. These charms are used to subdue the mountain spirits while the adept is travelling. Ritual steps are also mentioned.

(17) WELCH, HOLMES. "The Bellagio Conference on Taoist Studies." History of Religions 9 (Nov. 1969 and Feb. 1970):107-36.
    A report on the symposium on Taoist studies held at Bellagio, Italy, in September 1968. The discussion touched upon the following topics: relationships between philosophical Taoism and religious Taoism, relationships between science and Taoism, Taoist alchemy, Taoist canon, Taoist temples in Taiwan, translations of Taoist texts and Taoist researches at the present, and the differences between the T'ien-shih Tao and the Mao-shan Tao.

2.1.8 Sacred Animals, Trees, Plants

(1) DORÉ, HENRI. Researches into Chinese Superstitions (see 2.1.6[1]). Vol. 5, translated by M. Kennelly, pp. 657-734.
    Contains special references to the unicorn, phoenix, tortoise, and dragon. Other sacred animals and plants are the carp, crane, cock, stag, bat, peach, lotus, pine, jujube, bamboo, plum, willow, and yarrow.

(2) GRAHAM, DAVID CROCKETT. "Tree Gods in Szechwan Province." Journal of the West China Border Research Society 8 (1936):59-61.
    "The worship of trees is often seen in Szechwan, especially in sacred places such as Mt. Omei, Wa Shan, and the Yellow Dragon Gorge. . . . in the following instances the worshippers

and others definitely affirmed that the trees were gods, and
denied that worship was rendered because some spirits of gods
were living in the trees." A brief note citing instances personally observed by the author.

(3) LI WEI-TSU. "On the Cult of the Four Sacred Animals (<u>szu
ta men</u>) in the Neighborhood of Peking." <u>Folklore Studies</u> 7
(1948):1-94.
    The animals are fox, weasel, hedgehog, and snake. "The be-
lief in these four animals as sacred is very widespread amongst
the rural population in the Peking area." After a detailed discussion of the sacred forms and characteristics of these animals,
the author takes up the subject of magicians (<u>hsiang-t'ou</u>) as a
social institution: such magicians serve the family, or the
spirit, of a sacred animal, by means of which they can cure,
tell fortunes, etc. Should be read in conjunction with the
article by Owen, "Animal Worship Among the Chinese" (5).

(4) LING SHUN-SHENG. "Turtle Sacrifice in Ancient China."
<u>Academia Sinica, Bulletin of the Institute of Ethnology</u> (Taipei)
31 (1971):41-46 (English abridgement).
    Traces the use of turtles in sacrifice back into archaic
times (as indicated by evidence of Yin oracle bones). The turtle was one of the "four supernatural creatures" (the others
being unicorn, phoenix, and dragon), and it was valued especially for its divinatory power. The author traces many connections with turtle worship in the Pacific island region, as well
as on Taiwan itself, where today cakes in the shape of a turtle,
colored red, are commonly used in festivals and on other auspicious occasions. Unfortunately, there is only a summary in
English.

(5) OWEN, G. "Animal Worship Among the Chinese." <u>Chinese
Recorder</u> 18 (1887):249-55, 334-46.
    The "four intelligent animals" are the dragon, unicorn,
phoenix, and tortoise. The "five poisonous creatures" are
snakes, centipedes, scorpions, lizards, and toads. But most of
the article deals with five "common and very insignificant animals which have attained the dignity and importance of popular
gods. Their pictures hang in thousands of homes and are daily
honoured with incense, offerings and prostrations." These five
animals are the fox, weasel, hedgehog, snake, and rat. Author
discusses Taoist ideas underlying these cults and possession by
the spirits of these animals. This article should be consulted
in conjunction with that of Li Wei-tsu, "On the cult of the four
sacred animals in the neighborhood of Peking" (3).

(6) VISSER, M.W. de. <u>Dragon in China and Japan</u>. Amsterdam: Akademie van Wetenschappen te Amsterdam, 1913, 242 pp. Reprint. Weisbaden: M. Sändig, 1969.

The most thorough study of this basic Chinese symbol in English. The author identifies the dragon with the Indian, and especially the Buddhist <u>naga</u>. Quoting from the Chinese classics, the author discusses divination and geomancy, symbolism in ornaments, the connections of dragons with imperial symbolism, the transformations of the dragon and its function as causer of rain, thunder, and storm, and miscellaneous topics relevant to the subject. Chinese characters are provided. This is an interesting book, written in a nontechnical style, although some acquaintance with Chinese studies will be helpful to the reader.

(7) WATERBURY, FLORANCE. <u>Bird-Deities in China</u>. Ascona, Switz.: Antibus Asiae, 1952, 191 pp.

A book in five chapters. The first is on "the pervasiveness of animal-worship and the concept of the soul." The second deals with "some representations of anthropomorphized bird-forms" in the paleolithic, neolithic, and bronze ages. The third takes up "the widespread belief in a connection between birds and the spirit-world." The fourth discusses China through the Six Dynasties, and the fifth discusses "two representations of bird-deities from Christian churches of the European peninsula." This is an important (necessarily speculative) study in comparative religious symbolism centering on China. Illustrated with sixty-one plates.

2.1.9 <u>Pantheon</u>

(1) ALEXEIEV, BASIL. <u>Chinese Gods of Wealth</u>. Hertford, England: School of Oriental and African Studies; S. Austin & Sons, 1928, 36 pp., 24 plates.

Originally a lecture, then expanded to make a small book, the study deals with iconography and symbolism of this universal Chinese cult. Illustrated with twenty-four annotated plates.

(2) DAY, CLARENCE B. <u>Chinese Peasant Cults</u>. Taipei: Ch'eng Wen, 1969, 243 pp. (Orig. pub. Shanghai: Kelly & Walsh, 1946.)

A description of popular Chinese paper gods used for family worship. These consist of images and inscriptions engraved on papers. They were popular in rural China.

(3) DAY, CLARENCE. "The Cult of the Hearth." <u>China Journal</u> 10 (1929):6-11.

Interesting account of the author's visit to a peasant home near Hangchow on New Year's Eve to observe Kitchen God's rites.

Discusses the cult as found in some other areas as well. Illustrated with several pictures of paper gods.

(4) DORÉ, HENRI. Researches into Chinese Superstitions (see
2.1.6[1]). Vol. 6, translated by M. Kennelly, 233 pp.; vol. 9,
translated by D.J. Finn, 227 pp.
     Volume 6 describes the Three Pure Ones (San-ch'ing), the
Three Rulers (San-kuan), gods of literature (Wen-ch'ang and
Ku'ei-shing), and Kuan-ti. Doré mistakenly considers Kuan-ti
(Lord Kuan) a god of war. Actually, Kuan-ti is a protector-god
who delivers man from disasters and plagues. Volume 9 discusses
Yuan-shih T'ien-tsun (Lord of the Original Emperor), the Eight
Immortals, the Taoist temple guardian, and the deified Taoist
sages.

(5) FENG HAN-CHI. "The Origin of Yü-huang." Harvard Journal
of Asiatic Studies 1 (1936):242-50.
     The author repudiates the view of Western scholars (Weiger,
Doré, etc.) that the worship of the Jade Emperor began with
Emperor Chen-tsung (998-1022) of the Sung dynasty. On the basis
of documental evidence, Feng points out that the worship of this
popular divinity began in the eighth or ninth century and that
its genesis probably goes back several centuries earlier.

(6) KOEHN, ALFRED. "Harbingers of Happiness, the Door Gods of
China." Monumenta Nipponica 10 (1954):81-106.
     A light discussion of some popular deities as they are repre-
sented on ma-chang or chih-ma, i.e., cheap paper prints. Sample
prints are reproduced in black and white.

(7) THOMPSON, LAURENCE G. "The Community: Gods and Temples."
In Chinese Religion: An Introduction (see 1.1[14]), pp. 54-64.
     A description of divinities of Chinese folk religion in
Taiwan. Whereas not all of them are Taoistic, most of them are
related to the Taoist religion.

(8) WELCH, HOLMES H. "Taoist pantheon." In The Parting of the
Way (see 1.2.8[2]), pp. 135-41.
     Presents the prominent Taoist divinities: The Three Pure
Ones headed by the Lord of the Original Beginning (Yuan-shih
T'ien-tsun), Jade Emperor (Yü-huang), Queen of the West (Hsi-
wang mu), Lord Kuan (Kuan-ti), gods of moats and walls, gods
of the hearth, etc.

2.1.10 Authors on Folk Religion

(1) FREEDMAN, MAURICE. "Marcel Granet, 1884-1940, Sociologist."
In The Religion of the Chinese People (see 1.2.2[2]), pp. 1-29.
    An essay on the career of Granet as a sociologist of Chinese
religion and as a disciple of Durkheim.

(2) YU, DAVID C. "Chinese Folk Religion." History of Religions
12 (May 1973):378-87.
    A review of de Groot's The Religious Systems of China (see
1.2.1[3]) and Doré's Researches into Chinese Superstitions (see
2.1.6[1]). Whereas the interpretative schemes of both works
are repudiated, the factual data presented in them are viewed
as being useful for the theoretical understanding of Chinese
folk religion.

2.2 CONFUCIUS (551-479 B.C.) AND THE CONFUCIAN CULT

    See also 1.5, The Cult of Confucius

(1) The Analects of Confucius. Translated by Arthur Waley. London:
Allen & Unwin, 1938, 268 pp. Paperback reprint. New York: Random
House, Vintage Books, 1966.
    A collection of the "sayings" of Confucius as he was understood by
the Confucians of the late fourth century B.C. when the book was compiled. It was the intent of the translator to present the Confucius
of the Analects as he was actually depicted without being influenced
by the late commentators, particularly Chu Hsi (1130-1200). Waley's
explanations of terms are very useful: they prepare the reader to
enter into the atmosphere of China of the fourth century B.C. Most
of the terms are related to Chinese religion.

(2) CREEL, H.G. "Was Confucius Agnostic?" T'oung Pao 29 (1932):55-59.
    "The purpose of this paper is rather to offer some indication of the
inadequacy of the evidence underlying the current assumption of Confucian
agnosticism than to give an exposition of the religion of Confucius. . . .
It is, in fact, impossible to understand Confucius unless one recognizes
that for him, as surely as for the priests and prophets of Israel, ethics, politics, and the whole of life were inseparable from their cosmic
and religious background." The argument proceeds in careful philological style.

(3) De BARY, W. THEODORE; CHAN, WING-TSIT; and WATSON, BURTON, comps.
Sources of Chinese Tradition (see 1.4.1[3]), pp. 245-48.
    Two accounts of the miraculous birth of Confucius from the apocry-
phal literature.

(4) DUBS, HOMER. "Theism and Naturalism in Ancient Chinese Philosophy."
Philosophy East and West 9 (1959-60):163-72.
   The traditional picture of Confucius was formed in the Han period
and under the influence of Hsün Tzu's ideas. Hence he is made out to
be a naturalistic thinker rather than a theistic thinker. This essay
attempts to show that Confucius actually "carried the Duke of Jou's
theological teaching to its logical monotheistic conclusion. Monotheism is quite in harmony with Confucius' high ethics and his insist-
ence upon the highest of ideals."

(5) JASPERS, KARL. "Confucius." In Socrates, Buddha, Confucius, Jesus.
New York: Harvest, 1957, pp. 41-63.
   Places Confucius as one of the four "paradigmatic individuals" of
all human history. A brief but good summary of the Master's life,
teaching, and significance. Originally part of the eminent author's
history of world philosophy.

(6) KAIZUKA SHIGEKI. Confucius. Translated by Geoffrey Bownas.
London and New York: Macmillan, 1956, 192 pp.
   A short book by a leading Japanese scholar. In five chapters he
discusses the milieu, the early days, the Master's relationship to his
predecessors, his views, and his statesmanship. These are followed by
a concluding section on his death. The main contribution of the work
is to explain in some detail the social and political setting for the
formation of the thought of Confucius. May be somewhat technical for
students without background in Chinese history.

(7) LIU WU-CHI. Confucius: His Life and Time. New York: Philosophical
Library, 1955, 189 pp.
   "The first aim of my book is . . . to rediscover the historical K'ung
Ch'iu as he lived in those dark, restless days of decaying feudalism.
I have also endeavored to present the human K'ung Ch'iu. . . ." This
is a popular-style biography based on the traditional account of Ssu-
ma Ch'ien, with a liberal dash of the author's literary imagination.
The bibliography given is almost entirely Western, although the author
also used Chinese classics in the original. This treatment pays due
attention to the teachings of the Master; the author finds him no revolutionary as does Creel, but rather a "champion of feudal ideas." Best
read along with Creel's study "Was Confucius Agnostic?" (2) for scholarly balance.

(8) McCASLAND, S. VERNON; CAIRNS, GRACE E.; and YU, DAVID C.
"Confucius." In Religions of the World (see 1.1[10]), pp. 613-25.
   A summary of Confucius's views on man, propriety, education, govern-
ment, tao, and religion.

(9) MUNRO, DONALD J. "The Confucian Concept of Man." In The Concept
of Man in Early China. Stanford: Stanford University Press, 1969, pp.
49-83.

2. *Religious Thought*

Based on the view that the early Chinese concept of man--both
Confucian and Taoist--is founded upon man's natural equality, the
author proceeds to demonstrate that the natural equality in Confucianism refers to the evaluating mind man is endowed with at birth. Once
men are born with minds, however, they vary in morality and worldly
achievements because they differ in the applications of their individual minds. The evaluating mind is the human nature, which has its beginning, according to Mencius, in man's innate feelings of commisera-
tion, reverence and respect, shame and dislike, and approving and
disapproving. The author also persuasively points out that there is
basic agreement between Mencius and Hsün Tzu concerning human nature.
The prevalent view that Hsün Tzu attributes an evil nature to man represents the later commentators' misinterpretation of Hsün Tzu. The entire
book is stimulating; it also compares the Chinese view of human nature
with the classical Greek view.

(10) SMITH, D. HOWARD. "The Significance of Confucius for Religion."
In Chinese Religions (see 1.1[12]), pp. 32-44.
     The author points out the religious aspects of Confucius: T'ien
(Heaven), mandate of Heaven, tao, ritual, and benevolence (jen).
Smith feels that, giving religion a broader meaning, Confucius was
profoundly religious. However, the author's understanding of T'ien
as the supreme deity in the monotheistic sense (chap. 2) reflects his
own Judeo-Christian assumptions which were unknown to Confucius.

(11) TAKEUCHI TERUO. "Study of the Meaning of Jen Advocated by
Confucius." Acta Asiatica 9 (1965):57-77.
     Using the Analects as his source, the author finds that the impor-
tant term jen was used to express two different meanings: "humane or
sympathetic," and admiration for someone's "heroic personality or
superior individuality." He then attempts to trace the meaning from
usage in the Shih [Book of songs] and Shu [Book of history].

(12) WILHELM, RICHARD. Confucius and Confucianism. Translated by
George H. Danton and Annina Danton. New York and London: Harcourt,
Brace, & Co., 1931, pp. 3-95. Reprint. Port Washington, N.Y.:
Kennikat Press, 1970.
     The author is a well-known sinologist of the first half of the
twentieth century, a missionary who became converted, so to speak, to
Chinese culture (as evidenced by his famous translation of the I-ching).
This short book contains his translation (in English versions by the
Dantons) of the first biography of Confucius, by Ssu-ma Ch'ien, dis-
cussions of the life and teachings of the Master, and samples of
Confucian texts of the ancient period. A sound source for approaching
the subject, not as text-critical as the work of Creel, but with suf-
ficient modern critical judgment.

2.3 MENCIUS (372–289 B.C.)

(1) Mencius: A New Translation Arranged and Annotated. Translated
by W.A.C.H. Dobson. Toronto: University of Toronto Press, 1963,
215 pp.
   A translation made in the light of recent textual and philological
studies but intended for the general reader. Sections are rearranged
by topics to enhance readability.

(2) McCASLAND, S. VERNON; CAIRNS, GRACE E.; and YU, DAVID C. "Mencius."
In Religions of the World (see 1.1[10]), pp. 629–35.
   A brief discussion of Mencius's views of human nature, education,
government, and religion.

(3) WALEY, ARTHUR, trans. "Mencius." In Three Ways of Thought in
Ancient China. London: Allen & Unwin, 1939, pp. 115–95. Paperback
reprint. New York: Doubleday, 1956.
   Translations of selections from the Mencius with Waley's comments.
The selections deal with the goodness of human nature, the importance
of nourishing the spirit, the moral basis of the state, and mysticism.
Waley has rendered Mencius's thought into modern English.

(4) YEARLEY, LEE H. "Mencius on Human Nature: The Forms of His
Religious Thought." Journal of the American Academy of Religion 43
(1975):185–98.
   The author proposes that Mencius's understanding of human nature
is religious; he proceeds to articulate its religious meaning by using
and amplifying Joachim Wach's "theoretical expression" of religion,
which involves myths, doctrines, and dogmas. By applying the skills
of analytic philosophy, the author demonstrates how these three criteria are satisfied in Mencius's view of human nature.

(5) _____. "Toward a Typology of Religious Thought: A Chinese Example." Journal of Religion 55 (1975):426–43.
   A philosophical analysis of the religious thought of Mencius,
particularly of his conceptions of Heaven (t'ien). The author develops
a "typology" of religious thought. The author believes that Mencius's
religious ideas belong to a type which elucidates thought mainly for
the purpose of guiding moral action. The type "is guided by a concern
for the direct religious usefulness of whatever is thought about and
the desire actually to maintain rather than probe certain basic ten-
sions." Consequently, many questions, such as theodicy, are not an-
swered by Mencius. However, Mencius's type also forces Western religious thinkers to face issues such as the speculative construction
of abstract formulations merely to satisfy man's intellect.

2.4 HSÜN TZU (313-238 B.C.?)

(1) CHAN, WING-TSIT. "Hsün Tzu." In A Source Book in Chinese
Philosophy (see 1.4.2[1]), pp. 115-35.
  Comments and selections from the Hsün Tzu on the doctrine of Heaven,
the evil nature of man, and the rectification of names. Hsün Tzu's
view of Heaven is important for it presents a school of Confucianism
that holds a naturalistic view of Heaven while advocating the necessity
of rituals and worship.

(2) DOBS, HOMER H. Hsüntzu: The Moulder of Ancient Confucianism.
Taipei: Ch'eng-wen, 1966, 308 pp. (Orig. pub. London: Probsthain,
1927.)
  Chapter 5 deals with criticisms of metaphysics, chapter 8 with the
concept of li, and chapter 10 with music. These three chapters offer
us the religious perspective of Confucian elitism.

(3) FEHL, NOAH EDWARD. "Hsün Tzu." In Rites and Propriety in
Literature and Life (see 1.2.4[2]), pp. 151-212.
  Three chapters are devoted to Hsün Tzu's conception of li. According to this hard-headed "secularist" in pre-Ch'in China, li, in the
ultimate sense, is a religious concept because it implies the importance of rites which bind society and sensitize emotions. Fehl thinks
that Hsün Tzu anticipates Schleiermacher by over two millenia by emphasizing religion as primarily a response of feelings rather than intellect.

(4) Hsün Tzu: Basic Writings. Translated by Burton Watson. New York:
Columbia University Press, 1963, 177 pp. Reprinted in Basic Writings
of Mo Tzu, Hsün Tzu, and Han Fei Tzu. New York: Columbia University
Press, 1967, 452 pp.
  A translation of the basic writings of Hsün Tzu. Section 17 on
Heaven, section 19 on rites, and section 20 on music are particularly
related to Hsün Tzu's rational conception of religion.

(5) MACHLE, EDWARD J. "Hsün Tzu as a Religious Philosopher."
Philosophy East and West 26 (1976):443-60.
  A repudiation of the prevalent view that Hsün Tzu is a nonreligious
or antireligious thinker. Based on Hsün Tzu's understanding of shen
(spirit), the moral supremacy of Heaven, and man's ritual response to
Heaven, the author has argued his thesis cogently. The textual evidence to support his case appears to be strong. The paper is a vindi-
cation of Hsün Tzu's reputation as a secular philosopher.

(6) McCASLAND, S. VERNON; CAIRNS, GRACE E.; and YU, DAVID C. "Hsün
Tzu." In Religions of the World (see 1.1[10]), pp. 635-41.
  A summary of Hsün Tzu's views of human nature, education, govern-
ment and religion.

2.5   HAN CONFUCIANISM (206 B.C.-A.D. 220). ORIGINAL CONFUCIANISM;
      SCHOOLS OF YIN-YANG AND FIVE ELEMENTS; THE "I-CHING" [BOOK OF
      CHANGES]; THE "LI-CHI" [BOOK OF RITES] WHICH INCLUDES THE "TA-
      HSÜEH" [GREAT LEARNING] AND THE "CHUNG-YUNG" [DOCTRINE OF MEAN],
      THE "HSIAO-CHING" [CLASSIC OF FILIAL PIETY], TUNG CHUNG-SHU'S
      "CH'UN-CH'IU FAN-LU" [LUXURIANT GEMS OF THE SPRING AND AUTUMN
      ANNALS]: THEORY OF THE STATE, DOCTRINE OF PORTENTS, ANTHROPO-
      LOGICAL VIEW OF HEAVEN, MAN AS A MACROCOSM

      See 1.4.1 for the Religious Nature of the Chinese Empire. See
      1.4.2[1] for the text of Ch'un-ch'iu fan-lu.

(1) BALAZS, ÉTIENNE. "Political Philosophy and Social Crisis at the
End of the Han Dynasty." In Chinese Civilization and Bureaucracy.
Edited by A.F. Wright and H.M. Wright. New Haven: Yale University
Press, 1964, pp. 187-225.
      Discussion of three philosophers: Wang Fu, Ts'ui Shih, and Chung-
ch'ang T'ung. The author introduces their lives and thought with a
vivid description of their times. As Balazs points out, these three
men not only provide us with valuable information on their age, but
also engage our attention because "they prepared the way for intensely
active intellectual life that characterized the third century of our
own era." Interestingly written.

(2) BODDE, DERK. "Dominant Ideas in the Formation of Chinese Culture."
Journal of the American Oriental Society 162 (1942):293-99.
      Attempts to summarize "what has been the prevailing Chinese attitude
toward religion, toward the physical universe, and toward themselves."
The author reaffirms "the fundamental oneness and harmony of the Chinese
Weltanschauung. In the Chinese mind, there is no real distinction between the world of the supernatural, the world of nature, and the world
of man. They are all bound up in one all-embracing unity." A useful
summary for students, which has been more fully developed in the author's small book, China's Cultural Tradition: What and Whither? (New
York: Harper & Row, 1965).

(3) CHAN, WING-TSIT. "The Correspondence of Man and the Numerical
Categories of Heaven." In A Source Book in Chinese Philosophy (see
1.4.2[1]), pp. 280-82.
      A translation of Tung Chung-shu's description of the cosmic status
of man as the miniature of Heaven.

(4) FUNG YU-LAN. "Tung Chung-shu and the New Text School"; "Prognostication Texts, Apocrypha, and Numerology during the Han Dynasty." In A
History of Chinese Philosophy (see 2.1.7[11]) 2:7-87; 88-132.
      An in-depth treatment of the philosophical and religious thought of
the Han period based on the following elements: a) teaching of
Confucius and Mencius, b) the yin-yang school, c) the Five Elements
school, d) the Book of Changes, e) teaching of Tung Chung-shu,

f) Prognostication texts, g) Apocrypha, and h) numerology. The fusion
of these various elements has produced the unique architectonic system
characterized by the correlations of man, nature, state, seasons, directions, colors, etc.

(5) HU SHIH. Development of Logical Method in Ancient China. Shanghai:
Oriental Book Co., 1922, pp. 28-45. Reprint. New York: Paragon, 1965.
     A work that was very influential in the development of modern under-
standing of ancient Chinese thought. In its exposition of the methodology of the various schools of thought, the work throws light on many
other problems of the formative age of Chinese philosophy. The author
was one of the most distinguished scholars of this century, and the
present book, although an early product of his scholarship, fully
demonstrates his intuitive grasp of the essentials of a question and
his remarkable talents of analysis and exposition. Technical, but not
too difficult for students with some background in Chinese philosophy.

(6) IKEDA, SUETOSHI. "Origin and Development of the Wu-hsing." East
and West, n.s. 16 (1966):297-309.
     A brief study of "the problems of the Wu-hsing (five-elements) idea
before it was established"--in other words, its possible references in
oracle bones, bronzes, and classical texts, and the historical and
philosophical context of the theory. Author recognizes that "in ancient China where ideas in general are neither analytic nor systematic
but synthetic and integrated at their root, there cannot exist any
cosmic philosophy devoid of the religious element." Subject matter
is technical, but the article is written in an easily understood style.

(7) McCASLAND, S. VERNON; CAIRNS, GRACE E.; and YU, DAVID C. "Han
Confucianism." In Religions of the World (see 1.1[10], pp. 651-57.
     A summary of the thought of Tung Chung'shu (ca. 179-104 B.C.) re-
garding his theory of correspondence (Nature, virtues, yin-yang, five
elements, etc.), human nature, ethics, and the cycles of history.

(8) St. INA, MARIE de. "China's Contribution to the Spiritual
Foundation of Humanity." International Philosophical Quarterly 6
(1966):445-54.
     A discussion of the I-ching theme of "the creative receptive rela-
tionship," a rather subjective interpretation of ch'ien (Heaven) and
k'un (Earth). Author concludes that "primitive China has abundant
confidence in life. For her, earth was saturated with heaven, matter
with spirit, and the profane with the sacred."

(9) YAO SHAN-YU. "Cosmological and Anthropological Philosophy of Tung
Chung-shu." Journal of the North China Branch, Royal Asiatic Society
73 (1946):40-68.
     Following a brief biographical sketch of Tung Chung-shu, the author
deals with his philosophy of the cosmic order, the state, and the

individual man. He emphasizes that Tung's was a philosophy of paral-
lelism between Heaven and man. A good, adequate summary, written in
a not-too-technical style.

2.6 NEO-CONFUCIANISM

2.6.1 Influences of Buddhism and Taoism upon Neo-Confucianism

(1) CHANG, CARSON. "Buddhism as a Stimulus to Neo-Confucianism."
Oriens Extremus 2 (1955):157-66.
Discusses the three Chinese Buddhist schools and Yogācārya
(Consciousness Only school), then tries "to give a picture of
how the Confucian scholars lived and felt towards the monks who
introduced Buddhism into China." Finally, shows "how the concepts of Neo-Confucianism were related to Buddhism." A clear
and not-too-technical style.

(2) ____. "Buddhism as Stimulus to Neo-Confucianism." In
The Development of Neo-Confucian Thought. Vol. 1. New York:
Bookman Associates, 1957, pp. 113-35.
A revision of (1). Traces the influences of the Buddhist
schools of T'ien t'ai, Hua-yen, and, particularly, Ch'an (Zen)
upon Neo-Confucianism. Relationships between Neo-Confucian
concepts and Buddhist ideas are discussed: e.g., Buddhist concepts of nature (svabhāva), compassion (karunā), and trance
(samādhi) are compared to the Confucian ideas of human nature
(hsing), humanity (jen), and reverence (ching).

(3) FU, CHARLES WEI-HSUN. "Morality or Beyond: The Neo-
Confucian Confrontation with Mahāyāna Buddhism." Philosophy
East and West 23 (July 1973):375-96.
An analysis and evaluation of the Neo-Confucian criticisms
of Buddhism in the Sung (960-1279) and Ming (1268-1644) periods.
The author felt that Neo-Confucian criticisms are based upon
three principles: a) jen-yi (love manifested in terms of grad-
ations), b) sublime transcendence (kao-ming), and c) the "mean"
in everyday moral practice (chung-yung). He rightly points out
that most of the Neo-Confucian criticisms show their lack of
deep understanding of Buddhist philosophy, particularly of the
Mādhyamika school (Middle way). The article ends with an appeal
to modernize Buddhism by updating its concern for ethics and
society.

(4) FUNG YU-LAN. "Neo-Confucianism: The Cosmologists." In
A Short History of Chinese Philosophy. Edited by Derk Bodde.
New York: Macmillan, 1958, pp. 266-80.
A discussion of the Buddhist interpretation of Confucianism

by Li Ao and of the T'ai-chi t'u shuo [Explanation of the diagram of the supreme ultimate] by the neo-Confucianist Chou Tun-
yi (1017-1073). The latter work is Taoist in outlook. The
chapter includes the cosmology of Shao Yung (1011-1077), whose
interpretation of the Book of Changes reflects a great influence by religious Taoism.

(5) _____. "The Rise of Neo-Confucianism and Its Borrowing
from Buddhism and Taoism." In A History of Chinese Philosophy
(see 2.1.7[11] 2:407-33.
     A discussion of Li Ao (d. ca. 844), whose Buddhistic interpre-
tation of Confucianism anteceded neo-Confucianism. The book
Ts'an-t'ung ch'i [Three ways unified and harmonized], a work
of religious Taoism that has influenced neo-Confucianism, is
also treated.

(6) KIMURA, EIICHI. "The New Confucianism and Taoism." Cahiers
d'histoire mondiale 5 (1960):801-29.
     A general historical survey which shows "the formulation and
development of the old schools of Confucianism and Taoism as
distinct from the new schools which developed in Sung times."
A lucid summary in convenient length.

(7) LIU TS'UN-YAN. "Lin Chao-en (1517-1598)." T'oung Pao 53
(1967):253-78.
     Traces briefly the process of amalgamation of Buddhism with
Taoism and the further amalgamation of Confucian teachings with
these in Sung and Yüan times. Continues on into Ming, with a
detailed study of the eclectic scholar-preacher-healer of the
article's title, whom the author characterizes as "a Taoist-
inclined Confucianist who also knew something about Buddhism."
He was the founder of a sect--the San-chiao or Three Religions--
that continued to be very influential through the Ch'ing period.
May be somewhat too technical for nonspecialists.

2.6.2 School of Principle ("Li") Represented by Ch'eng I (1033-1107)
and Chu Hsi (1130-1200). Correlations between the Supreme
Ultimate (T'ai-chi) and the Ultimate of Non-Being ("Wu-chi"),
between Principle and Material Force ("ch'i"); the Cosmicization
of the Four Virtues Including "jen" (Goodness); Doctrine of Evil
as Due to the Presence of Material Force in Man; Influences of
Buddhism: Hua-yen (Flower-garland) School's theory of the
Correspondence between Principle and Affairs ("shih"), Doctrines
of the Buddha-nature of Man, Meditation, Enlightenment; Influences of Taoism: Spontaneity ("tzu-jan"), Alternation between
Passivity and Activity, Noninvolvement and Involvement

(1) BRUCE, J. PERCY, trans. Philosophy of Human Nature by Chu
Hsi. London: Probsthain, 1922, 336 pp.
    Translation, with annotations, of Books 42-48 of Chu Hsi's
Complete Works, including discussion of the Nature and the
Decree (hsing and ming), Mind (hsin), the Feelings (ch'ing),
Moral Law (tao), Law (li), and other key terms in Chu Hsi's
thought. A basic work for understanding the moral and meta-
physical views of the Sung School of Principle (li).

(2) BRUCE, J. PERCY. "Theistic Import of Sung Philosophy."
Journal of the North China Branch, Royal Asiatic Society 49
(1918):111-27.
    Discusses neo-Confucian metaphysics, especially the thought
of Chu Hsi, and concludes that it is definitely theistic. This
article is a brief presentation of what Bruce later published
as a book, Philosophy of Human Nature by Chu Hsi (1). A careful piece of scholarship written in lucid style.

(3) CHAN, WING-TSIT. "Chu Hsi's View of Spiritual Beings and
His Criticisms of Buddhism." In A Source Book in Chinese
Philosophy (see 1.4.2[1]), pp. 643-53.
    This section is about Chu Hsi's interpretation of the spiri-
tual forces (shen-kuei) and the concept of the soul (hun-p'o).
He holds the view that although the material force (ch'i) of a
man eventually disintegrates after death, it does not disinte-
grate completely at once. Therefore it can exert some influence
upon the living when the descendants perform the rituals of
ancestor worship. Chu Hsi criticizes Buddhism as follows:
a) it neglects the principles of the five human relationships,
b) it confuses principle with consciousness or movement, and
c) it negates the objective world.

(4) CHENG CHUNG-YING, trans. Tai Chen's Inquiry into Goodness.
Honolulu: East-West Center Press, 1971, 176 pp.
    Translation, with introductory essay, of one of the chief
works of an early Ch'ing philosopher, who opposed Chu Hsi's
views with a form of "rationalistic monism." The introduction
is almost as long as the translation and offers a good background
and analysis for the latter. Not too technical.

(5) McCASLAND, S. VERNON; CAIRNS, GRACE E.; and YU, DAVID C.
"Neo-Confucianism." In Religions of the World (see 1.1[10]),
pp. 657-69.
    An introduction to neo-Confucianism from the Sung to the
Ch'ing period, with reference to Ch'eng Hao, Ch'eng I, Chu Hsi,
Wang Yang-ming, and the Confucians of the Ch'ing period. A de-
lineation of the differences between the School of Principle
and the School of Mind, as well as criticisms of these two
schools by the more positivist-minded Ch'ing Confucians.

(6) NEEDHAM, JOSEPH. "Chu Hsi." In Science and Civilization
in China (see 2.1.6[7]) 2:472-93.
    Needham, combining his scientific expertise with sinological
learning, interprets Chu Hsi's li as pattern or principles of
organization and ch'i as matter-energy. The author considers
Chu's philosophy organismic, anticipating the organismic phi-
losphy of Whitehead by eight centuries.

2.6.3 School of Mind, Represented by Ch'eng Hao (1032-1085), Lu
Hsiang-shan (1139-1193), and Wang Yang-ming (1472-1529). Mind
is Principle ("li"); Innate Knowledge of the Good ("liang-chih")
as Man's Original Mind; Unity of Theory and Practice; Influences
of Ch'an (Zen) Buddhism: Subjectivity, Antirationalism

(1) ARAKI, KENGO. "Confucianism and Buddhism." In The Unfolding
of Neo-Confucianism. Edited by W.T. DeBary. New York: Columbia
University Press, 1975, pp. 39-62.
    A historical and philosophical study of the relationship be-
tween the mind school of neo-Confucianism and Ch'an Buddhism in
the late Ming period. It points out that the confluences between these two schools are a pervasive cultural and intellectual
phenomenon of the day. Whereas Wang Yang-ming himself consciously denied the place of Buddhism in Confucianism, the late Ming
Confucian school of Mind openly appropriated Ch'an thought and
advocated reciprocity between Confucianism and Buddhism.

(2) CHAN, WING-TSIT. "How Buddhist Is Wang Yang-ming?"
Philosophy East and West 12 (1962):203-15.
    Using entirely Chinese sources, the author argues that Wang
is not a Buddhist as he has been understood by Chinese and
Japanese writers. On the other hand, although Wang considered
himself a spokesman for neo-Confucianism, it is undeniable that
there are Buddhist elements in his thought, particularly Ch'an
(Zen) idioms and stories.

(3) _____. "Lu Hsiang-shan the Idealist"; "Translator's
Comments on the Philosophical Development of Wang Yang-ming
in Relation to his Biography." In A Source Book in Chinese
Philosophy (see 1.4.2[1]), pp. 572-87; 654-67.
    The pages on Lu Hsiang-shan contain comments and a transla-
tion of his writings. The original sources provide information
showing the polemics between Lu and Chu Hsi, a friend. The
selections on Wang Yang-ming are from his Inquiry on the Great
Learning, which embodies the essential points of his thought:
doctrine of the mind and the innate knowledge of goodness; importance of will over intellect; identity between the internal
and the external, between knowledge and action.

(4) ____. "Wang Yang-ming: A Biography." Philosophy East
and West 22 (Jan. 1972):64-74.
   The first biographical article in a Western language on Wang
Yang-ming, based on Chinese and Japanese sources. It emphasizes
Wang's career as a civil administrator and military commander.
Wang formulated his important philosophical ideas during his
busy years as a governmental official: identity between mind
and principle at the age of 37, unity between theory and action
at 38, innate knowledge at 49. The influences of Buddhism and
Taoism on his thought are also discussed.

(5) CHANG, CARSON. Wang Yang-ming, Idealist Philosopher of
Sixteenth Century China. New York: St. John's University Press,
1962, 102 pp.
   The author gives the gist of Wang's philosophy as well as its
place in neo-Confucianism. Chapter 1 provides a biography of
Wang. The author views Wang's philosophy as intuitionism.

(6) CHING, JULIA. To Acquire Wisdom: The Way of Wang Yang-ming.
New York: Columbia University Press, 1976, 373 pp.
   This is a philosophical study of Wang Yang-ming, although it
has many religious implications, since Wang's thought emphasizes
the importance of will, man's innate knowledge of the good and
the primacy of practice. It culminates with Wang's ideal of
"beyond good and will" as the ultimate monistic principle. It
includes a translation of seven short essays and twenty-five
poems. But for many misprints, this work is a fine contribution
to the study of Wang Yang-ming.

(7) TANG CHUN-I. "The Development of the Concept of Moral Mind
from Wang Yang-ming to Wang Chi." In Self and Society in Ming
Thought. Edited by W. Theodore DeBary. New York: Columbia
University Press, 1970, pp. 91-120.
   A study of Wang Yang-ming's liang-chih (original mind or
knowledge) which, according to the author, came into being as
a result of Wang's synthesis between Chu Hsi's and Lu Hsiang-
shan's concepts of the mind. Wang Chi (1498-1583), a close
disciple of Wang Yang-ming, further developed his master's
"original mind" by emphasizing the notion that the original mind
knows neither good nor evil. Wang Chi's distinction between the
original mind and the ideas of good and evil appears to be a de-
parture from Wang Yang-ming's "original mind" and bears some re-
semblance to the Taoist concept of Nothing (wu).

(8) ____. "Liu Tsung-chou's Doctrine of Moral Mind and Prac-
tice and His Critique of Wang Yang-ming." In The Unfolding of
Neo-Confucianism (see 2.6.3[1]), pp. 305-31.
   An original study of the late Ming neo-Confucianist Liu

Tsung-chou (1578-1645) in relation to his philosophical differences with Wang Yang-ming and the different schools originated
by Wang.   Liu Tsung-chou's principal tenet is that the moral
will (the will to be good) is prior to knowledge of the good
(Wang Yang-ming's original mind or knowledge).   Hence from Liu's
point of view, Wang Yang-ming's doctrine of liang-chih (original
knowledge) has made the moral will posterior to knowledge.   Coming from the tradition of the school of mind, Liu also advocated
the doctrine of the original mind, but for him it is simultane-
ously pure knowing, pure willing, and pure feeling in the immediate sense without involving an object.   This is the creative
will (sheng-i) that must precede all actions of goodness.   The
author's contention is that much of Liu's argument for the primacy and priority of moral will is actually implied in Wang
Yang-ming's thought.   But it was Liu who made the moral will
the ontological aspect of man, thus establishing the metaphysical basis of morality.   This is a difficult essay, but it is
important in that it faithfully presents the religious and
spiritual dimensions of neo-Confucianism, which have so far been
neglected or distorted by modern interpreters in the West.

(9) TU WEI-MING.   Neo-Confucian Thought in Action: Wang Yang-
ming's Youth (1472-1509).   Berkeley and Los Angeles: University
of California Press, 1976, 222 pp.
    A detailed historical and biographical study of the early
life of Wang Yang-ming.   It emphasizes his spiritual and personal crises, his continual wrestling with Taoism and Buddhism
(Ch'an), and his final acceptance of Confucianism.   The best
Western biography of Wang.

2.7   LAO TZU, CHUANG TZU, LIEH TZU

(1) FU, CHARLES WEI-HSÜN.   "Creative Hermeneutics: Taoist Metaphysics
and Heidegger."   Journal of Chinese Philosophy 3 (1976):115-43.
    This essay attempts to appropriate Heideggerian hermeneutics for an
understanding of the Tao-tê ching, based on the author's conviction
that both Heidegger and Lao Tzu use the same kind of poetic-philosophi-
cal language.   Whether the author's "five steps" of hermeneutization
is Heideggerian or not, his real intent is to demonstrate that the Tao
(both the unnameable and the unnameable as named) in the Tao-tê ching
is essentially ontological or trans-ontological (pre-ontological); it
is not meant as the explanation of cosmic origin.   The author uses the
works of Chuang Tzu and the commentaries by Wang Pi and Kuo Hsiang as
the literary sources for his interpretation of the Tao, although he
relies most heavily on Chuang Tzu.   This is a lucid attempt to make
the philosophy of Lao Tzu systematic and clear.   It also contains a
concise and useful textual explanation of the interpretations of Tao
by Chuang Tzu, Wang Pi, and Kuo Hsiang.

2.7.1   <u>Lao Tzu (Sixth or Fourth Century B.C.)</u>

See also 1.3(2)

(1) CHAN, WING-TSIT, trans. <u>The Way of Lao Tzu</u>. Indianapolis:
Bobbs-Merrill, 1963, 285 pp.
  Extensive consultation was made for the translation. Each
chapter is followed by a comment as well as detailed notes.
Three introductory essays treat the influence of the <u>Tao-tê
ching</u> upon neo-Taoism, Buddhism, and neo-Confucianism, and pro-
vide some biographical material. The translator believes that
Tao is not mysterious.

(2) CHEN CHUNG-HWAN. "What Does Lao-tzu Mean by the Term
'Tao'?" <u>Tsinghua Journal of Chinese Studies</u>, n.s. 4 (1964):
150-61.
  Examines the usage of this key term in the <u>Tao-tê ching</u>.
Useful for clarifying differing senses of the word.

(3) CHEN, ELLEN MARIE. "Is There a Doctrine of Physical
Immortality in the <u>Tao-tê ching</u>?" <u>History of Religions</u> 12
(1973):231-49.
  The author maintains that there is a belief in physical immortality in the <u>Tao-tê ching</u>. While critical of the cult of
physical immortality, she is opposed to the rigid dichotomy between philosophical Taoism and Taoist religion as held by many
Western and Chinese writers.

(4) CREEL, HERRLEE G. "What is Taoism?"; "On Two Aspects in
Early Taoism"; "On the Origin of <u>Wu-wei</u> (Taking no Action)."
In <u>What is Taoism? and Other Studies in Chinese Cultural History</u>.
Chicago: University of Chicago Press, 1970, pp. 1-24; 25-47;
48-78.
  The author, in the first two essays, argues for the distinction between philosophical Taoism and religious Taoism and de-
fends the view that they did not belong to the same tradition.
Creel takes issue with Maspero (11), who believed that even from
the very beginning Taoism and the search for physical immortality were inseparable. It should be noted that Creel's argument
is predicated upon a prior distinction between contemplative
Taoism and purposive Taoism. According to this distinction,
religious Taoism belongs to purposive Taoism. In chapter 4,
Creel, by collating the lost book <u>Shen Pu-hai</u> (the title is the
name of its author, who died in 337 B.C., an early administrator
of the Legalist School), presents the thesis that the concept of
<u>wu-wei</u> was derived from the Legalist School. According to this
school, <u>wu-wei</u> means that the ruler only reigns but does "nothing" with reference to specific political actions. Both the

Tao-tê ching and the Chuang Tzu, for Creel, adopted this Legalist concept, and it was absorbed into Taoist philosophy. Creel
is challenging the prevalent view which attributes the origin
of wu-wei to Lao-Tzu and the Chuang Tzu. Much of the argument
depends upon the dating of the Tao-tê ching and of the Chuang
Tzu.

(5) HURVITZ, LEON. "Recent Japanese Study of Lao-tzu: Kimura
Eiichi's Roshi no Shin Kenkyu." Monumenta Serica 20 (1961):
311-67.
    A thorough, critical review of Kimura Eiichi's Roshi no shin
Kenkyu [New studies on Lao Tzu] (1959), a major examination of
text and authorship by a leading authority. The article includes Hurvitz's English rendering of the Japanese version of
text as established by Kimura. Hurvitz's conclusion is that
the work is "an unsuccessful attempt on the part of a philolo-
gist to arrive by philological means at the description of a
system of thought."

(6) JAN YÜN-HUA. "Problems of Tao and Tao Tê Ching." Numen
22 (1975):208-34.
    A critical review of Chinese scholars' debates on the Tao-
tê ching and Taoism in the 1950s in the People's Republic of
China. It concerns the discussions between Fung Yu-lan and his
opponents. Fung's new opinion on the Tao of the Tao-tê ching
is that it is the forces of essence (ching-ch'i) or the breath
of life; hence Tao is materialistic. Fung further says that
the ancient Taoists were concerned primarily with how to pre-
serve the self, and this motivated them to be interested in
medicinal science such as the art of breath control. The opponents of Fung, however, disagree with him by arguing for the
idealistic bent of the Tao-tê ching and Taoism. This is based
on their conviction that the Tao is the Non-being (wu) which
transcends time and space. The essay also points out the likely
relation between ancient Taoists and Chinese shamans.

(7) _____. "Short Bibliography of the Silk Manuscripts on
Taoism." Newsletter, Society for the Study of Chinese Religion
1 (March 1976):4-7.
    A bibliographical explanation of the silk manuscripts of the
Han dynasty, discovered in 1973-74 at Ma-wang-tui, Changsha.
In addition to the two versions of the Lao Tzu and the four
lost texts of the Huang-ti Ssu-ching, other items found are
also specified. An additional bibliography of articles by
mainland Chinese scholars on the silk manuscripts is provided.

(8) LAU, D.C., trans. Tao-tê Ching. Baltimore: Penguin, 1963,
191 pp.

A translation of the classic into simple and clear language
which does not fall into mysticism. In the introduction, Lau
attacks the association of the cyclical view (rise and fall,
wealth and poverty, etc.) with the Tao-tê ching. He believes
that the book teaches holding fast to submission. This is different from the teaching that one must be submissive in order
to rise again.

(9) LAU, D.C. "Treatment of Opposites in Lao Tzu." Bulletin
of the School of Oriental and African Studies 21 (1958):344-60.
    One of the still too few serious attempts to bring a sophis-
ticated analysis to this text, as opposed to the never-ending
production of translations. Cites five divergent views on Lao
Tzu's treatment of opposites: 1) "development and decline form
a circular process"; 2) "in a conflict between opposites the
lower will overcome the higher"; 3) "opposites are interde-
pendent"; 4) "Heaven, though it shows no favoritism, is on the
side of good people"; and 5) "the higher always begins from the
lower and . . . the process of development is always gradual."
The article continues with a perceptive critique of these views.

(10) LIEBENTHAL, WALTER. "Lord Atman in the Lao-tzu."
Monumenta Serica 27 (1968):374-80.
    Suggests the possibility of Upanishadic influence on Lao-tzu,
based on an analysis of several troublesome terms and passages
in the text compared with their analogs in Sanskrit texts, particularly that of the Bṛhadāraṇyaka Upaniṣad. Not conclusive,
but an interesting revival of older theories as to Indian influence on pre-Han thought. Technical.

(11) MASPERO, HENRI. "On Lao Tzu and Chuang Tzu." In Le
taoisme. Paris: Civilisations du sud, 1950, pp. 227-42.
    A discussion of the mysticism of these two Taoists. For the
author, philosophical and religious Taoism were historically inseparable. Le taoisme, together with Maspero's Les religions
chinoises, was translated into English by Frank A. Kierman, Jr.
under the title Taoism and Chinese Religion (Amherst: University
of Massachusetts Press, 1981), 578 pp.

(12) MUNRO, DONALD J. "Taoist Concept of Man." In The Concept
of Man in Early China (see 2.2[9]), pp. 117-39.
    While the early Taoists, like the early Confucianists, be-
lieved that all men are naturally equal, they do not view natural equality in terms of the evaluating mind, as the Confucianists do. The Taoists believe that natural equality lies
in man's original nature or Tao, which is unitary and undivided.
To return to Tao, man must give up the evaluating mind which,
according to the Taoists, belongs to the ephemeral part of the

human endowment. The Taoist term te refers both to the produc-
tive and nourishing qualities of Tao in man and that which is
received from Tao. In either case, te involves the operation
of Tao in man.

(13) SMITH, CARL. "A Heideggerian Interpretation of the Way of
Lao Tzu." Ching Feng 10 (1967):5-19.
    Three sections discuss 1) the Way of fundamental thought to
Being and Tao, 2) Being and Non-Being in Heidegger and Taoism,
3) the Way of Inaction (wu-wei) and the "Letting Be" of
Heidegger. The author notes that "Non-Being is a fundamental
concept in both. . . ." An interesting essay, not especially
technical in style.

(14) TING NAI-TUNG. "Laotzu's Criticism of Language." Etc. 19
(1962):5-38.
    Despite the author's stated intention "to study the semantic
ideas in the Tao-te ching," this article is a broader treatment
than that statement implies. It also includes brief discussions
of Confucian and Legalist ideas for the purpose of contrast.
One of the more rewarding analyses of the purport of this text.

(15) WALEY, ARTHUR, trans. The Way and Its Power (see 1.2.8[1]).
    Waley's translation was done with the intent of taking the
reader to the China of the fourth century B.C. Hence the archaic
and the magical aspects of the Chinese tradition are clearly
discernible in his work. The translation is preceded by an introduction in which Taoism and its contemporary rival schools
are delineated.

(16) WELCH, HOLMES H. "Tao-te ching." In The Parting of the
Way (see 1.2.8[2]), pp. 18-87.
    An interpretation of some of the basic ideas of the Tao-te
ching in a modern Western context. The author's purpose is to
make the Tao-te ching intelligible to modern readers.

2.7.2 Chuang Tzu (ca. 399-295 B.C.)

(1) CHAN, WING-TSIT. "Chuang Tzu." In A Source Book in Chinese
Philosophy (see 1.4.2[1]), pp. 177-210.
    A translation of chapter 2, "The Equality of Things," and
chapter 6, "The Great Teacher," plus selections on the meaning
of Tao, vacuity (hsü), mind, and transformation.

(2) CREEL, HERRLEE G. "The Great Clod." In What is Taoism?
And Other Studies in Chinese Cultural History (see 2.7.1[4]),
pp. 25-36.

A philological and philosophical analysis of the meaning of the "Great Clod" (ta-k'uai) in the Chuang Tzu. By pointing out that the "Great Clod" refers to the Tao, Creel tells us that the Tao in Taoism should not be understood as Logos or God.

(3) FINAZZO, GIANCARLO. Notion of Tao in Lao Tzu and Chuang. Taipei: Mei Ya Publication Co., 1968, 198 pp.
Careful examination of this key term, with relation to the general philosophy of Lao Tzu and Chuang Tzu, and as related to many other important terms in these texts. A brave and not unsuccessful attempt to lift the study of ancient Chinese thought to a new level.

(4) GRAHAM, A.C. "Chuang Tzu's Essay on Seeing Things as Equal." History of Religions 9 (Nov. 1969-Feb. 1970):137-59.
An analytical exposition and translation of the second chapter of the Chuang Tzu, "Ch'i-wu lun," with emphasis on the linguistic nature of Chuang Tzu's arguments. The main thrust of the chapter is that a philosopher, by the very fact of applying reason, is dependent on a perspective which may contradict another perspective, whereas the man of tao can embrace all because he has no perspectives.

(5) HANSEN, JUL. "Analysis of Autumn Floods in Chuang Tzu." In Invitation to Chinese Philosophy. Edited by A. Naess and A. Hunnay. Oslo: Universitetsforlaget, 1972, pp. 113-40.
"Interpretation and analysis of the theory of knowledge expounded in the dialogue between the Sea-Spirit and the River-Lord in chapter 17 of Chuang Tzu's 'Autumn Floods.'" A rare attempt at sophisticated philosophical analysis of an ancient Chinese text. Lucidly written.

(6) LEGGE, JAMES, trans. "Writing of Chuang Tzu." In Texts of Taoism. New York: Julian, 1959, pp. 175-672. (Orig. pub. in Sacred Books of the East, vols. 39 and 40. London: Oxford University Press, 1891.)
A meticulous translation accompanied by extensive notes. Legge also wrote an introduction which contains commentary on each of the thirty-three chapters.

(7) MERTON, THOMAS. Way of Chuang Tzu. New York: New Directions, 1965, 159 pp.
Selected thoughts of Chuang Tzu in English versions derived by Merton from several Western translations, and shaped by his poetic talent. These "renderings," as well as the substantial introductory material, are valuable especially because Merton strongly empathizes with his Chinese predecessor as a mystic. Despite its brevity and selectivity, all in all the best introduction to Chuang Tzu in English.

(8) WALEY, ARTHUR, trans. "Chuang Tzu." In Three Ways of
Thought in Ancient China (see 2.3[3]), pp. 2-79.
     A most readable and interesting translation of selected pas-
sages of the Chuang Tzu. Waley translated only those sections
which he understood with certainty. His understanding of Chuang
Tzu is clearly reflected in the following quote concerning
Chuang Tzu's attitude toward magic, religion, and philosophy:
"We shall not be surprised to find these three sometimes overlapping, and shall not necessarily put the consolations of magic
on a lower footing than those of philosophy or religion."

(9) WARE, JAMES, trans. The Sayings of Chuang Chou. New York:
New American Library, 1963, 240 pp.
     A readable translation of the complete work of Chuang Tzu,
but Ware has the habit of translating the subtle Taoist terms
into straightforward concepts. Hence, for instance, Tao becomes "God," hsü (vacuity) becomes "uncomittedness," wu (awaken-
ing) becomes "perfect wisdom."

(10) WATSON, BURTON, trans. Chuang-Tzu: Basic Writings. New
York: Columbia University Press, 1964, 148 pp.
     A translation of eleven chapters of the Chuang Tzu.

(11) _____. The Complete Works of Chuang Tzu. New York:
Columbia University Press, 1968, 397 pp.
     A translation of all thirty-three chapters of the Chuang Tzu
in modern expression. The introduction offers comparison of
the various English translations of the same text. The most
readable and reliable English translation of the book.

(12) WU, JOHN C.H. "Wisdom of Chuang Tzu." International
Philosophical Quarterly 3 (1963):5-36.
     Contains sections on what we know of Chuang Tzu's life, his
notion of the Tao, life, death and dreams, etc. According to
Wu, "Chuang Tzu is a mystic through and through." This is a
deeply empathetic study by a learned Catholic layman who is
thoroughly versed in the Chinese text.

2.7.3 The "Lieh Tzu"

(1) GILES, LIONEL, trans. Taoist Teachings from Lieh Tzu.
Wisdom of the East Series. London: John Murray, 1912, 121 pp.
2d ed., 1947.
     A small, popular book containing seven chapters from the
text, the "considerable nucleus" of which the translator considers to be "older than the genuine parts of Chuang Tzu."
Despite the disagreement on this point by later scholars (cf.

Graham's view), the translation itself is careful and lucid, with brief but helpful notes in the form of comments interspersed between the lines.

(2) GRAHAM, A.C., trans. The Book of Lieh Tzu. London: John Murray, 1960, 183 pp.
    A complete translation of the Lieh Tzu. According to Graham, the book of Lieh Tzu is the product of A.D. 300, representing the second wave of Taoism. The most valuable aspect of the book is the collection of ancient legends, stories, and marvelous takes which reflect a pre-Confucian tradition.

2.7.4 Alchemy: External Alchemy (Elixirs) and Internal Alchemy (Hygiene, Meditation, Diet, Sex Techniques)

See 1.8.1 and 1.8.2 for Taoist Alchemists and Hygienists between the Second and the Seventh Centuries A.D.

(1) WARE, JAMES R., trans. "God and Cinnabar"; "The Genie's Pharmacopoei"; "The Yellow and the White." In Alchemy, Medicine, Religion in China of A.D. 320 (see 1.8.2[3]), pp. 68-96; 177-99; 261-78.
    Chapter 4 describes recipes for the making of elixirs; chapter 11 describes plants and "excresences" to be gathered as ingredients of medicines; chapter 16 delineates recipes for the production of gold and silver to be taken as elixirs. The preparation of elixirs is essentially a religious ritual, preceded by a purification rite of one hundred days, and must take place in a sacred mountain.

2.8 DOCTRINE OF HUANG-LAO: MYTHOLOGIZATION OF HUANG-TI (YELLOW EMPEROR) AND LAO TZU

(1) KALTENMARK, MAX. "Lao Tzu Deified." In Lao Tzu and Taoism (see 1.3[3]), pp. 109-13.
    A brief account of the mythicizing of Lao Tzu in the Han period and afterwards.

(2) RIEGEL, JEFFREY B. "A Summary of Some Recent Wenwu and Kaoku Articles: Mawangtui Tombs Two and Three." Early China 1 (1975):10-15.
    A report, based on articles published in Wenwu [Ancient relics] and Kaoku [Archaeological studies] on the discovery of Han silk manuscripts buried in tombs two and three (second century B.C.) at Ma-wang-tui, Ch'angsha, in 1973-74. It discusses, in particular, the two copies of the Lao-tzu and the manuscripts of the lost texts identified by the mainland scholars as the Four Books of the Yellow Emperor (Huang-ti ssu-ching).

(3) WARE, JAMES R., trans. "Yellow Emperor"; "Lao Tzu." In Alchemy, Medicine, Religion in China of A.D. 320 (see 1.8.2[3]), pp. 59, 122-23, 137, 174, 201, 215-17, 302; 128-30, 174, 201, 229-30, 256-57, 267, 313, 324-25.

These pages contain materials on the legendary Yellow Emperor and Lao-Tzu which appeared in the Han period (202 B.C.-A.D. 220). This offers us a classical example of what religious Taoism was in the Han period. Most of the essentials of religious Taoism are touched upon (e.g., shamanism, alchemy, physical immortality, Taoist sects, political rebellions, revealed scriptures, and messianism). Some of the terms rendered by Ware should be read with reservations: the tao is translated as the Divine Process of God, tao-shih (Taoist adept or priest) as the processor, hsien (the immortal) as genie, chen-jen (true man) as God's Man, ch'ang-seng (longevity) as fullness of life. But in spite of these terms, Ware has rendered an adequate translation of a very important and difficult book, the "inner chapters" of the Pao-p'u tzu.

2.9 IMMORTALS ("HSIEN")

(1) GILES, LIONEL, trans. A Gallery of Chinese Immortals. Wisdom of The East Series. London: John Murray, 1948, 127 pp.

Biographies of adepts who have attained the status of hsien, taken from a wide range of Chinese literature. Popular style, but reliable because the translator was a leading English sinologist.

(2) NEEDHAM, JOSEPH. "The Achievement of Immortality." In Science and Civilisation in China (see 2.1.6[7]) 2:139-54.

A discussion of the aims of physical immortality as pursued by individuals under the topics of a) respiratory techniques, b) heliotherapeutic techniques, c) gymnastic exercises, d) sexual techniques, e) hagiography of immortals, f) hsien and organic philosophy. Needham seems to believe that China is the only country where physical immortality became a central cultural motif. He also feels that the two paradoxical themes of Taoism are inseparable: the mystic naturalism of the hermit-philosophers and the cultic practices of the shaman-magicians. This view would make the separation of religious Taoism from philosophical Taoism untenable.

(3) WARE, JAMES R., trans. "Genii." In Alchemy, Medicine, Religion in China (see 1.8.2[3]), pp. 33-52.

Arguments in defence of the existence of immortals based on the argument that the invisibility of immortals does not disprove their existence. According to Ko Hung, there are three classes of immortals: heavenly immortals who raise their bodies into the void; earthly immortals who reside in famous mountains; "corpse-free" immortals who slough off their bodies after death. Many of the human-transformed immortals belong to the third class of immortals.

(4) YETTS, W. PERCEVAL. "Chinese Isles of the Blest." Folklore 30
(1919):35-62.
     First briefly explains the concept of tao, then the term hsien
(immortal). Descriptions of the isles are quotes from Lieh Tzu,
Shih-chi, Shih chou chi [Record of the ten islands], and Han Wei Ts'ung
Shu [Collected books of the Han and Wei dynasties]. Comparisons are
drawn between Chinese notions and similar conceptions in Indian, Greek,
and Celtic lore. Author feels, however, that the Chinese idea is not
borrowed but is indigenous; he explains the historical background in
Ch'in and early Han. A good summary, interestingly written.

2.10 CONCEPT OF REVEALED SCRIPTURES

(1) CHAO WEI-PANG. "Secret Religious Societies in North China in the
Ming Dynasty." Folklore Studies 7 (1948):95-115.
     The material here is mostly translated or adapted from a book called
Criticizing the Heterodoxy in Detail (P'o-hsieh Hsing-pien) in four
chuan by a district magistrate of early Ch'ing times who came into
possession of various scriptures of secret societies published by them
at the end of the Ming period. He reproduced these and criticized each
one individually. There is much valuable detail. The syncretic nature
of the secret societies is noted, as is the dominance of millenarianism.
Not too technical.

(2) KALTENMARK, MAX. "Sacred Texts and Revelations." In Lao Tzu and
Taoism (see 1.3[3]), pp. 139-43.
     A brief account of the Taoist canon, particularly the T'ai-p'ing
ching [Scripture of the supreme peace], the Shang-ch'ing ching [Scrip-
ture of the heaven of superior purity], the Huang-t'ing ching [Scrip-
ture of the yellow court], and the Ling-pao ching [Scripture of the
marvelous jewel].

(3) WELCH, HOLMES H. "Interior Gods Theology." In The Parting of the
Way (see 1.2.8[2]), pp. 105-12.
     According to Welch, the interior gods theology constituted a school
of Taoism, but according to Kaltenmark, the interior gods theology reflects the ideas derived from the first and second collections of the
Taoist canon, respectively called the Tung-chen and the Tung-hsüan.
These scriptures advocate the belief that man's body is inhabited by
thirty-six thousand gods and that man is a microcosm. Following
Kaltenmark, our opinion is that the interior gods theology is a common
doctrine of Taoism, not a particular Taoist school.

2.11 SCHOOLS OF YIN-YANG AND THE FIVE ELEMENTS

(1) FUNG YU-LAN. "The Yin-Yang School and Early Chinese Cosmology."
In A Short History of Chinese Philosophy (see 2.6.1[4]), pp. 129-42.
     Fung views the Yin-Yang school and the Five Elements school as the
common heritage of both Confucianism and Taoism. In this chapter he
particularly wishes to point out the occult aspect of both schools,
which preceded Confucianism and Taoism but eventually became incorporated into religious Taoism.

(2) HUGHES, E.R. "Yin-Yang and the Five Elements." In Chinese
Philosophy in Classical Times. London: J.M. Dent & Sons, 1942, pp.
212-25. Rev. ed., 1954.
     Superior translations of brief excerpts from several important texts
including Ssu-ma Ch'ien's estimate of Tsou Yen (305-ca. 240 B.C.), two
chapters from the Kuan Tzu, a bit of the Lu-shih Ch'un-chiu, the Yueh
Ling from the Li Chi, and the Hung-fan from the Shu-ching.

(3) NEEDHAM, JOSEPH. "Fundamental Ideas of Chinese Science." In
Science and Civilisation in China (see 2.1.6[7]) 2:216-345.
     A masterful study of the theories of yin-yang forces, the Five
Elements, and the Book of Changes, in the light of modern natural science. Needham's thesis is that whereas the Chinese worldview of correspondence (correlations) is basically scientific, it did not stimulate
the rise of modern science because the Confucian bureaucracy did not
provide those conditions which would have been conducive to such a
rise. Needham calls the Chinese worldview "coordinative thinking,"
namely, thinking in terms of concepts that can be placed side by side
in a pattern.

2.12 THE APPENDIXES OF THE "I-CHING"

(1) FUNG YU-LAN. "The Appendixes of the Book of Changes." In A
History of Chinese Philosophy (see 2.1.7[11]) 1:379-95.
     An explanation of the origins of the trigrams and hexagrams in
relation to early Chinese divination and politics. These appendixes
reflect a synthesis of ideas from the Tao-tê ching, the doctrine of
yin-yang, and the divination of prognostication.

(2) _____. "The Yi Scripture Amplifications and the Chung Yung."
In The Spirit of Chinese Philosophy. Translated by E.R. Hughes.
Boston: Beacon, 1967, pp. 81-111. (Orig. pub. London: Kegan Paul,
Trench Trubner Co., 1947.)
     According to Fung, the contents of the Amplifications of the "I-
ching" (Hsi-tzu) and the Chung-yung [Doctrine of mean], ordinarily con-
sidered as Confucian literature, were actually influenced by Taoism.

2.14   The Tai-p'ing ching   2.14

(3) WEI TAT. An Exposition of I-ching. Taipei: Institute of Cultural
Studies, 1970, 564 pp.
   A large book that presents a serious study of the classic. Its
major parts offer line-by-line and paragraph-by-paragraph analysis of
the ch'ien hexagram, the k'un hexagram, and the rest of the hexagrams.
This is preceded by a hundred pages of introductory material on the
work as a whole, its history and its component parts, with many diagrams and charts. What may be considered as the author's naivete in
textual-critical matters does not detract from the value of his interpretations and analyses. One can actually begin to comprehend the
I'ching through the assistance of this work.

2.13   THE "HUAI-NAN TZU"

(1) CHAN, WING-TSIT. "Taoism of Huai-nan Tzu." In A Source Book in
Chinese Philosophy (see 1.4.2[1]), pp. 305-8.
   A translation of three short cosmological essays of the Huai-nan
Tzu [Prince of Huai-nan]. Its Taoist motif was later incorporated
into neo-Confucianism.

(2) FUNG YU-LAN. "The Cosmology of the Huai-nan Tzu." In A History
of Chinese Philosophy (see 2.1.7[11]) 1:395-99.
   Translation of a collection of excerpts on cosmology that suggest
a Taoist origin.

(3) WALLACKER, BENJAMIN E. Huai-nan Tzu, Book Eleven: Behavior,
Culture, and the Cosmos. New Haven: American Oriental Society, 1962,
88 pp.
   A work of careful scholarship in the best tradition of philological
sinology. The actual translation of the text occupies only about half
of the work, the rest being devoted to problems of commentaries, filia-
tion, technical terms, etc. Best used by advanced students.

2.14   THE "TAI-P'ING CHING" [SCRIPTURE OF SUPREME PEACE]

(1) YU YING-SHIH. "Life and Immortality in the Mind of Han China."
Harvard Journal of Asiatic Studies 25 (1964-65):80-122.
   The author traces the transformation of the otherworldly hsien
(immortal) to this-worldly hsien in the context of the immortality
cult of the Han dynasty. Although this essay is not a direct exposition of the important Taoist scripture, T'ai-p'ing ching, it quotes
several passages from this book and discusses one of its central ideas:
the paramount duty of Taoists to seek immortality drugs and recipes
for the sovereign. The T'ai-p'ing ching was composed in the middle
of the second century A.D.

2.15 NEO-TAOISM

(1) BALAZS, ÉTIENNE. "Nihilistic Revolt or Mystical Escapism." In
Chinese Civilization and Bureaucracy (see 2.5[1]), pp. 226-54.
    "The whole history of 3rd-century ideas, as far as moral and intel-
lectual matters were concerned, is epitomized by the development that
led from the 'criticism by the pure' to 'pure talk,' which in turn became nothing but pure talk." The author characterizes "the two categories of nihilistic revolt and mystical escapism--the libertarians
and the libertines." The article is a thorough and lucid discussion
of the main currents of Taoist-inspired thought and behavior during
the post-Han century.

(2) CHAN, WING-TSIT. "Neo-Taoism." In A Source Book in Chinese
Philosophy (see 1.4.2[1]), pp. 314-35.
    A comprehensive introduction followed by translation of selections
of three neo-Taoists. These selections attempt to show the influences
of neo-Taoism upon Chinese Buddhism and neo-Confucianism.

(3) CH'EN, KENNETH K.S. "Neo-Taoism and the Prajñā School During the
Wei and Chin Dyansties." Chinese Culture 1 (1957):33-46.
    Discusses the prajñā sūtras and various Chinese translations, the
different groups of Buddhist interpreters of these texts during the
fourth and fifth centuries, the neo-Taoist ch'ing-t'an (pure conversations) movement and the rationalist wing of neo-Taoism. Notes
affinities between neo-Taoism and prajñā Buddhism, and describes the
method of ko-i or interpreting Buddhist concepts in the light of
Chinese thought. Although the subject matter is technical, this essay
is written for general readers.

(4) CHUAN TSENG-KIA. "Yuan Chi and His Circle." T'ien Hsia Monthly
9 (1939):469-83.
    An interesting discussion of the so-called Seven Sages of the Bamboo
Grove (Three Kingdoms period, third century A.D., state of Wei), based
on the extant contemporary sources. A good summary of the ideas and
the lifestyle of eccentrics of the time, whose philosophical leanings
were towards Taoism.

(5) FUNG YU-LAN. "Neo-Taoism." In A Short History of Chinese
Philosophy (see 2.6.1[5]), pp. 217-54.
    Fung discusses neo-Taoism in terms of the two schools: the meta-
physical and the romantic. The former emphasizes "mysterious learning"
(hsüan-hsüeh), whereas the latter prefers "pure conversations"
(ch'ing-t'an).

(6) _____ . "Neo-Taoism during the Period of Disunity." In A History
of Chinese Philosophy (see 2.1.7[11]) 2:168-236.
    Contains selected translations as well as expositions of the writings
of Wang Pi (226-249), Hsiang Hsiu (fl. 250), and Kuo Hsiang (d. 312).

(7) _____ . "The Mystical School." In The Spirit of Chinese Philosophy
(see 2.12[2]), pp. 130-55.
   A discussion of neo-Taoism in the period of Political Disunion (265-
589), with emphasis on how the neo-Taoists modified the meaning of being and non-being of the Lao Tzu and the Chuang Tzu. The second half
of the chapter deals with the influences of neo-Taoism upon the Buddho-
Taoists of this period.

(8) GULIK, R.H. van. Hsi K'ang and His Poetical Essay on the Lute.
Tokyo: Sophia University, 1941, 133 pp. New ed., rev. Rutland, Vt.:
C.E. Tuttle Co., 1969.
   The subject of this monograph is one of the most famous characters
of the post-Han century (223-262 A.D.). While his essay on the lute
(ch'in-fu) is given careful study and translation, the book also discusses his biography, his accomplishments as poet and philosopher, and
his reputation as a musician. The author is a distinguished sinologist. The work may be too technical for students withoug considerable
background.

(9) HOWARD, RICHARD CAMPBELL. "Hsi K'ang's Essays on Nurturing Life."
Master's thesis, Columbia University, 1949, 89 pp.
   A translation of Hsi K'ang's essay, Nurturing Life, together with
Hsiang Hsiu's (ca. 221-300) Objections and Hsi K'ang's Reply. Hsi
K'ang, one of the Seven Bamboo Sages of the period, combined neo-
Taoism with the cult of physical immortality and the art of medicine.
His thought anticipated the religious Taoism of Ko Hung in the next
century. The translations are preceded by an introduction that de-
scribes the various strands of movements associated with religious
Taoism.

(10) LIEBENTHAL, WALTER, trans. "T'ang Yung-t'ung: Wang Pi's New
Interpretation of the I Ching." Harvard Journal of Asiatic Studies
10 (1946):124-61.
   "Authorized translation" of an important article by a leading
Chinese authority. The subject is the most influential of the interpre-
tations of this classic work, written in the early third century A.D.
Liebenthal remarks that "two attainments, namely the destruction of Han
Byzantinism and the propagation of a worldview that dared to interpret
the world as a whole, make Wang Pi one of the great pioneers of philosophy in China." Technical, for advanced students of Chinese thought.

(11) LINK, ARTHUR E. "The Taoist Antecedents of Tao-an's Prajñā
Ontology." History of Religions 9 (1969-1970):101-215.
   A discussion of the appropriation of neo-Taoist thought by the
Buddho-Taoist Tao-an (312-385) and his colleagues. For example, pen-
wu (original non-existence) was used to explain Prajñāpāramitā
(Transcendental Wisdom).

2.16 RELIGIOUS TAOISM OF KO HUNG (284-363)

(1) De BARY, W. THEODORE; CHAN, WING-TSIT; and WATSON, BURTON, comps.
"Ko Hung." In Sources of Chinese Tradition (see 1.4.1[3]), pp. 298-305
(vol. 1, pp. 258-65 in paperback reprint).
    Translation of excerpts from the Pao-p'u tzu [Philosopher who em-
braces simplicity], which deal with topics such as physical immortality,
alchemy, and the merit system.

(2) WARE, JAMES R., trans. Alchemy, Medicine, Religion in China of
A.D. 320 (see 1.8.2[3]).
    A complete translation of the inner chapters of the Ko Hung. All
divergent trends of religious Taoism in the fourth century may be found
in this work.

2.17 TAOIST MESSIANISM

(1) SEIDEL, ANNA K. "The Image of the Perfect Ruler in Early Taoist
Messianism: Lao Tzu and Li Hung." History of Religions 9 (1969-70):
216-47.
    Presents a documentary analysis of the image of the Taoist ruler of
the late Han dynasty and the concept of the "perfect lord of Li Hung"
in Taoist literature of the period of Political Disunion. The entire
article deals with the rebellious Taoist against the Confucian estab-
lishment of the Chinese state.

2.18 THEORY OF TAOIST ALCHEMY: EXTERNAL ALCHEMY (ELIXIRS) AND
      INTERNAL ALCHEMY (YOGA, HEALTH, DIET, SEX TECHNIQUES)

      See 1.8 for Taoist Alchemists between the Second and Seventh
      Centuries A.D.

(1) DAVIS, TENNEY L. "Dualistic Cosmogony of Huai-nan Tzu and Its
Relation to the Background of Chinese and European Alchemy." Isis
25 (1936):327-40.
    "The dualistic doctrine of yin-yang furnished a medium in which
alchemy could flourish." The author gives a number of non-Chinese examples of the doctrine of "Two Contrasts." Certain passages in the
Huai-nan Tzu contain references to yin-yang. Author concludes "that
alchemy came to Europe from China, probably through the agency of the
Arabs in the eighth or ninth century." Written in easily intelligible
style.

(2) DAVIS, TENNEY L., and CH'EN KUO-FU. "Shang-yang Tzu: Taoist Writer
and Commentator on Alchemy." Harvard Journal of Asiatic Studies 7
(1942-43):126-29.

A description of the life and work of a fourteenth-century alchemist,
Chen Chih-hsü, who was also known by his Taoist name Shang-yang Tzu.
He wrote an alchemical treatise entitled Chin-tan-ta-yao [Essentials
of the Elixir] which, according to the authors, agrees essentially with
the European alchemical theory. This article also includes brief biographies of three Taoist associates of Shang-yang Tzu.

(3) HO PENG-YU; LIM, BEDA; and MORSINGH, FRANCIS. "Elixir Plants."
In Chinese Science. Edited by Shigeru Nakayama and Nathan Sivin.
Cambridge: MIT Press, 1973, pp. 153-202.
   Translation of a text that was probably, according to the translators, "composed by an anonymous Taoist adept some time between the
years 1324 and 1443." The text consists of 69 verses, which are here
translated, in a tour de force, in English rhyme and rhythm. For each
plant, name identification is made in scientific terms, with brief comments on pertinent matters such as the plant's place in the Chinese
pharmacopoeia or the alchemical tradition. Despite its subject, the
article is not too technical.

(4) HO PENG-YU, and NEEDHAM, JOSEPH. "Theories of Categories in Early
Medieval Chinese Alchemy." Journal of the Warburg and Courtauld
Institutes 22 (1959):173-210, 2 plates, 1 table.
   Best studied after reading the translation of the Ts'an T'ung Ch'i
by Wu and Davis (see 1.8.1[2] and 2.6.1[4]). This article is a study
of the Tshan Thung Chhi Wu Hsiang Lei Pi Yao [Arcane essentials of the
similarities of the five (substances) in the kinship of the three].
It is "a Thang (Tang) text with a Sung commentary which strongly indicates a derivation from the philosophical ideas of a famous Han scholar
and thinker, Tung Chung-shu (179-104 B.C.)." The various sections
following the introduction discuss sources and dating, and offer a complete translation of the text and its commentary, followed by discussion of same. Chinese character list furnished. An important article,
quite technical.

(5) MASPERO, HENRI. "Alchemy and Physical Immortality." In Le taoisme
(see 2.7.1[11]), pp. 116-47.
   A discussion of the internal and external alchemy and their relations to practices such as diet, breathing, sexual art, and gymnastics.

(6) NEEDHAM, JOSEPH, and LU GWEI-DJEN. Science and Civilisation in
China (see 2.1.6[7]). Vol. 5, Spagyrical Discovery and Invention:
Magisteries of Gold and Immortality, 1974, 510 pp.
   Needham and his team have not only summarized and evaluated practically all the writings on Chinese alchemy and religious Taoism written
in the Chinese and Western languages in the twentieth century, but have
also brought new insights on this fascinating and abstruse topic. This
book mainly deals with a) theory and practice of alchemy (both external
and internal), b) the scientific and technological basis of alchemy,

c) the religio-mythological symbols of alchemy and Taoism, d) the
liturgical meaning of religious Taoism, insofar as it throws light on
alchemy and the Taoist vision of physical immortality, and e) comparison of Chinese alchemy with Western alchemy. There are many quotes
from the Taoist sources, a number of them newly translated by the authors, and a 155-page bibliography on Chinese alchemy and religious
Taoism with titles in Western languages. This is definitely a ground-
breaking work.

(7) SIVAN, NATHAN. Chinese Alchemy: Preliminary Studies. Cambridge:
Harvard University Press, 1968, 339 pp.
    The author has translated a representative alchemical work of the
seventh century A.D., Tan-ching yao-cheuh [Essential formulas from the
alchemical classics] by Sun Ssu-mo (581-682). As a trained chemist,
Sivin has rendered the alchemical concepts into chemical terms while
at the same time preserving the cosmological outlook of Taoism. This
book also includes a chapter on the problems relating to the study of
Chinese alchemy, a chapter on the tradition of the Tan-ching yao-cheuh,
and a section on the "biography" of author Sun Ssu-mo.

(8) WARE, JAMES, trans. Alchemy, Medicine, Religion in China (see
2.7.4[1]).

(9) YETTS, W. PERCEVAL. "Notes on Flower Symbolism in China." Journal
of the Royal Asiatic Society, 1941, pp. 1-21.
    Although the subject matter is not specifically religious, the sym-
bolism involves ideas found throughout Chinese religious art and literature. This is a good treatment of two of the many numerical categories
--the Four Seasons and the Twelve Months--as they are expressed in
flower symbolism. Easily intelligible style, despite its philological
approach.

2.19   TAOIST SECTARIAN TEACHINGS

2.19.1   Teaching of the Celestial Master Sect "T'ien-shih Tao"
         See also 1.9.2

         (1) SCHIPPER, K.M. Taoism: The Liturgical Tradition. Un-
         published paper. Paris: École pratique études, 77 pp.
             The author is a Dutch scholar who was a practising Taoist
         priest for five years in Taiwan. This paper is an eye-witness
         account of the practice and belief of Taoist temples in Taiwan
         associated with the T'ien-shih Tao. The author mentions the
         various functions of the different members of the Taoist tem-
         ple and points out the importance of the incense burner as the
         symbol of the religious community. This paper offers us much
         information not accessible to outsiders. Available from its
         author.

(2) WELCH, HOLMES H. "The Bellagio Conference on Taoist Studies" (see 2.1.7[17]), pp. 123-36.
    A summary of Schipper's paper (1).

2.19.2 Teaching of the Sect of the Preservation of the True Nature ("Ch'üan-chen Chiao")

See also 1.9.1

(1) CHAN, WING-TSIT. "Ch'üan-chen Sect." In Religious Trends in Modern China (see 1.1[3]), pp. 148-51.
    A brief presentation of the beliefs and practice of the Ch'üan-chen Sect.

2.19.3 Beliefs of the Taoist Lay Groups

(1) De BARY, W. THEODORE; CHAN, WING-TSIT; and WATSON, BURTON, comps. Sources of Chinese Tradition (see 1.4.1[3]), pp. 630-40 (omitted in paperback reprint).
    This section contains an introduction to popular religious cults and translations of the following Taoist scriptures: The Treatise of the Most Exalted One on Moral Retribution, The Silent Way of Recompense, Questions and Answers on the Way of Pervading Unity (I-Kuan Tao), and Methods of Religious Cultivation.

(2) YU, DAVID C. "A Buddho-Taoist Sect in Modern China." History of Religions 11 (1971):157-60.
    A review of Lo Hsiang-lin's Chinese-language monograph, The Spread of the Chen-k'ung Chiao in South China and Malaya (1962). Lo's book shows that even in the twentieth century, lay Taoist groups were still active in China.

2.20 BELIEFS OF THE SECRET SOCIETIES

See also 1.10

(1) De BARY, W. THEODORE; CHAN, WING-TSIT; and WATSON, BURTON, comps. Sources of Chinese Tradition (see 1.4.1[3]), pp. 649-59 (omitted in paperback reprint).
    Gives introduction to the origins and development of the secret societies and their relationship with religious Taoism; includes a translation of society documents dealing with ethics and its membership.

2. Religious Thought

2.20   2.20 Beliefs of the Secret Societies

(2) GRAHAM, DAVID C. "Original Vows of Kitchen God." Chinese Recorder
61 (1930):781-88.
    Translation of what Graham calls "a Taoist sacred book." He remarks
that "the conception of the vows of the Kitchen God is probably an imi-
tation of the vows of the Buddhist God, Amitābha." A good introduction
to Taoist ideas as they are propagated at the popular level, with theological explanations and warnings about punishments for sinners.

2.21 TWENTIETH-CENTURY CONFUCIAN RELIGIOUS THOUGHT

2.21.1 Rationalist School of Fung Yu-lan (1895-), Following the School of Principle with Taoist Emphasis

    (1) CHAN, WING-TSIT. "Development of Rationalistic Neo-
    Confucianism." In Religious Trends in Modern China (see
    1.1[3]), pp. 43-53.
        Fung Yu-lan is here viewed as the leader of the new Ration-
    alist school. The author believes that by applying the logic
    of Western philosophy, Fung has transformed the School of
    Principle into a system of realism in the classic sense.

    (2) _____. "Fung Yu-lan." In A Source Book in Chinese
    Philosophy (see 1.4.2[1]), pp. 751-62.
        Selections are from Fung's Hsin li-hsüeh [The new rational
    philosophy], which represents his own system. It discusses
    four formal concepts: principle (li), material force (ch'i),
    evolution of tao, and the great whole (ta-t'ung).

2.21.2 Idealist School of Hsiung Shih-li (1885-1968) Following the School of Mind of Neo-Confucianism with Buddhist Emphasis

    (1) CHAN, WING-TSIT. "Hsiung Shih-li." In A Source Book in
    Chinese Philosophy (see 1.4.2[1]), pp. 763-72.
        Selections from Hsiung's Hsin wei-shih lun [New doctrine of
    consciousness-only], with comments. This work represents
    Hsiung's efforts to synthesize the School of Mind of neo-
    Confucianism with Yogācāra School.

    (2) _____. "The Idealist School of Neo-Confucianism." In
    Religious Trends in Modern China (see 1.1[3]), pp. 31-43, 126-
    35.
        The author explains the process of contraction (hsi) and
    expansion (p'i), or matter and mind as the structure of con-
    sciousness which constitutes the basis of Hsiung's idealism.
    The author believes that Hsiung's philosophy is the Confucian-
    ization of Buddhism. Nevertheless, Hsiung claimed to be a

Confucianist under the influence of the Book of Changes and
the writings of Wang Fu-chih (1619-1692).

2.21.3 Beliefs of the Intellectuals

(1) CHAN, WING-TSIT. "The Religion of the Intellectuals."
In Religious Trends in Modern China (see 1.1[3]), pp. 217-64.
    A lucid account of the great debate on the fate of religion
among the intellectuals during the first half of the century.
The author thinks that Chinese intellectuals hold a common
view of religion as a) sanction of ethics, b) fulfillment of
human nature, c) the realization of Principle (Tao, Thusness,
or Li). Summarizes the Confucian idea of religion as expressed
by such thinkers as Chu Hsi, Fung Yu-lan, and Hsiung Shih-li.

(2) CHENG CHUNG-YING. "Dialectic of Confucian Morality and
Metaphysics of Man." Philosophy East and West 21 (1971):111-23.
    Argument for the structure of religious consciousness in
Confucian morality. The term "religious consciousness" involves
"an ultimate concern with an ultimate reality that defines a
goal for the transformation of man." Confucian morality is compared with Kant's categorical imperative, Hume's empirical moral
theory, and Sartre's existential thought.

(3) LIU SHU-HSIEN. "The Religious Import of Confucian Philosophy: Its Traditional Outlook and Contemporary Significance."
Philosophy East and West 21 (1971):157-75.
    A defense for the presence of the transcendent in Confucian
philosophy based on such statements as "that which is unfathom-
able in the operation of yin and yang is called spirit (shen)."
The author recognizes the "functional monism" in Confucianism
in contrast to the Western religions of "pure transcendence."
The paper suggests that the contemporary process philosophy in
the West is moving closer to the spirit of Confucian philosophy.

2.22 RELIGION OF MAO TSE-TUNG (1893-1976)

(1) FU, CHARLES WEI-HSÜN. "Confucianism, Marxism-Leninism and Mao."
Journal of Chinese Philosophy 1 (1974):119-51.
    This essay does not purport to establish the religiosity of Maoism,
but because it views Maoism as the pursuit of the moral concern of
Marxism-Leninism and because it propounds the view that Maoism emphasizes the primacy of praxis over theory, it is indirectly concerned
with Maoism as a spiritual movement. It attempts in the first part
to point out the dilemma in Marxism concerning whether it is a scientific truth or a practice. It then presents the thesis that Maoism

2. Religious Thought

has solved the dilemma by making Marxism (or Leninism) a "programmatic ideology," i.e., a revolutionary practice.   It concludes with the view that much of the moral interest in Maoism was in fact derived from Confucianism; however, it emphasizes the difference between Confucian morality, based on personal choice and a universal concept of human nature, and the Maoist morality based upon coercion and a class conception of human nature.   This is the first successful endeavor in English to see the continuities between traditional Chinese thought and Mao's ideology, and Western thought and Maoism.

(2) MAO TSE-TUNG.   Poems of Mao Tse-Tung.   Translated by Wong Man. Hong Kong: Eastern Horizon Press, 1966, 95 pp.
   This is a translation of twenty-seven peoms of Mao written between 1925 and 1958.   Some of them are considered to have religious meaning because there are: a) frequent allusions to legendary divinities and mythological figures of traditional China, and b) expressions of archetypal themes (good vs. evil, victory after long suffering, homology of man, etc.) which appear to be universal in man's religions.   Mao's poems reflect a continuation of classic Chinese poetry, but there is much greater trust in man's ability to change himself and the world. There is a defiance against nature's cruelty and man's intransigence. The English translation is well done.

(3) _____ .   Ten More Poems of Mao Tse-tung.   Hong Kong: Eastern Horizon Press, 1967, 33 pp.
   These ten poems were written between 1949 and 1963, but were not published until New Year's Day, 1964.   The translation retains much of the original mood.   The name of the translator is not given.

(4) MUNRO, DONALD J.   The Concept of Man in Contemporary China.   Ann Arbor: University of Michigan Press, 1977, 248 pp.
   Although this work is not directly concerned with religion, it has profound implications about what religion is or might be in Maoist China, for it analyzes the spiritual dimension of man as infinitely malleable in terms of the cultivation of mind and morality.   The author emphasizes the relationship between the traditional Confucian interest in the cultivation of the mind and the Maoist emphasis upon the transformation of the human nature in terms of the socialistic values and virtues.   Munro then moves on to discuss the function of the government in terms of the concept of fosterage.   It is the duty of the state, at both the formal and informal levels, to nurture the people in the direction of continuous socialistic and moral transformation.   The Maoist educational process emphasizes the identity between one's public and private life, as well as the inseparability of scientific-technological skills and moral and ideological consciousness.   The concept of equality in Maoist China is also discussed in terms of equality of opportunity, equality of distribution, and equality of status.   The entire book involves a sustained comparison concerning the nature of

man between the liberal-democratic tradition of the West, Soviet
Marxism, and contemporary Maoism. It concludes with a discussion of
the weaknesses and strengths of the Maoist concept of man. This book
is a companion volume of the author's The Concept of Man in Early China
(see 2.2[9]). Both works should be read by anyone who has a serious
scholarly interest in the continuities and discontinuities between contemporary and traditional China concerning her spiritual, moral, and
intellectual life.

(5) WAKEMAN, FREDERIC, Jr. History and Will: Philosophical Perspectives of Mao Tse-tung's Thought. Berkeley and Los Angeles: University
of California Press, 1973, 392 pp.
      This work in the formal sense is a study of the intellectual influ-
ences on Mao's thought. But it in many instances discloses the spiritual and volitional dimensions of Mao's thought that can be called religious even within the perspective of nontranscendent Marxism.
Although the book falls within the genre of contemporary Chinese intellectual history, the real intent of its author is to demonstrate
that Maoist Marxism is a religion, both in the practical and theoretical sense. It traces both the Western and Chinese philosophical influences upon Mao, although in the final sense the latter outweigh the
former. The Western traditions that have shaped Mao's thought are neo-
Kantianism, socialistic idealism, and Marxism-Leninism. The Marxist
teleological view of history in Mao's thought was made less determin-
istic by his emphasis on the human will which allows man to be the maker
of history. Mao's emphasis upon the human will and the necessity of
changes in history is traceable to a long line of traditional Chinese
thinkers, including the authors of the Book of Changes and Wang Yang-
ming.

2.23 CHINESE WORLDVIEW

(1) CHAN, WING-TSIT. "Individual in Chinese Religions." In The Status
of the Individual in East and West. Edited by Charles A. Moore.
Honolulu: University of Hawaii Press, 1968, pp. 181-98.
      This essay is a lucid summary of certain basic, universal charac-
teristics of the Chinese worldview and religious thought. The author
singles out three topics for detailed consideration: the goal, the
way to the goal, and "the position of the individual in relation to
ultimate reality. . . ." As to the first, the "ultimate goal (of the
Chinese) is simply the survival of the individual and the realization
of his nature." As to the second, "each of the three religions has
its own way, but in each case the way can be summed up in one word,
namely, vacuity (hsü) in Taoism, calmness (ting) in Buddhism, and sincerity (ch'eng) in Confucianism." As to the third, "in all the three
systems . . . the solution of the apparent conflict between the one
and the many is essentially the same, namely, that each involves the

other." A good survey of the essentials of Chinese religious thought.
Nontechnical.

(2) CHEN, ELLEN MARIE. "The Unity Way: Taoism-Ch'an and Christianity."
China Notes 15 (1977):6-10.
    A short but stimulating comparison between the Taoist-Ch'an world-
view and the Christian worldview. Although the title appears to emphasize unity, the essay in actuality accentuates the basic differences
between Taoism-Ch'an and Christianity. The former emphasizes the un-
conscious, the descent into the abyss, the cultivation of no-mind, the
embracing of the impersonal, and the exaltation of the weak; whereas
the latter emphasizes the conscious, the ascent to God, the transformation of world through action, the absoluteness of divine personhood,
and the adoration of power.

(3) CHENG CHUNG-YING. "Religious Reality and Religious Understanding
in Confucianism and Neo-Confucianism." International Philosophical
Quarterly 13 (1973):33-61.
    Attempts to demonstrate the truly religious character of Confucian-
ism and neo-Confucianism, something which the author feels has not
generally been appreciated "because we do not generally take a suffi-
ciently theoretical perspective on problems of religion and develop a
grasp of possible alternatives to already established perspectives. . . ."
He emphasizes a type of religious thinking which presents "the ultimate
and the total" as "the existential fulfillment of the rational through
a process of embodying the practical and the moral." According to the
author, it is Confucianism and neo-Confucianism that "provide a most
rich and suggestive example" of this type. The balance of the essay
is devoted to explicating this view. A rare attempt to understand the
Confucian tradition as religious in the profound, rather than the
superficial, sense.

(4) SMITH, HUSTON. "Transcendence in Traditional China." Religious
Studies 2 (1969):185-96.
    A discussion on the characteristics of the transcendent in early
Confucianist and Taoist classics. The author criticizes the prevalent
view held by students of Chinese religion/philosophy that there is a
lack of the transcendent in Chinese thought. Both Western and Chinese
scholars tend to equate Chinese mysticism with agnosticism or religious
functionalism. Four aspects of Chinese transcendence are pointed out:
1) it provides the grounds for the social norms; 2) it is the root or
source of man and nature; 3) it assures the individual that the cultivation of virtue is self-rewarding; 4) it encourages an endless cultivation of virtue in man's lifespan.

3. Authoritative Texts

3.1 CONFUCIAN RELIGION

3.1.1 Bibliography

(1) De BARY, W. THEODORE, and EMBREE, AINSLEE T., eds.
"Confucian Classics." In A Guide to Oriental Classics. New
York: Columbia University Press, 1964, pp. 120-31.
   An annotated bibliography of both primary and secondary
sources.

3.1.2 "Ta-hsüeh" [The great learning]

(1) BAHM, ARCHIE. The Heart of Confucius. New York and Tokyo:
Walker & Weatherhill, 1969, 159 pp.
   Despite its perhaps unfortunate title, this book is a good
introduction to the study of two of the Confucian Four Books,
the Chung Yung--which Bahm calls Genuine Living--and the Ta
Hsüeh--which Bahm calls Great Wisdom. They are presented in
honesty as "interpretations," reflecting the fact that Bahm is
not actually translating the texts from the Chinese, but utilizing existing translations for his own purposes. These "interpretations," and the long introduction that precedes them, are
valuable because Bahm is an experienced scholar in comparative
philosophy, with a long-term interest in Chinese thought. Their
very lack of strictly sinological expertise may enable him to
give us new perspectives on these texts, although the student
should at the same time consult one or more standard versions,
such as those by Legge (3) or Hughes (see 3.1.3[3]).

(2) CHAN, WING-TSIT. "The Great Learning." In A Source Book
in Chinese Philosophy (see 1.4.2[1]), pp. 84-94.
   A translation of the text as edited by Chu Hsi (1130-1200)
with his commentary. The introduction preceding the text is
instructive.

(3) "The Great Learning." Translated by James Legge. In The
Chinese Classics (see 1.2.7[4]) 1-2:354-81.
   A scholarly translation of the classic with extensive notes.

3.1.3   "Chung-yung" [The doctrine of the mean]

(1) CHAN, WING-TSIT.   "The Doctrine of the Mean." In A Source
Book in Chinese Philosophy (see 1.4.2[1]), pp. 95-114.
    A conscientious translation of the text as edited by Chu Hsi
with commentary.

(2) "The Doctrine of the Mean." Translated by James Legge.   In
The Chinese Classics (see 1.2.7[4]) 1-2:382-434.
    A faithful translation of the text with extensive notes.

(3) HUGHES, ERNEST R.   "The Great Learning" and the "Mean-in-
Action." New York: Dutton, 1943, 176 pp.
    A readable translation by an able scholar based upon an older
text (pre-Chu Hsi). Both the philosophical and philological
grounds are fully considered.

(4) KU HUNG-MING, trans. Conduct of Life. London: John Murray,
1906, 60 pp. Reprint. Taipei: privately published, 1956.
Also in The Wisdom of China and India, ed. Lin Yutang (New York:
Random House, 1942), pp. 843-64.
    A translation of Chung-yung by a Chinese literatus of the old
school who, however, was thoroughly versed in Western learning
as well. Ku's translation gives the text a more religious interpretation than others, and is obviously the product of a profound understanding of the deeper meanings. It is also a more
poetic version that is entirely free from scholarly apparatus.

3.1.4   The Analects

(1) The Analects of Confucius. Translated by Arthur Waley (see
2.2[1]).
    A collection of the "sayings" of Confucius as he was under-
stood by the Confucians of the late fourth century B.C. when
the book was compiled. It was the intent of the translator to
present the Confucius of the Analects as he was actually depicted
without being influenced by the late commentators, particularly
Chu Hsi. Waley's explanations of terms are very useful: they
prepare the reader to enter into the atmosphere of China of the
fourth century B.C. Most of the terms are related to Chinese
religion.

(2) CHAN, WING-TSIT.   "Analects." In A Source Book in Chinese
Philosophy (see 1.4.2[1]), pp. 18-48.
    Selections of translation with emphasis upon the humanism of
Confucius. Commentary stresses the neo-Confucian interpretations
of the text.

3.   Authoritative Texts

(3) <u>Confucian Analects</u>. Translated by James Legge. In <u>The Chinese Classics</u> (see 1.2.7[4]) 1-2:137-354.
A translation based upon careful scholarship with extensive notes.

3.1.5   "The Book of Mencius"

(1) <u>The Book of Mencius</u>. Translated by Wing-tsit Chan. In <u>A Source Book in Chinese Philosophy</u> (see 1.4.2[1]), pp. 51-83.
A translation of selections showing the idealistic philosophy of Mencius with commentary.

(2) <u>The Book of Mencius</u>. Translated by James Legge. In <u>The Chinese Classics</u> (see 1.2.7[4]) 1-2:125-502.
A faithful translation with exhaustive notes dealing with contemporary Chinese thought.

(3) <u>Mencius</u>. Translated by D.C. Lau. Baltimore: Penguin, 1970, 288 pp.
The latest translation of this text by a scholar with the ideal combination of thorough native scholarship and Western methodological expertise. Lau is also an excellent English stylist, which is the final ingredient in production of what may be regarded as the new standard translation.

(4) <u>Mencius: A New Translation Arranged and Annotated</u>. Translated by W.A.C.H. Dobson (see 2.3[1]).
A translation made in the light of recent textual and philological studies but aimed for the general reader. Sections are rearranged by topics to enhance readability.

(5) <u>The Sayings of Mencius</u>. Translated by James R. Ware. New York: New American Library, Mentor, 1900, 173 pp.
A popular translation. The translator has the habit of rendering the key concepts into hyphenated terms. For example, <u>jen</u> (humanity) is translated as "man-at-his-best."

(6) WALEY, ARTHUR, trans. "Mencius." In <u>Three Ways of Thought in Ancient China</u> (see 2.3[3]), pp. 115-95.
Translations of selections with Waley's commentary. The selections deal with the goodness of human nature, importance of nourishing the spirit, moral basis of the state, and mysticism. Waley has rendered Mencius's thought into readable modern English.

3.1.6 "I-ching" [Book of changes]
See also 1.2.7

(1) WILHELM, HELLMUT. Changes: Eight Lectures on the "I-ching."
Translated by Cary F. Baynes. New York: Bollingen, Pantheon
Books, 1960, 111 pp.
  Eight chapters on the history and meaning of the Book of
Changes covering: 1) origin of the book, 2) meaning of polarity,
3) trigrams and hexagrams, 4) the appendices of the book, 5) interpretations of the book by scholars since the Sung dynasty,
6) use of the book in divination. The author's thesis is that
the Book of Changes is essentially symbolic and mythical; it is
a reflection of the human psyche. In Chinese history, whenever
Confucianism dominated the intellectual scene, this book became
more studied; the Chinese felt the need to plunge into their
psychic life when their cultural life was controlled by rationalism.

3.1.7 "Shih-ching" [Book of songs]

(1) The Book of Songs. Translated by Arthur Waley (see 1.2.7[1]).
  A translation of two hundred and ninety songs accompanied by
the author's commentary. Helpful for an understanding of the
rituals, folklore, and society of pre-Confucian China.

(2) CREEL, HERRLEE G. The Birth of China (see 1.2.5[2]), pp.
254-75.
  The author discusses the bronze inscriptions as the earliest
historical records of China. He also presents the literary
sources that were eventually embodied in the Shu-ching [Book of
history], Shih-ching [Book of songs], I-ching [Book of changes],
and I-li [Book of etiquette and ceremony]. Although these works
in the present form were set down in the late Chou or early Han
dynasty, they tell of the culture and history of Shang and Chou,
particularly the latter.

3.1.8 "Shu-ching" [Book of history]

(1) CREEL, HERRLEE G. The Birth of China (see 1.2.5[2]). See
also 3.1.7[2].

(2) "Shoo King" [Shu-ching]. In The Chinese Classics (see
1.2.7[4]) 3:735 pp.
  History covering the periods of Shun, Yü, Shang, and Chou,
with strong Confucian interpretation by the redactors.

3.1.9   "Li-chi" [Book of rites]

>   (1) Li-chi. Translated by James Legge. Edited by Ch'u Chai
> and Winberg Chai (see 1.4.2[4]).
>   The introduction (pages ix-lxxx) explains the origin of I-li,
> Chou-li, and Li-chi as well as the four basic elements of the
> Li-chi: a) interpretation of the rites, b) institution of the
> rites, including a discussion of the purpose of mourning and of
> sacrificial rites, c) philosophical essays which include two
> famous treatises known as Ta-hsüeh [Great learning] and Chung-
> yung [Doctrine of mean], and d) anecdotes about Confucius and
> his disciples together with conversations between Confucius and
> his disciples.

3.1.10 "Hsiao-ching" [Classic of filial piety]

>   (1) Hsiao-ching. Translated by Mary L. Markra (see 1.4.2[2]).
>   This book contains both the translation of the text and the
> original text in Chinese. The translation is faithful and ac-
> curate. The footnotes are useful for an understanding of Han
> Confucianism. The text explains why ancestor worship is neces-
> sary.

3.1.11 "Po-hu-t'ung" [The comprehensive discussion in the White Tiger
        Hall]

>   (1) CHAN, WING-TSIT; AL FARUQI, ISMA'IL RAGI; KITAGAWA, JOSEPH
> M.; and RAJU, P.T., comps. "White Tiger Hall." In The Great
> Asian Religions (see 1.1[2]), pp. 130-31.
>   Translation of two excerpts showing the relationship between
> religion, rites, and music.

>   (2) THOMPSON, LAURENCE G., ed. "Po-hu-t'ung." In The Chinese
> Way in Religion (see 1.1[15]), pp. 34-45.
>   Excerpts from the Po-hu-t'ung, translated by Tjan Tjoe-som
> (Tseng Chu-sen) and published by E.J. Brill (Leiden, 2 vols.,
> 1949 and 1952). This material describes the five household
> deities, the gods of earth and millet, divination, and the
> cosmology of the Five Elements. This work represents the
> syncretism of Confucian religion in the Han dynasty.

3.1.12 "Ch'un-ch'iu fan-lu" [Luxuriant gems of the spring and autumn
        annals]

>   (1) "Ch'un-ch'iu fan-lu," by Tung Chung-shu. In A Source Book
> in Chinese Philosophy (see 1.4.2[1]) and in Sources of Chinese

3. *Authoritative Texts*

3.1.13   3.1 Confucian Religion

Tradition (see 1.4.1[3]), pp. 174-75, 178-83, 187-88, 217-20.
    This work reflects what is generally referred to as Confucian
metaphysics in which ethics, politics, religion, and cosmology
are fused.

3.1.13 "Lu-shih Ch'un-ch'iu" [Spring and autumn annals of Mr. Lu]

    (1) "Lu-shih Ch'un-ch'iu." In Sources of Chinese Tradition
    (see 1.4.1[3]), pp. 221-26 (vol. 1, pp. 206-10 in paperback
    reprint).
    This excerpt deals with the duties of the emperor during
the first month of the year regarding his personal conduct,
law and administration, sacrifice, music and dance, propitious
acts, and taboos. The entire book is an "almanac" explaining
the "dos" and "don'ts" that should be followed each month: it
shows the interaction between religion, astronomy, politics,
and ethics.

3.1.14 "T'ai-chi-t'u shuo" [Diagram of the supreme ultimate explained]

    (1) CHAN, WING-TSIT. "An Explanation of the Diagram of the
    Great Ultimate." In A Source Book in Chinese Philosophy (see
    1.4.2[1]), pp. 460-64.
    A translation of the short metaphysical essay by the neo-
Confucianist, Chou Tun-yi (1017-1073), which exerted great influence upon both neo-Confucianism and Taoism. Introduction
and commentary are provided.

    (2) FUNG YU-LAN. "Diagram of the Supreme Ultimate Explained."
    In A History of Chinese Philosophy (see 2.1.7[11] 2:435-42.
    Translation of the short essay with full explanation. Fung
believes that Chou Tun-yi's essay resembles an earlier Taoist
essay (T'ang dynasty). In substance, Chou's essay is more
Taoist than Confucian.

3.2 TAOIST RELIGION

3.2.1 Taoist Canon

    See also 2.10, Concept of Revealed Scriptures

    (1) De BARY, W. THEODORE, and EMBREE, AINSLEE T., eds. "Taoist
    Writings." In A Guide to Oriental Classics (see 3.1.1[1]), pp.
    132-37.
    Annotated bibliography on the Tao-tê ching and the Chuang-
Tzu, including secondary sources on these two texts.

92

(2) LIU TS'UN-YAN. "The Compilation and Historical Value of
the Tao-tsang." In Essays on the Sources for Chinese History.
Edited by Donald Leslie, Colin MacKerras, and Wang Gungwu.
Canberra: Australia National University; Columbia: University
of South Carolina, 1973, pp. 104-19.
  A brief and concise presentation of the history of the compilation of the Taoist canon from the Sung to the Republic period.
The present Tao-tsang was completed in 1445 during the Ming
dynasty, totalling 5,305 chüan. A more simplified edition
called Tao-tsang chi-yao was compiled in 1906. A general summary of the contents of Tao-tsang is provided.

(3) NEEDHAM, JOSEPH, and LU GWEI-DJEN. Science and Civilisation
in China (see 2.1.6[7]). Vol. 5, Spagyrical Discovery and
Invention: Magisteries of Gold and Immortality, 1974, Bibliography A, pp. 314-64.
  This portion contains many titles of the Taoist canon (Tao-
tsang): their Chinese titles, transliterations, English meanings of the titles, authors and dates. Information concerning
partial or complete translations of some of these works in
Western languages is also given.

(4) ŌBUCHI, NINJI. "On Ku Ling-pao ching." Acta Asiatica 27
(1974):33-56.
  A study of the manuscripts of the Ling-pao ching discovered
in 1900 at Tun-huang, probably copied during the mid-eighth
century A.D. Compilation of this group of scriptures was attributed to Lu Hsiu-ching (406-477). In comparing the manuscripts with those in the Tao-tsang, Ōbuchi found considerable
discrepancies between them. A highly technical essay, for
specialists only.

(5) SCHIPPER, KRISTOFER M. Concordance de Houang-t'ing King:
Nei-king et Wai-king. Paris: Publications de l'École française
d'Extrême-Orient, 1975.
  A French edition of the different Chinese versions of the
inner and outer chapters of the "Yellow Court Canon," a fourth
century A.D. internal alchemistic text produced by the Mao-shan
sect. Includes indexes to important terms that appear in these
chapters. An introduction is also provided.

(6) _____. Concordance du Tao-tsang. Paris: Publications de
l'École française d'Extrême-Orient, 1975.
  A French catalog of 1,487 titles of the Taoist canon.

(7) SCHIPPER, KRISTOFER M., trans. Le "Feng-teng": Rituel
taoïste. Paris: Publications de l'École française d'Extrême-
Orient, 1975.

3. *Authoritative Texts*

Schipper provides a photographic reproduction of the ritual
text of Feng-teng [Division of the lamps], a translation, and
an introduction. The text consists of a sequence of three rituals involving the lighting and distribution of lamps in the
sanctuary. The origin of this ritual can be traced to the fifth
century A.D.

(8) STRICKMANN, MICHEL. "Taoist Literature." Encyclopaedia
Britannica. 15th ed. Chicago and London: Encyclopaedia
Britannica, 1974, 17:1051-55.
   A brief and expert explanation of the major sections of the
Taoist canon by a specialist. It presents the revelations to
Yang Hsi that became the Shang-ch'ing ching, the first section
of the Tao-tsang; and the Lin-Pao literature that emphasizes
the divinities of the T'ien-tsun and became the second major
section of the Tao-tsang. The Sang-huang ching constitutes
the third major section. According to the author, "The continuing study of the Taoist Canon in its wider historical context
can radically alter many established conceptions of both Chinese
religion and Chinese society."

(9) WELCH, HOLMES H. "Taoist Canon." In "The Bellagio Conference on Taoist Studies" (see 2.1.7[17]), pp. 129-31.
   A brief discussion of the composition of the Taoist canon
as well as popular Taoist scriptures.

3.2.2 "Tao-tê ching"

See also 2.7.1, Lao Tzu

(1) BAHM, ARCHIE J. "Tao Teh King" by Lao Tzu. New York:
Frederick Unger, 1958, 126 pp.
   Highly original interpretation. Useful discussion by the
author includes a notable section in which the concept of Tao
is compared with other similar-seeming concepts in world
philosophy and religion.

(2) CHANG CHUNG-YUAN, trans. Tao: A New Way of Thinking.
New York: Harper & Row, 1975, 223 pp.
   A translation of the Tao-tê ching with a commentary following each chapter. Two thinkers are frequently discussed in
order to elucidate the meaning of the Taoist classic: Heidegger
and Nishida, a modern Japanese philosopher. Chinese and Western
aesthetic theories regarding art and poetry are also utilized.
In the introduction the translator says: "Heidegger is the only
Western philosopher who not only intellectually understands Tao,
but has intuitively experienced the essence of it as well."

(3) WU, JOHN C.H., trans. <u>Lao Tzu: Tao Teh Ching</u>. New York:
St. John's University Press, 1961.
   A translation from the Wang Pi edition, which gives what might
be called a "middle way" interpretation, one that would be ac-
ceptable to most Chinese scholars. Chinese text facing English.

3.2.3   The "Chuang-tzu"

See 2.7.2

3.2.4   The "Lieh-tzu"

See 2.7.3

3.2.5   "I-ching" [Book of changes]

See 1.2.7, Earliest Classics and 2.12, The Appendixes of the
I-ching

3.2.6   "Lu-shih Ch'un-ch'iu" [Spring and autumn annals of Mr. Lu]

See 3.1.13, The Doctrine of the Mean

3.2.7   "Huai-nan Tzu" [Prince of Huai-nan]

See also 2.13

(1) MORGAN, EVAN, trans. <u>Tao, the Great Luminant</u>. Taipei:
Chinese Materials and Research Aids Service Center, 1966, 287
pp. (Orig. ed. London: Kegan Paul, 1934.)
   Translations of eight essays from the <u>Huai-nan Tzu</u>, together
with forty-five pages of introductory matter, separate "eluci-
dations and analyses" of the translated essays, and notes. The
material is of the greatest interest and importance in our attempt to understand the cosmological and metaphysical views of
at least one school of ancient Chinese thought. The translation has been criticized rather severely, but it certainly is
adequate to give students a good general idea of these trends
of thought.

(2) MORGAN, EVAN. "The Taoist Superman." <u>Journal of the North
China Branch, Royal Asiatic Society</u> 54 (1923):229-45.
   "Superman" is Morgan's translation of "the ideal man of Taoist philosophy (<u>chih jen</u>)," while "the Perfect Man" (<u>chen jen</u>)
denotes "the one next in order. . . . Both have a higher standing than the Confucian words for Sage and Princely Man. For

the former move in the realm of the spirit and the latter two
in the realm of the senses." Derived from author's study of
the Huai Nan Tzu. A useful discussion of the ideal goal sought
by the Taoist religious philosopher (as distinct from the seeker
after immortality--hsien).

3.2.8   "T'ai-p'ing ching" [Scripture of supreme peace]

(1) YU YING-SHIH. "Life and Immortality in the Mind of Han
China" (see 2.14[1]).
    The author traces the transformation of the otherworldly
hsien (immortal) to the this-worldly hsien in the context of
the immortality cult of the Han dynasty. Although this essay
is not a direct exposition of the important Taoist scripture,
T'ai-p'ing ching, it quotes several passages from this book and
discusses one of its central ideas: the paramount duty of Taoists to seek immortality drugs and recipes for the sovereign.
The T'ai-p'ing ching was composed in the middle of the second
century A.D.

3.2.9   "Pao-p'u tzu" [The philosopher who embraces simplicity]

See 2.16, Religious Taoism of Ko Hung

3.2.10   "Ts'an-t'ung ch'i" [Three ways unified and harmonized]

See also 1.8.1, Wei P'o-yang

(1) FUKUI, KŌJUN. "A Study of Chou-i Ts'an-t'ung-ch'i." Acta
Asiatica 27 (1974):19-32.
    A critical study of the evolution of this Taoist alchemical
work. According to Fukui, this text is an internal alchemical
manual, composed in the second century A.D. But the present
version was derived from a copy which existed in the tenth
century A.D.

(2) LIU TS'UN-YAN. "Lu Hsi-hsing and His Commentaries on the
Ts'an-t'ung ch'i." Tsinghua Journal of Chinese Studies 7
(1968):71-98.
    Attempts to prove that it is probable that the famous work,
Ts'an-t'ung ch'i, was actually a treatise (couched in esoteric
language) on "dual-cultivation"--i.e., "restoring one's vigour
through sexual connexion"--rather than a treatise on alchemy,
or, at least, that "there is little doubt that this was how the
Taoist philosophers of the Sung-Yüan period saw it, and so it
was with Lu Hsi-hsing, a great Taoist scholar of the Ming

times." An important study, which will be sticky going, however, for nonspecialists.

3.2.11 "Tan-ching yao-chueh" [Essential formulas from the alchemical
        classics]
        See 2.18, Theory of Taoist Alchemy

3.2.12 "Yin-fu ching" [The Secret accord scripture]

        (1) CHAN, WING-TSIT; AL FARUQI, ISMA'EL RAGI; KITAGAWA, JOSEPH
        M.; and RAJU, P.T., comps. The Great Asian Religions (see
        1.1[2]), pp. 171-72.
           A translation of this short scripture composed in the early
        seventh century. It teaches people how to take advantage of
        the secret course of Nature in order to gain benefits.

3.2.13 "T'ai-i chin-hua tsung-chih" [Secret of the golden flower]

        (1) WELCH, HOLMES H. "The Bellagio Conference on Taoist
        Studies" (see 2.1.7[17]), pp. 120-23.
           Describes the life of Liu Hua-yang and the nature of his
        text.

        (2) WILHELM, RICHARD, trans. The Secret of the Golden Flower.
        Translated from German by C.E. Baynes. New York: Harcourt,
        Brace & World, 1962, pp. 3-65.
           A translation of a seventeenth-century Taoist scripture con-
        cerning internal alchemy. The work contains Buddhist elements.

3.2.14 "Hui-ming ching" [Scripture of consciousness and life]

        (1) WILHELM, RICHARD, trans. (see 3.2.13[2]), pp. 69-78. C.J.
        Jung's commentary, pp. 81-137.
           A translation of the short scripture composed by Liu Hua-
        yang, a Buddhist monk of the eighteenth century. This work
        on internal alchemy is highly syncretistic. It embodies
        Buddhist and Confucian ideas, although remaining essentially
        a Taoist work.

3.2.15 "Kung-kuo-ko" [System of merits and demerits]

        (1) WEIGER, LEON. "Kung-Kuo-Ko." In A History of Religious
        Beliefs and Philosophical Opinions in China. Translated by

3.2.16

E.C. Werner. New York: Paragon, 1969, pp. 579-88. (Orig.
pub. Hsien Hsien Hopei, China: Mission Press, 1927.)
    A translation of the text attributed to Lu Tung-pin of the
eighth century. This work is strongly influenced by Confucian
and Buddhist ethics. Emphasis is on merits and demerits.
Other items include family relations, business ethics, the
immortals, and self-cultivation.

3.2.16   "T'ai-shang kan-yin p'ien" [Treatise on the Most Exalted One
         on influence and response]

         (1) CHAN, WING-TSIT; AL FARUQI, ISMA'EL RAGI; KITAGAWA, JOSEPH
         M.; and RAJU, P.T., comps. The Great Asian Religions (see
         1.1[2]), pp. 172-75.
             A translation of one of the most popular religious tracts
         in China. A work of the thirteenth century, it exemplifies
         the thought of the religion of the "three teachings," although
         its language is Taoist.

3.2.17   "Yin-chih wen" [Silent way of recompense]

         (1) CHAN, WING-TSIT; AL FARUQI, ISMA'EL RAGI; KITAGAWA, JOSEPH
         M.; and RAJU, P.T., comps. The Great Asian Religions (see
         1.1[2]), pp. 175-77.
             A translation of a popular religious tract attributed to
         Wen-chang, a Taoist divinity of literature. The work, composed
         no earlier than the thirteenth century, contains a list of in-
         junctions and meritorious actions.

3.3 MAOIST RELIGION

(1) MAO, TSE-TUNG. "Talks at the Yen-an Forum on Literature and Art."
In Selected Works of Mao Tse-tung. Vol. 3. Peking: Foreign Languages
Press, 1965, pp. 69-97.
   These are addresses Mao gave in 1942. They reflect the Maoist religion at its best. He argues that the Chinese Communist Revolution
is a people's revolution. "People" refers to the peasants, workers,
and soldiers who were exploited in the past. Unless the intellectuals
identify themselves completely with the masses, their writings and artistic creations could not contribute significantly to the Revolution,
and the only way to do so is to live among the peasants, workers, and
the soldiers. The intellectuals must first of all learn from the
masses before they can be revolutionaries. They cannot learn from
the masses merely through thinking and studying. Mao's view that the
intellectuals' conversion to Communism requires their submission to

3. Authoritative Texts

the masses makes Maoisn highly ethical and self-denying. It is a
religion of asceticism.

4. Popular Literature

4.1 FOLKTALES

(1) EBERHARD, W., ed. <u>Folktales of China</u>. Chicago: University of Chicago Press, 1965, 267 pp.

A translation of a collection of seventy-nine tales related to supernaturalism, magic, and fantasy from the beginning of Chinese history to the present. Sources of these tales are indicated in "Notes to the Tales" near the end of the book.

(2) EBERHARD, WOLFRAM. <u>Guilt and Sin in Traditional China</u>. Berkeley: University of California Press, 1967, 141 pp.

A sociological study of the Chinese attitudes toward sin and guilt based upon the popular literary genre of <u>shan-shu</u> (books for moral improvement). The author's thesis is that the Chinese were very much conscious of sin (violation of a divine code) and guilt, whereas the awareness of shame is only a secondary phenomenon. His view, therefore, is opposite to the predominant Western view that the Chinese did not have a dominant concept of sin. However, the author does point out that among the Confucian elites the notion of shame played a more important part, due to their strong sense of moral obligation to the community as Chinese leaders. It should be noted that the <u>shan-shu</u> literature was strongly influenced by the Buddhist concept of retribution and its mythological accounts of the underworld. Such literature was generally despised by the Confucian elite. Hence, insofar as the <u>shan-shu</u> literature reflecting the Chinese sense of sin and guilt is concerned, it is only applicable to the masses.

(3) _____. <u>Studies in Chinese Folklore and Related Essays</u>. Bloomington: Indiana University Press, 1970.

Parts 1 and 2 of this collection contain essays on the folklore of Chekiang province and on that of China in general. They were all published more than three decades prior to their collection in this volume, most of them in German before World War II. The author is an eminent folklorist and sinologist who has been a pioneer in many kinds of sociological study of China, and of the study of comparative cultures. The essays are written in a nontechnical style, easily intelligible to the nonspecialist.

(4) GILES, HERBERT, trans. <u>Strange Stories from a Chinese Studio</u>.
4th rev. ed. Shanghai: Kelly & Walsh, 1936, 488 pp.
    Translation of a famous collection of tales of the remarkable and
supernatural by P'u Sung-lin, entitled <u>Liao-chai chih</u>, dating from the
early Ch'ing (seventeenth century). These give us a good insight into
a variety of notions of the Chinese relating to religious and quasi-
religious subjects. Appendix I is the translation of a popular text
of the "hellfire and damnation" sort, detailing the punishments sinners
may expect in purgatory. For a partial version of this latter piece,
see Thompson's <u>Chinese Way in Religion</u> (see 1.1[15]), pp. 186-95.

(5) YANG HSIEN-YI, and YANG, GLADYS, trans. <u>Man Who Sold a Ghost:</u>
<u>Chinese Tales of the Third-Sixth Centuries</u>. Peking: Foreign Languages
Press, 1958.
    Stories of the supernatural are prominent in this excellent collec-
tion. From these enjoyable tales one may learn of the many common notions about ghosts, magic, immortals, and other aspects of religion as
these were understood by the people of post-Han, pre-T'ang times.

(6)_____. <u>Stories about Not Being Afraid of Ghosts</u>. Peking: Foreign
Languages Press, 1961.
    Disregarding the polemical preface which tells us that this is a
work which utilizes stories about not being afraid of ghosts as satire
and allegory referring to the "ghosts" of present-day "imperialism"
and "reactionaries," we may enjoy it as a good sampling of common
Chinese notions about the supernatural during traditional times.

4.2 <u>SHORT STORIES</u>

(1) BIRCH, CYRIL, trans. <u>Stories from a Ming Collection</u>. Bloomington:
Indiana University Press, 1958, 205 pp.
    A translation of six stories from the collection entitled <u>Stories</u>
<u>Old and New</u> [Ku-ching shiao-shuo], first published in the early 1620s,
edited by Feng Meng-lung. Many of these stories existed as early as
the Sung period (960-1279). These six stories deal with such themes
as the ungrateful husband and the virtuous wife, retribution, friend-
ship between two men, and immortality.

(2) BISHOP, JOHN L. "A Bibliography of Translation into Western
Languages of <u>San-yen</u> Stories (Three Collections of Tales)." In <u>The</u>
<u>Colloquial Short Story in China</u>. Cambridge: Harvard University Press,
1956, pp. 127-35.
    A bibliography of the short stories from the three Chinese collec-
tions that have been translated into Western languages.

(3) DE MORANT, G.S., trans. <u>Chinese Love Tales</u>. Garden City: Halcyon
House, n.d., 161 pp.

A translation of seven short stories originally published in the
seventeenth century--one from the collection entitled Wonders New and
Old [Chin-ku ch'i-kuan] and six from the Hsing-shih heng-yen [Tales to
arouse the world].

(4) DIEN, ALBERT E.   "The Yuan-hun Chi (Account of Ghosts with Griev-
ances): A Sixth-Century Collection of Stories." In Wen-lin: Studies
in the Chinese Humanities.   Edited by Chow Tse-tsung. Madison:
University of Wisconsin Press, 1968, pp. 211-28.
    An introduction to a collection of short stories dealing with the
theme of retribution, i.e., the returning of ghosts to seek justice.
The author is of the opinion that although these stories were told in
the Buddhist milieu, the belief in retribution by ghosts is a pre-
Buddhist conception in China.   In these stories, the final arbitrator
is neither Buddha nor Bodhisattva, but Heaven (T'ien) or Ruler-above
(Shang-ti).   The author thinks that the motif of retribution by ghosts
was a popular Confucian belief, but in these stories it was taken up
by Buddhists and developed into a genre of religious literature.

(5) HSIA CHIH-CH'ING.   "Society and Self in the Chinese Short Story."
In The Classic Chinese Novel. New York: Columbia University Press,
1968, pp. 229-321.
    A discussion of several short stories from the three seventeenth-
century collections: Ku-chin hsiao-shuo [Stories of old and new],
Ching-shih t'ung-yen [Tales to warn the world], Hsing-shih heng-yen
[Tales to arouse the world].   Hsia believes that it is the love stories
in these collections that best reflect realism. But even in these
stories self-fulfillment and social demand are in constant tension.
This essay can be read as a good introduction to traditional Chinese
short stories.

(6) Van OVER, RAYMOND, ed.   "Short Fiction." In Taoist Tales.   New
York: New American Library, Mentor Book, 1973, pp. 21-145.
    A collection of short stories with supernatural and magical elements.
The adjective of the title, Taoist, is misleading, for most of these
stories are miraculous tales, imaginative and earthy, read and enjoyed
by the common people regardless of their religious preferences.   The
"Divine Panorama" (pp. 121-45) is not a story but a spiritual travelogue
of the ten courts in the subterranean world, where the souls of the dead
are judged and purged before they are reborn.   The editor does not identify the bibliographical sources of these stories except the ones taken
from the Chuang Tzu. Most of the stories were composed during the Ming
and Ch'ing periods.

(7) WANG CHI-CHEN, trans.   Traditional Chinese Tales. New York:
Greenwood Press, 1976, 225 pp. Annotated bibl. (Orig. pub. Columbia
University Press, 1944.)
    An expert translation of twenty traditional short stories composed

in various periods from the sixth to the sixteenth century. Thirteen stories in the collection involve ghosts and demons and are representative of Chinese supernatural tales. Most of the authors are identified.

4.3 NOVELS

(1) EDWARDS, E.D. Chinese Prose: Literature of the T'ang Dynasty. London: Probsthain. Vol. 1 (1937), "Religion," pp. 49-59. Vol. 2 (1938), "Tales of the Supernatural," pp. 28-34; "Translations," pp. 35-393.

In this work we have many examples of the religious ideas of T'ang times as revealed in fiction, as well as the translator's commentary. Scholarly production, but easily intelligible to the nonspecialist.

(2) HSIA CHIH-CH'ING. The Classic Chinese Novel (see 4.2[5]).

A lucid and scholarly discussion of the following six classic novels: The Romance of the Three Kingdoms, The Water Margin, Chin P'ing Mei (Golden Lotus), Journey to the West, The Scholars, Dream of the Red Chamber. The best introductory study of the Chinese novel.

(3) WILLIAMS, Mrs. E.T. "Some Popular Religious Literature of the Chinese." Journal of the North China Branch, Royal Asiatic Society 33 (1900-1901):11-29.

The material discussed is mainly of the tract type, which the author remarks "stamp[s] the Chinese as an essentially religious people." The article contains numerous excerpts in translation so that one gets a good sense of the motifs and style.

4.3.1 "San-kuo chih yen-i" [Romance of three kingdoms]

(1) BREWITT-TAYLOR, C.H., trans. Romance of Three Kingdoms. 2 vols. Taipei: Ch'eng-wen Publishing Co., 1969. (Orig. pub. Shanghai: Kelly & Walsh, 1925.) 1:638 pp.; 2:623 pp.

A complete translation of a fourteenth-century novel by Lo Kuan-chung. It describes the three rival kingdoms in the Three Kingdoms period (220-265) when religious Taoism prevailed.

4.3.2 "Shui Hu Chuan" [Water margin]

(1) BUCK, PEARL SYDENSTRICKER, trans. All Men Are Brothers. 2 vols. New York: John Day, 1968, 1279 pp. (Orig. pub. 1933.)

A complete translation of the seventy-chapter version without the epilogue. It is a fourteenth-century novel attributed to Shih Nai-an, but the story takes place in the preceding century. It depicts a group of brave and righteous individuals who were

driven to banditry because of the corruption of government
officials.

(2) JACKSON, J.H., trans. Water Margin. 2 vols. New York:
Paragon, 1968, 917 pp. (Orig. pub. Shanghai: Commercial Press,
1937.)
    A translation of the seventy-chapter edition with some
abridgement.

4.3.3 "Hsi-yu chi" [Journey to the west]

(1) CHAN PING-LEUNG. "Chinese Popular Water-gods Legends and
the Hsi-yu Chi." In Essays in Chinese Studies Presented to
Professor Lo Hsiang-lin. Hong Kong: University of Hong Kong
Press, 1970, pp. 299-317.
    The author argues that the prominent characters of the novel
Hsi-yu chi, such as Monkey, Pigsy, Sandy, and Tripitaka, are
actually marine divinities which have their counterparts in
early Chinese mythology. He points out, for example, that the
Monkey hero Sun Wu-k'ung is simply another form of the ancient
marine god Wu-chih-ch'i, who has the appearance of a monkey.
Although this essay raises several points for further research
concerning the literary sources of the Hsi-yu chi, further docu-
mentation is needed to prove its basic thesis.

(2) HSIA, C.T., and HSIA, T.A. "New Perspectives on Two Ming
Novels: Hsi-yu Chi and Hsi-yu Pu." In Wen-lin: Studies in
the Chinese Humanities (see 4.2[4]), pp. 229-45.
    The first part of the essay deals with the literary device
of the Hsi-yu chi in terms of the relationship between comedy
and mythological reality. "Comedy" should be understood in the
Buddhist sense: phenomenon is emptiness, and emptiness is phenomenon. The second part of the essay deals with the Hsi-yu Pu
[Supplement to the Hsi-yu chi] by Tung Yueh (1620-1686), which
uses the literary device of a dream to present the Monkey's
predicament.

(3) WALEY, ARTHUR, trans. Monkey. New York: Grove, 1958,
305 pp. (Orig. pub. New York: John Day Co., 1943.)
    A translation of thirty of the one hundred chapters of the
sixteenth-century novel by Wu Ch'eng-en. It tells about Monkey
Sun Wu-k'ung, who escorted Hsuan-tsang (596-664) on his journey
to India to collect Buddhist scriptures.

(4) YU, ANTHONY C. "Heroic Verse and Heroic Mission: Dimensions of the Epic in the Hsi-yu Chi." Journal of Asian Studies
31 (August 1972):879-97.

The author identifies the novel <u>Hsi-yu chi</u> as belonging to
the literary genre of epic, resembling Homer's <u>Odyssey</u>. A common element of the epic is the fusion between fantasy and truth,
as seen in the <u>Hsi-yu chi</u>. The article also emphasizes the integral relationship between the poems and prose in the novel:
the poems augment the narrative forces of the prose.

(5) _____. <u>The Journey to the West</u>. Vol. 1. Chicago:
University of Chicago Press, 1977, 530 pp.
     The first complete translation of the famous sixteenth-
century novel in English. The translator emphasizes the integral relation between the verse and the prose portions of the
novel. The importance of the internal alchemy and its allegorical meaning are fully explicated. The present volume begins
with an informative introduction to the work as a whole, its
origin, history and style, followed by a translation of the
first twenty-five chapters with annotations. (Vols. 2-4 published 1978, 1980, 1983 [1983 also in paperback].)

(6) _____. "The Monkey's Tale." <u>University of Chicago Magazine</u>
70 (1977):10-21.
     A translation of chapter 27 of <u>The Journey to the West</u> with
a brief introduction to the novel. Chapter 27 involves the epi-
sode of the female White-Bone-Spirit who attempts to eat the
flesh of Monk Tripitaka and who is finally destroyed by Monkey
Sun Wu-k'ung. Monkey Sun is tentatively banished by his master,
Tripitaka, because of what he did to the White-Bone-Spirit.

(7) _____. Religion and Allegory in the <u>Hsi-yu Chi</u>. Presented
to the session on Chinese religion, American Academy of Religion
annual meeting, 1974, 37 pp. (typescript).
     This essay deals primarily with the view that the novel <u>Hsi-
yu chi</u> emphasizes the importance of the internal cultivation
("internal alchemy") as pursued by esoteric Taoism. This aspect is particularly evidenced in the poetic portion of the
novel. Thus the three pilgrims--Monkey, Pigsy, Sandy--who safe-
guard Tripitaka are allegorical representations of the Taoist
immortals. The "journey to the West" is but an allegory of the
internal cultivation of the Taoists. The author also points
out some of the poems in the novel that are actually derived
from the Taoist canon (<u>Tao-tsang</u>).

4.3.4 "Feng-shen yen-i" [Investiture of the gods]

(1) GRUBE, WILHELM, and MUELLER, HERBERT, trans. <u>Die
Metamorphosen der Götter</u>. 2 vols. Leiden: E.J. Brill, 1912,
657 pp.

Translations of chapters 1-46 by Grube and a summary of chapters 47-100 by Mueller. There has been no English translation of this popular sixteenth-century novel.

(2) LIU TS'UN-YAN. Buddhist and Taoist Influences on Chinese Novels. Vol. 1, The Authorship of the Feng-sheng yen-i. Wiesbaden: Otto Harrassowitz, 1962, 326 pp.

A thorough investigation of the origins of gods as presented in this novel. Most of these divinities pertain to Buddhism or Taoism. The author of this novel is Lu Hsi-hsing, a priest of the Ch'üan-chen school of Taoism.

(3) _____. "Buddhist Sources of the Novel Feng-sheng Yen-i." Journal of the Hong Kong Branch, Royal Asiatic Society of America 1 (1960-61):68-97.

A brief summary of the author's findings taken from the work done for his book, Buddhist and Taoist Influences on Chinese Novels (2). As the Feng-shen Yen-i is the single most influential book in so far as the modern popular pantheon is concerned, this article is important. Despite the technical difficulties of the original study, the article is not difficult for non-specialists.

4.3.5   "Chin P'ing Mei"

(1) EGERTON, CLEMENT, trans. The Golden Lotus. 4 vols. New York: Paragon, 1959, 1:387 pp.; 2:276 pp.; 3:385 pp.; 4:375 pp. (Orig. pub. London: Routledge, 1939.)

A complete translation of the famous sixteenth-century novel attributed to Wang Shih-cheng (1526-90). It deals with the life of a merchant-official Hsi-men Ch'ing and his six wives. Although eroticism is a dominant theme in the novel, its author shows that it may awake one's desire for salvation.

(2) KUHN, FRANZ, trans. Chin P'ing Mei: The Adventurous History of Hsi Men and His Six Wives. Translated from German by Bernard Miall. New York: Putnam's, 1940. 2 vols.:863 pp.

A translation of forty-nine of the one hundred chapters of the novel. The Buddhist motif is seen in the last chapter where the only son of Hsi-meng Ch'ing becomes a monk in order to redeem the sins of his father.

4.3.6   "Hsü Chin P'ing Mei" [Sequel to Chin P'ing Mei]

(1) _____. Flower Shadows Behind the Curtain (Ko-lien hua-ying), translated from German by Vladimir Kean. New York: Pantheon, 1969, 432 pp.

This is a translation of the <u>Ko-lien hua-ying</u>, which is an
abridged edition of the <u>Hsü Chin P'ing Mei</u>, a seventeenth-cen-
tury novel. This story tells of the lives of Hsi-men Ch'ing's
monk son and his mother. Filial love and retribution dominate
the scenes. It also describes the Tantric rite of sexual union
as a symbol of Nirvāṇa.

4.3.7 "Hung-lou meng" [Dream of the red chamber]

(1) KNOERLE, JEANNE. <u>Dream of Red Chamber: A Critical Study</u>.
Bloomington: University of Indiana Press, 1972, pp. 121-48.
    This is one of the rare critical studies of a major Chinese
work of fiction. The chapter in question attempts a brief analysis of the religious elements of the novel in the traditional
frame of reference of the Three Religions. The author's general
view is that this work "is not basically a religious or philosophical novel," but she offers some interesting observations
of the religious and philosophical elements found therein.

(2) KUHN, FRANZ, trans. <u>The Dream of the Red Chamber</u>. Translated from German by Florence and Isabel McHugh. New York:
Random House, 1958, 582 pp.
    A translation of fifty of one hundred and twenty chapters of
the novel which describes the gradual decline of the prominent
Chia household. The protagonist, Pao-yü, is caught between
loyalty to family expectations and personal freedom. His final
resolution is the entrance into monkhood.

(3) WANG CHI-CHEN, trans. <u>Dream of the Red Chamber</u>. New York:
Twayne, 1958, 574 pp.
    An adapted and abridged translation.

(4) _____. <u>Dream of the Red Chamber</u>. New York: Doubleday,
1958, 329 pp.
    A further abridged translation of forty chapters. Only
chapter one is complete.

4.4 POETRY

(1) DAVIS, A.R. "The Double Ninth Festivals in Chinese Poetry: A
Study of Variations upon a Theme." In <u>Wen-lin: Studies in the Chinese
Humanities</u> (see 4.2[4]), pp. 45-64.
    A literary description of the poetic meaning of the festival of the
Double Ninth (the 9th of the 9th month of the lunar calendar), based
on the poems of T'ao Yuan-ming (365-427), Li Po (701-762), Po Chu-i
(772-846), and others. The author emphasizes the theme of impermanence

underlying the festivals of the Double Ninth, as well as the feelings of community among the Chinese poets.

(2) HAWKES, DAVID. "The Supernatural in Chinese Poetry." In The Far East: China and Japan. Edited by D. Grant and M. Maclure. Toronto: University of Toronto Press, 1961, pp. 311-24.

Discusses "this religion of poets which has nothing to do with Confucianism and Buddhism, which has much in common with Taoism and yet is much older," and asserts that "it was the Old Religion which supplied the Chinese poet with his mythology--the religion of the witch, or medium, or shaman." A revealing article by a professor of Chinese at Oxford and the excellent translator of the most famous example of that "Old Religion" in literature, the Ch'u Tz'u [Songs of the south].

4.5 SONGS

(1) FUJINO, IWATOMO. "On Chinese Soul-Inviting and Firefly-Catching Songs." Acta Asiatica 19 (1970):40-57.

Similarity between the Chinese soul-inviting songs (chao-hun ko), the most famous example of which is to be found in the Ch'u Tz'u, and the firefly-catching songs popular in both China and Japan. The author proves that the firefly is in fact considered a soul, often transformed from blood: "We may say that there is every likelihood that the firefly-catching song was also originally a song for calling souls." The final transformation is of the firefly-catching songs into children's songs. This is a fascinating article, fully documented, with Chinese characters given.

(2) LING SHUN-SHENG. "Kuo Shang and Li Hun of the Nine Songs and the Ceremonies of Head-Hunting and Head-Feast." Academia Sinica, Bulletin of the Institute of Ethnology 9 (1960):451-61 (English abridgement).

The author utilizes anthropological data to interpret the last two of the Nine Songs (in reality these are nos. 10 and 11 of those songs) as texts used in services for the ghosts of slain enemies whose heads had been taken by Pu and Yüeh tribespeople of the ancient state of Ch'u, thus partly corroborating and partly modifying earlier interpretations, especially by Waley and Hawkes.

(3) WALEY, ARTHUR, trans. The Nine Songs (see 1.2.1[5]). Excerpts reprinted in The Chinese Way in Religion (see 1.1[15]), pp. 36-38.

A small book in which the dean of English translators (of this century) gives translations of the Nine Songs (traditionally attributed to the poet Ch'ü Yuan of the third century B.C.), with commentary on the deities whom the shamans served, and a general introduction dealing with the subject of shamanism, particularly from the "semi-barbarian" feudal state of Ch'u in ancient China. This latter, although

only a brief essay, is still one of the few important discussions of
the subject in English.

5.   Arts, Architecture, Music

5.1   ARTS

(1) AYSCOUGH, FLORENCE. "The Symbolism of the Forbidden City, Peking."
Journal of the North China Branch, Royal Asiatic Society 61 (1930):
111-26.
   A journey through portions of the Imperial Palace, taking special
note of the innumerable symbolic ornaments, decorations, and arrange-
ments. Written in the typically vivid style of the author, it makes
an interesting introduction to the importance of symbolism in Chinese
state religion. The sources for her article are slides she made from
photos taken by the Japanese in 1900 at the time of the flight of the
Chinese court during the "Boxer" uprising.

(2) BACHHOFER, LUDWIG. A Short History of Chinese Art. London: B.T.
Batsford, 1944, 129 pp. Illus.
   A discussion of neolithic pottery, Shang bronzes, sculpture from
Shang to the seventeenth century, and painting up to the eighteenth
century. Ample illustrations.

(3) BULLING, A. The Meaning of China's Most Ancient Art: An Inter-
pretation of Pottery Patterns from Kansu (Ma Ch'ang and Pan-shan) and
Their Development in the Shang, Chou, and Han Periods. Leiden: E.J.
Brill, 1952, 150 pp.
   After an introduction explaining the intention and importance of
the study, there are six chapters dealing with individual motifs, and
the conclusion. Four short appendixes give details on fine points.
Bulling contends that "not only the geometrical patterns of Kansu and
China, but also those of Western Asia, India, and Europe were connected
with cosmology, time-reckoning, and the stars. . . . The patterns are
symbols of a universal religious conception, which spread slowly from
its centre in Western Asia to the outer fringes of the ancient world."
In her conclusion she states: "I hope that this study will show that
the peoples who used the patterns had an integrated vision of the universe. According to the doctrine of the unity of the macrocosm and
the microcosm, in which they believed, to every region, and to every
single individual were assigned a particular place and a special function as part of the whole. The patterns, far from being haphazardly
chosen for their aesthetic value, reflected cosmic harmonies and

movements. . . ." This is a stimulating attempt at demonstrating the participation of the prehistorical Chinese in a worldwide cosmology and symbolism, which makes it highly controversial for most sinologists.

(4) CAHILL, JAMES F. "Confucian Elements in the Theory of Painting." In The Confucian Persuasion. Edited by Arthur F. Wright. Stanford: Stanford University Press, 1960, pp. 115-40.
    The author points out that students of Chinese painting have generally neglected the Confucian ideas of painting. This essay presents a theory of art criticism on the basis of the neo-Confucianism of the Sung period. Painting or calligraphy should reflect elements such as sincerity, virtue, blandness, li (principle or order). Cahill is particularly concerned with the wen-jen-hua (literati painting) of the Sung period.

(5) CAMMANN, SCHUYLER. "The Magic Square of Three in Old Chinese Philosophy and Religion." History of Religions 1 (1961):37-80.
    A study of the symbolic meaning of "nine" in the ancient diagram of Loshu (Lo River writing). Nine is the expression of the center of the cosmos, and T'ai-i (the Supreme One) is the religious counterpart of the cosmic symbol.

(6) _____. "Magical and Medicinal Woods in Han China." History of Religions 3 (1964):292-99.
    A study of belt-toggles (chui-tzu), based on the collection of C.F. Bieber. The belt-toggles not only serve the practical function of holding items at the belt, but are also regarded as amulets and talismans. Certain woods were selected for this use, apparently with four considerations uppermost: 1) auspicious connotations of the wood which gave the charm its power, 2) medicinal qualities ascribed to the wood, 3) practicability of working the wood with ease, 4) its availability. The article describes the woods used and the reasons they were considered auspicious. This is an interesting essay which may easily be understood by nonspecialists.

(7) _____. "Significant Patterns on Chinese Bronze Mirrors." Archives of the Chinese Art Society of America 9 (1955):43-62. 13 plates.
    Deals with myths and symbols as found on mirrors from Han to T'ang times. A very useful summary of the main concepts of the Chinese worldview, including those of popular religion, during that age. May be read to complement Cheng's "Yin-yang Wu-hsing and Han Art" (10). Lucid style.

(8) _____. "Types of Symbols in Chinese Art." In Studies in Chinese Thought. Edited by A.W. Wright. Chicago: University of Chicago Press, 1953, pp. 195-231.
    A descriptive study of nine groups of symbols (e.g., t'ao-t'ieh masks, cosmic symbols) in Chinese society from ancient to modern times.

This essay can be used as an introduction to the relation between
arts and religion in China.

(9) CHANG KWANG-CHIH. "Changing Relationships of Man and Animals in
Shang and Chou Myths and Art." Academia Sinica, Bulletin of the
Institute of Ethnology 16 (1963):133-46.
   Tries to show the "functional place" of the dominant zoomorphic
motifs of archaic art in Shang and Chou "religious and ritualistic
life in particular and in their cultural and social life in general."
Proceeds with an illuminating discussion of kinship, kingship, and the
religious reflections of changes in these matters as shown in art
motifs during the three periods of Shang, Early Chou, and Late Chou.
An important contribution to our understanding of archaic religion.
Intelligible to nonspecialists.

(10) CHENG TE-KUN. "Yin-yang Wu-hsing and Han Art." Harvard Journal
of Asiatic Studies 20 (1957):162-86. 9 plates (27 figs.).
   Points out that it is the doctrine "based on the fundamental theories of the Two Forces and the Five Power-Elements of Nature" that "is
the backbone of Han thought, and its influence in the shaping of Han
art was indeed tremendous." The article is devoted to discussion of
the main features of this school and its influences on the art of the
period. Thus, he takes up the subjects of Tsou Yen, supposed founder
of the school, the influence of its doctrines on Ch'in and Han emperors,
and then--in considerable detail--specific influences in the symbolism
of Han art. Nontechnical and informative.

(11) CHOW FONG, and YEH CHENG. "A Brief Report on the Excavation of
Han Tomb No. 1 at Ma-wang-tui, Ch'ang-sha." Artibus Asiae 35 (1973):
15-24. Illus.
   A translation of a Chinese article published in 1972 by Wen-wu
Publishers, Peking, on the 1972 discovery of the artifacts buried in
the Han tomb of second century B.C. Among the things found is a silk
brocade, placed on top of the casket of Lady Tai, which depicts the
religious scenes familiar to the aristocrats of the Han dynasty.
Colored photographic reproductions of many items are provided.

(12) EASTLAKE, F. WARRINGTON. "Equine Deities." Transactions of the
Asiatic Society of Japan 11 (1883):260-85.
   Concerned with demonic animals of the netherworld, especially the
horse-faced and bull-headed devils. Interesting comparative study between Chinese examples and those of India and the ancient West. A
typical late-nineteenth-century philological approach.

(13) EBERHARD, WOLFRAM. "Topics and Moral Values in Chinese Temple
Decorations." Journal of the American Oriental Society 87 (1967):
22-32.
   After a brief historical summary of temple decoration, the author

5. Arts, Architecture, Music

discusses data from field investigation of some fifty temples in Taiwan
and several in Hong Kong. He also interviewed two temple painters.
His analysis indicates that there were five general types of scenes
depicted: purely religious, filial piety, historical, symbolic representations, and scenes from novels and plays. After discussion of each
of these types in turn, there is a final section offering a number of
conclusions. This is a pioneering attempt to study popular values in
China from a novel source. In conjunction with this article one should
further consult Schuyler Cammann's critique, "On the Decoration of
Modern Temples in Taiwan and Hong Kong" and Eberhard's "Rejoinder to
Schuyler Cammann," Journal of the American Oriental Society 88 (1968):
785-90; 790-92.

(14) ENCYCLOPAEDIA BRITANNICA. The Romance of Chinese Art. Garden
City, N.Y.: Garden City, 1936, 192 pp. Illus.
   A collection of essays by recognized authors on arts such as em-
broidery, wood carving, screens, and ivory carving.

(15) GROUSSET, RENÉ. Chinese Art and Culture. Translated by Haakon
Chevalier. New York: Orion, 1959, 22 + 331 pp.
   This is a chronological approach to Chinese art with emphasis upon
the relationship between art and religion. It deals mostly with the
period from Han to Sung.

(16) HENTZE, CARL. Chinese Tomb Figures: A Study in the Reliefs and
Folklore of Ancient China. London: E. Goldston, 1928, 112 pp. 114
plates.
   An extensive monograph on the symbolism of the ming-ch'i, pottery
figures excavated from Han to T'ang tombs. Chapters deal with "the
soul's survival and the origin of tomb figures," "the bird of fire,"
"human and animal figures," "exorcists, guardians and spirits, pro-
tectors of tombs," and styles. All of Hentze's work is subject to
serious criticism by sinologists, but is at the same time stimulating
and suggestive for the same reasons which have caused the criticism--
the author's attempts to integrate Chinese symbolism and cultural development into a universal schema.

(17) _____. "Gods and Drinking Serpents." History of Religions 4
(1965):179-208. Illus.
   A typical work of this author, who has spent a lifetime trying to
show that the symbolism of Chinese artifacts must be understood in the
light of comparative ethnology. Opposition to his thesis has been
based in part upon what strictly sinological scholars consider his
too-frequently fanciful or at least unsubstantiated conclusions, and
in part upon what Hentze correctly diagnoses as a tendency of sinology
"to construct a wall isolating the culture of ancient China from every
other culture." This article examines Chinese and other objects for
their expressions of archaic myth.

(18) LAUFER, BERTHOLD. Chinese Pottery of the Han Dynasty. Leiden:
E.J. Brill, 1909, 339 pp. Reprint. Rutland, Vt.: C.E. Tuttle Co.,
1962.
    A major work of one of the greatest scholars of this century, this
is a study of many aspects of Chinese culture of the Han period through
comparison of mortuary pottery with literary and pictorial sources.
Laufer was a universal scholar who united the methods of comparative
ethnography, philology, and other sciences, and this book is a fine
example of the fruitful results of this approach. May be too detailed
for any but serious students.

(19) _____. Diamond: A Study in Chinese and Hellenistic Folk-Lore.
Chicago: Field Museum of Natural History, 1915, 75 pp.
    A comparative study of the sort for which this author was noted,
based upon his incredible erudition in many languages and his ability
to synthesize disparate sources. For serious students.

(20) _____. Jade: A Study in Chinese Archaeology and Religion.
Chicago: Field Museum of Natural History, 1912, 370 pp. Reprint.
South Pasadena, Calif.: P.D. & Iona Perkins, 1946.
    Based upon author's expedition to Tibet and China, 1908-10, in the
course of which he acquired an extensive collection of Chinese artifacts for the Chicago Field Museum. The present monograph utilizes
the jades of this collection to construct a picture of culture in
general and religion in particular of ancient China, in the erudite
and creative manner peculiar to Laufer. Written long before the systematic excavation of the last Shang capital at Anyang, the author's
conclusions must, of course, be studied in the light of our present
knowledge. Nevertheless, the work retains considerable importance.
For serious students.

(21) LING SHUN-SHENG. "Origin of the Ancestral Temple in China."
Academia Sinica, Bulletin of the Institute of Ethnology 7 (1959):
177-84 (English summary). Illus.
    Author utilizes archaeological and anthropological evidences long
used by scholars. He concludes in part: "Our study of the ancestral
temple in ancient China not only gives support to the hypothesis of
Kuo Mo-jo, Granet, and Karlgren who all consider the temple to have o-
riginated from the Earth Altar, but also has disclosed the fact that the
miao and shê in ancient China, marae (me'ae) in Polynesia, and Sar in
Melanesia are identical as to form, name, and function." He supports
the theory of Kuo and Karlgren that the character for ancestor, tsu,
was a phallic picture, and holds "that both shê and tsu originated
from the worship of male and female genital organs."

(22) _____. "The Sacred Enclosures and Stepped Pyramidal Platforms
of Peiping." Academia Sinica, Bulletin of the Institute of Ethnology
16 (1963):83-100. Illus. Bibl.

"In the ancient religions of China, the gods and spirits which were generally worshipped were divided into four classes, namely, Shang-ti (the Supreme Being), Heavenly Gods, Earthly Gods, and Human Ghosts. Sacrifices were made to these supernatural beings either at a tan (raised platform or altar) or a shan (level spot or court). . . . Every tan was built on a shan, but there were shans without a tan on them." They "were unsheltered and all sacrifices were made in the open." The balance of the article discusses the tan and shan preserved in the great Forbidden City of Peking, with a detailed historical account of their origins and development. Too detailed for nonspecialists.

(23) NOTT, STANLEY CHARLES. Chinese Jade Throughout the Ages: A Review of Its Characteristics, Decoration, Folklore, and Symbolism. 2d ed. Tokyo and Rutland, Vt.: C.E. Tuttle, 1962, 193 pp. Illus. (Orig. pub. London: Scribner, 1937.)
A good survey which includes much on religious symbolism in general and as found in jades, and the ritual use of the latter. By a leading authority. Profusely illustrated. It is rather too encyclopedic for easy reading, but not too technical.

(24) RAWSON, PHILIP, and LEGEZA, LASZLO. Tao: The Eastern Philosophy of Time and Change. New York: Avon, 1973, 128 pp. 67 plates, 129 "documentary illustrations and commentaries."
This is a visual as well as conceptual introduction to Taoist ideas. It breaks new ground in demonstrating the pervasive influence of Taoism in Chinese art and especially in the extent to which erotic expressions of those ideas prevail. A fascinating book that gives the profundity of the Taoist views its full due.

(25) SALMONY, ALFRED. Antler and Tongue: An Essay on Ancient Symbolism and Its Implications. Ascona, Switz.: Artibus Asiae, 1954, 39 pp. Illus.
The author, a noted art historian, has studied the meaning of the peculiar objects excavated from central China (around Ch'ang-sha) that feature men and animals with antlers and extended tongues. His monograph ranges widely in scope, surveying what is known of the evolution of these two motifs in prehistoric times and in many ancient cultures, including medieval Europe. One of his conclusions is especially interesting: "that the Chinese use of stag antlers and extended tongues is of Indian origin." This is significant, if true, because the Chinese objects antedate by several centuries the historically verified arrival of direct Indian influence (i.e., Buddhism) in China. Somewhat detailed, but lucidly written, and well illustrated.

(26) SICKMAN, LAURENCE, and SOPER, ALEXANDER. "Painting and Sculpture." In The Art and Architecture of China. Baltimore: Penguin, 1956, pp. 1-211. 156 plates, pp. 1-156.
A discussion of painting and sculpture in the socio-religious milieu, with attention to the lives of painters and artists.

(27) SMITH, G. ELLIOT. "Dragons and Rain Gods." Bulletin of the John Rylands Library 5 (1918-20). Illus.
    Treats the subject as a universal symbol, the material on China being only a part of an elaborate assemblage of evidences from all parts of the world. Important as one of the few serious efforts to integrate a basic Chinese idea into the worldviews of all ancient cultures. Necessarily speculative, but very stimulating. Too detailed for casual reading, but intelligible enough for nonspecialists.

(28) SOWERBY, ARTHUR de CARLE. Nature in Chinese Art. New York: John Day, 1940, 203 pp.
    A collection of articles on the place of animals, birds, fishes, and flowers in Chinese paintings, sculptures, and carvings. Their symbolic meaning is briefly indicated. Two articles by H.E. Gibson on animal life and argicultural life as depicted in the Shang writings are included.

(29) SPEISER, WERNER. The Art of China. Translated by George Lawrence. New York: Crown, 1960, 257 pp.
    Contains an elucidation of Chinese arts (tomb painting, ceramics, bronze, sculpture, lacquer, painting) in the context of the changing society. Geography, religion, and politics are emphasized.

(30) SULLIVAN, MICHAEL. "The Heritage of Chinese Art." The Legacy of China. Edited by Raymond Dawson. Oxford: Clarendon Press, 1964, pp. 165-233.
    This essay begins with a historical survey of the Western attitude toward Chinese art, then proceeds to introduce bronze, jade, textile, lacquer, enamels, ceramics, and painting and calligraphy. It concludes with a discussion of the attitudes of the Chinese toward art. It can be used as an introduction to Chinese art.

(31) _____. "The Magic Mountain." Asian Review 51 (1955):300-10.
    On the significance of mountains in Chinese culture. Mountains are the abode of cosmic forces, the ch'i of yin and yang, places where the fungus of immortality (ling-chih) grows, and, of course, the dwelling places of immortals. Special mention is made of mountains in Chinese painting (the author is an Asian art historian). This is easy reading, as it was originally delivered in the form of a popular lecture.

(32) TOMITA, KOJIRO, and CHIN KAIMING. "Portraits of Wu Ch'üan-chieh, Taoist Pope in Yüan Dynasty." Bulletin of the Museum of Fine Arts 44 (1946):88-95. Illus.
    Report on a seventeenth-century copy of a horizontal scroll painting entitled Fourteen Portraits of Wu Ch'üan-chieh (1268-1346) of the Yüan Dynasty. Gives a brief biography of Wu, an account of earlier versions of this painting, and details about each of the fourteen portraits. Interesting evidence concerning the career of a Taoist priest-scholar. The illustrations are reduced small photos of the portraits.

(33) WATERBURY, FLORANCE. Early Chinese Symbols and Literature. New
York: Weyhe, 1942, 164 pp. 77 plates.
  Discusses the various animal themes found in the archaic Chinese
bronzes, and attempts to understand their symbolism. The author says
she "began this study with no preconceived theories as [to] the sig-
nificances of the symbolic animals. The premises were only two:
I. All the symbolic animals are auspicious. II. The Earth, or Life-
cult, and the Cult of Ancestral Piety, are so profound, so pervasive,
and so interwoven, that in cases of doubtful symbolism we are justified
in trying to find a connection between the symbol and one or both of
these ancient indigenous conceptions." It should be noted that this
study was undertaken at the very beginning of the serious work on late
Shang by means of the Anyang excavations and that apparently the only
archaeological information derived therefrom available to the author
was H.G. Creel's popularizing book, The Birth of China (see 1.2.5[2]).
Nevertheless, it is a stimulating and suggestive effort.

(34) WHITE, WILLIAM CHARLES. Chinese Temple Frescoes. Toronto:
University of Toronto Press, 1940, 230 pp.
  The book is divided into two main parts: the first is a general
introduction of eleven short chapters, and the second is on the three
frescoes themselves, of which the first is of the Paradise of Maitreya,
the second of the Lord of the Northern Dipper, and the third of the
Lord of the Southern Dipper. The three frescoes came from temples in
southern Shansi. The book has much valuable information about religious ideas and symbolism. It is illustrated with excellent plates.

(35) YETTS, W. PERCEVAL. "The Eight Immortals." Journal of the Royal
Asiatic Society, 1969, pp. 773-807.
  "The purpose of this article is to give the generally accepted tradition surrounding this group of eight as exemplified in the works of
Chinese artists and craftsmen." The author combines his own "notes
upon a large number of objects of art" with extracts from Lieh-hsien
Chuan [Stories of immortals], from which he also takes woodcuts of the
subjects for illustrations. A good summary of popular Chinese ideas,
written in an easily understandable style.

(36) _____. "Pictures of a Chinese Immortal." Burlington Magazine 9
(1921):113-21.
  A study of Lu Tung-pin, one of the Eight Immortals, with three
illustrations: 1) a rubbing of an incised design of a stele at Yo-chou
near the entrance to Lake Tung-t'ing, 2) a portrait of painting on silk
attributed to Chang Lu (purported grandson of the founder of the T'ien-
shih Tao, d. 220), 3) a painting on paper in the British Museum. An
interesting, brief monograph.

5.2 ARCHITECTURE

(1) PRATT, JAMES BISSETT. "Buddhist Temples in China." In The
Pilgrimage of Buddhism. New York: Macmillan, 1928, pp. 305-24.
    This chapter discusses Chinese Buddhist architecture and sculpture.
It gives a graphic description of typical temple architecture and art.
It also shows regional differences regarding temple architecture. In
central and northern China, the Buddhist temples reflect pure Buddhist
designs and art, whereas in West and South China they reflect Taoist
architectural and artistic influences. Special remarks are made concerning the Taoist temple, Lao Chuin Tung (Cave of Lao Tzu) and the
famous Buddhist temples in the Western Hills near Peking.

(2) PRIP-MOELLER, JOHANNES. Chinese Buddhist Monasteries: Their Plan
and Its Function as a Setting for Buddhist Monastic Life. Hong Kong:
Hong Kong University Press, 1967, 396 pp. (Orig. pub. Oxford: Oxford
University Press, 1937.)
    A firsthand study, in great detail, by a Danish architect, of the
architecture of Buddhist monasteries. About one hundred pages are devoted to the architecture of the monastery Hui chu Ssu [Wisdom-dwelling
temple] in Pao Hua Shan, Kiangsu.

(3) SICKMAN, LAURENCE, and SOPER, ALEXANDER. "Architecture." In The
Art and Architecture of China (see 5.1[26]), pp. 205-334. Plates, pp.
157-90.
    A historical presentation of architecture from the Shang to the
Ch'ing dynasty with special attention to the architecture of early
periods up to the T'ang dynasty. Japanese architecture of the Nara
period is utilized in order to elucidate the T'ang architecture.

(4) SIREN, OSWALD. "Chinese Architecture." In Romance of Chinese Art
(see 5.1[14]), pp. 20-51.
    A summary of types of Chinese building construction with emphasis
upon both the wooden buildings and the stone structures. The project-
ing and curved roof in historical China is traced to a southeast Asian
origin. Buddhist architecture is also discussed.

(5) SOOTHILL, WILLIAM E. The Hall of Light: A Study of Early Chinese
Kingship. Edited by Dorothea Hosie and G.F. Hudson. London:
Lutterworth, 1951, 289 pp.
    Although this book is not primarily on architecture, it is closely
concerned with the architecture of the Ming-t'ang [Hall of light], the
imperial hall dedicated to Heaven. According to Soothill, the architecture of the Ming-t'ang symbolizes the worship of the celestial stars
or Ursa Major. As the Northern Dipper rules the celestial world, so
the emperor rules the terrestrial world.

(6) WANG SUNG-HSING. "Taiwanese Architecture and the Supernatural."
In Religion and Ritual in Chinese Society (see 1.1[19]), pp. 183-92.
   A discussion of the architectural provisions for the worship of
ancestors, gods, and ghosts in Taiwanese residential houses both on
the farm and in the fishing villages. The central place of worship
is the family hall, cheng-t'ing, which is the joint property of all
branches of the family and represents the agnatic solidarity.

5.3 MUSIC

(1) BRUNET, JACQUES, ed. "China." In Oriental Music: A Selected
Discography. New York: Foreign Area Materials Center, 1971, pp.
66-71.
   Gives a brief introduction of various kinds of Chinese musical in-
struments and a list of records issued in Europe and America, and in
Hong Kong and Peking.

(2) GULIK, R.H. van. The Lore of the Chinese Lute. Rutland, Vt.:
Charles Tuttle, 1969, 271 pp.
   Provides history of the development of the Chinese musical instru-
ment, the ku-ch'in (lute), with samples of its tunes, and discusses
the Confucian, Taoist, and Buddhist understanding of the ku-ch'in.

(3) LEVIS, JOHN H. Foundations of Chinese Musical Art. New York:
Paragon, 1963, 233 pp. (Orig. pub. Peiping: H. Vetch, 1936.)
   The author emphasizes the relationships between Chinese language
and melody and between Chinese poetry and music. The five, seven, and
twelve scales of Chinese music are analyzed. He concludes with a comparison of Chinese and Western music.

(4) WIANT, BLISS. The Music of China. Hong Kong: Chung Chi College,
Chinese University of Hong Kong, 1965, 161 pp.
   The book deals with the relationships between music and five areas
of Chinese society: a) government, b) literature, c) nature, d) daily
life, e) religion. Samples of folk songs and Buddhist chants, as well
as instrumental folk tunes, are provided. Forty Chinese folk musical
instruments are itemized.

6. Social, Economic, and Political Developments

6.1 THE RELIGIOUS DIMENSION OF CONFUCIANISM AS A SOCIOPOLITICAL INSTITUTION

See 1.6 for ancestor cult and family. See 1.5 for the cult of Confucius. See 5.2 for the Hall of Light. See 1.4.1 for emperor as Son of Heaven

(1) EBERHARD, WOLFRAM. "Confucius as a Revolutionist and a Critic of Morals." In Moral and Social Values of the Chinese (see 1.1[5]), pp. 401-11.

The article expresses two central ideas: 1) Confucius intended to be a king to realize his political philosophy based upon his work, Spring and Autumn Annals, and 2) Confucius was much interested in the folk religion associated with the shao music in his day (The Analects, VII, 13), or, to further develop the second idea, Confucius was in favor of a refined folk religion in which the primitive elements (e.g., sexual rituals) have been sublimated.

(2) _____. "The Political Function of Astronomy and Astronomers in Han China." In Chinese Thought and Institutions. Edited by John King Fairbank. Chicago: University of Chicago Press, 1957, pp. 33-70.

The author formulates the view, based on Han documents, that astronomy and astrology, as well as calendar-making, were instituted primarily for a political reason, namely, the security of the imperial dynasty. Hence science became subordinated to politics.

(3) HSU, FRANCIS L.K. Under the Ancestors' Shadow. New York: Columbia University Press, 1948, 317 pp.

An anthropological study of a district called Western Town, with 80,000 inhabitants, in Yunnan Province of southwest China in the early 1940s. The author attempts to show the integral function of religion in the community. The ancestor cult is portrayed in great detail, and different types of rituals related to life and death are described. Some of the rituals and divinities are of Taoist and Buddhist origin, because the Confucian ancestor cult has incorporated both Taoist and Buddhist elements.

(4) KALTENMARK, MAX.   "Religion and Politics in China in the Ts'in
and the Han." Diogenes 34 (1961):18-46.
   About the religious functions of the emperor. Traces religious
etymologies of characters in the title huang-ti and the use of this
title by the First Emperor. Discussion of relevant theories such as
the Five Elements and the Five Virtues, etc. In ancient China, "to
govern was, above all, a magico-religious function. . . ." Finally,
there is a discussion of imperial sacrifices, particularly those of
the Han emperor Wu. A useful summary, not technical in style, but
romanizations are in the French forms rather than one of the English
systems.

(5) URBAN, GEORGE, ed.   The Miracles of Chairman Mao.   London: T.
Stacey, 1971, 131 pp.
   A collection of excerpts from Chinese newspaper articles in English
on the effectiveness of Maoism. The purpose is to show how Marxism-
Leninism is fused with traditional Confucianism. These excerpts indicate the religious dimension of Chinese Communism. The editor's introduction reflects Western judgment and a fear of racial confict.

(6) YANG, C.K.   "The Functional Relationship between Confucius' Thought
and Chinese Religion." In Chinese Thought and Institutions (see
6.1[2]), pp. 269-90.
   An analysis of the religious elements in Confucianism and a conceptual clarification made between "diffused religion" and "special
religion." Because Chinese religions were diffused, i.e., lacking
priesthood and centralized organization, they were generally unable
to protect themselves against Confucian state control.

(7) _____ .   "Religious Aspects of Confucianism in Its Doctrine and
Practice." In Religion in Chinese Society (see 1.1[20]), pp. 244-77.
   A discussion of the relationship between Confucianism and theism,
fate, ancestor worship, and divination, between supernaturalism and
the civil service examination, and of the supernatural status of the
literati-officials.

6.2   STATE CONTROL OVER BUDDHIST, TAOIST, AND POPULAR RELIGIOUS
      INSTITUTIONS
      See also 1.4.2 for religious rivalries

(1) CH'EN, KENNETH K.S.   "Chinese Communist Attitudes Toward Buddhism
in Chinese History." China Quarterly 22 (Apr.-June 1965):14-30.
   Explains that Communist writers hold essentially the same view of
Buddhist contributions to Chinese culture as writers in the pre-
Communist era.

(2) _____ . "Political Life." In The Chinese Transformation of
Buddhism. Princeton: Princeton University Press, 1973, pp. 65-124.
    This book might have been subtitled "Buddhism and Chinese Culture
in the T'ang," as that is its main subject. The author surveys five
specific aspects of T'ang culture as these are influenced by Buddhism:
ethical, political, economic, literary, and educational and social.
Written by an established scholar which does not impede the flow of
the lucid prose, this is a work that is strongly recommended for students who have some background in Buddhism and Chinese history.

(3) _____ . "Suppression of Buddhism"; "Control of Buddhism." In
Buddhism in China (see 1.9.1[1]), pp. 226-33; 253-57.
    An account of the suppression of Buddhism in 845 and a description
of the government offices which controlled Buddhist monasteries by
means of the registration and certification of monks.

(4) _____ . "On Some Factors Responsible for the Anti-Buddhist Persecution under the Pei-ch'ao." Harvard Journal of Asiatic Studies 17
(1954):261-73.
    During the post-Han period, Buddhism was differently treated by the
dynasties in the North and South. In the South, "what antagonism there
was . . . was expressed mainly in debates and intellectual arguments.
Under the Northern dynasties, however, force and persecution were re-
sorted to on two notable occasions, the first under Wei Wu-ti in 446
and the second under Chou Wu-ti in 574-577. . . . I shall attempt to
discuss some of the factors that were probably responsible for the
developments in the north." A lucid historical analysis, not too
technical.

(5) EBERHARD, WOLFRAM. "Temple Building Activities in Medieval and
Modern China." In Moral and Social Values of the Chinese (see 1.1[5]),
pp. 423-77.
    A study of the relationship between temple constructions and po-
litical, economic, and social conditions in China from 600 A.D. to the
twentieth century. Buddhist, Taoist and Confucian temples in central
China are included in this study, based upon information from local
gazettes. Among the findings are: 1) periods of high building activities corresponded to periods of economic growth in the said regions;
2) the peak building periods were 850-1000, 1100-1400, 1500-1700;
3) after 1300, the majority of Buddhist temples were constructed in
the cities; 4) the periods in which there was major construction of
Buddhist temples were also the periods in which there was major construction of Taoist temples; 5) before 1250, an average temple holding
was about 300 mou, but after this date the average holding was reduced
to between 20 and 30 mou.

(6) FORTE, ANTONINO. Political Propaganda and Ideology in China at
the End of the Seventh Century: Inquiry into the Nature, Authors and

Function of the Tunhuang Document S. 6502 Followed by an Annotated Translation. Naples: Instituto Universitario Oriental, 1976, 312 pp.
A study of the Buddhist text that serves as a basis for the legitimacy of the reign of Empress Wu Chao (reigned 683-705), who founded the short-lived dynasty of Chou (690-705). The author identifies the long-lost Tun-huang manuscript S. 6502 as the text entitled Commentary on the Meaning of the Prophecy about Shen-huang in the Great Cloud Sutra (Ta-yün ching Shen-huang Shou-chi i-shu). It was composed by a group of nine monks who claimed that Empress Wu Chao was the incarnation of Maitreya, the last Buddha to descend upon the earth in the present aeon. In addition to Buddhist ideas, this commentary also contains Confucian and Taoist ideas for the legitimization of Empress Wu. An annotated translation of the commentary is also provided.

(7) GROOT, J.J.M. de. Sectarianism and Religious Persecution in China (see 1.10.1[2]) 1:7-259.
Deals with the state policy toward religious sects and institutions under Confucian bureaucracy, primarily during the Ch'ing period (1644-1911).

(8) HSIAO KUNG-CHUAN. "Heretical Sects." In Rural China: Imperial Control in the Nineteenth Century. Seattle: University of Washington Press, 1960, pp. 229-35.
Explains concisely and with many historical examples why the state maintained constant surveillance over religious activities among the populace, and the political reasons for its repression of sectarian religion.

(9) HURVITZ, LEON. "'Render Unto Caesar' in Early Chinese Buddhism." Sino-Indian Studies: Liebenthal Festschrift, edited by K. Roy, vol. 5, nos. 3-4 (1957):80-114.
A famous incident in the history of Chinese Buddhism was the decree issued by Huan Hsuan, Emperor of Eastern Tsin in 403 A.D., "that no Buddhist cleric was to be compelled to make the outward signs of respect to secular authority." He was persuaded to this decision by the venerable patriarch of Lu-shan, Hui-yuan. The background is thoroughly discussed, and the latter part of the article gives the translation of Hui-yuan's later rationalization of this position. Nontechnical.

(10) MATHER, RICHARD. "The Conflict of Buddhism with Native Chinese Ideologies." Review of Religion 20 (1955-56):25-37.
Delineates the differences between Buddhism on the one hand, and Taoism and Confucianism on the other, with respect to metaphysics, morality, and socio-economic issues in China from the fourth to the tenth century.

(11) NAKAMURA, HAJIME. "Religion's Struggle against the State and Its Defeat." In Ways of Thinking of Eastern Peoples: India-China-Tibet-Japan. Edited by Philip P. Wiener. Honolulu: East-West Center Press, 1964, pp. 271-74.

6.2   6.2   State Control over Religious Institutions

A brief discussion of the need for Buddhist and Taoist institutions
to support the Confucian State for the sake of their survival.

(12) NAQUIN, SUSAN. Millenarian Rebellion in China: The Eight Trigrams Uprising of 1813 (see 1.10.1[3]).
    A detailed historical study of the Eight Trigrams (Pa-kua) uprising
in 1813 in Northeast China. In addition to presenting the organization
and ideology of this sect, the study concentrates on the planning and
the execution of the event by the leaders of the Eight Trigrams, also
known as the White Lotus Sect, particularly the "invasion" of the
Forbidden City in Peking and the occupation of the districts in Honan
by the rebels. The author describes the uprising from beginning to
end with penetration and a sense of drama. It also unfolds the social
and economic background of the leaders and their followers. Included
is a microscopic analysis of other similar peasant uprisings in the
Ch'ing dynasty. It confirms the opinion that despite the great rebellious potentiality of the peasants and the enthusiasm of the rebel
leaders, these uprisings were destined to fail, due to weak leadership,
lack of strong organization and discipline, as well as the support of
the Chinese intellectuals. This is an in-depth study of a memorable
event.

(13) OVERMYER, DANIEL L. Folk Buddhist Religion (see 1.10.1[4]).
    A study of the White Lotus Sect and its related groups from the
sixteenth century to modern times. It investigates the spontaneous
movements of Chinese popular religious groups in the context of social
and political history. The basic thesis is that although many of these
sects were antigovernment and hoping for the imminent coming of a new
political era, they on the whole should be viewed as religious groups,
based upon the meaning of "religion" understood in the popular Chinese
sense. In supporting his interpretation, the author has introduced
many popular Chinese sources such as Pao-chuan [Precious scrolls] and
biographies of religious founders, which offer us a picture of Chinese
folk religion and life. In addition to Chinese sources, the author
discusses important secondary Japanese sources on Chinese folk religion, a rare treat in a Western publication. A pioneering work.

(14) REISCHAUER, EDWIN O., trans. "Ennin's Diary: The Record of a
Pilgrimage to China in Search of the Law." In The Chinese Way in
Religion (see 1.1[15]), pp. 87-96.
    Ennin was a famous ninth-century Japanese monk who visited T'ang
China and recorded his impressions. He tells of having witnessed the
persecutions of Buddhism (844-846) during the reign of Emperor Wu-tsung,
who favored religious Taoism.

(15) WELCH, HOLMES. "Buddhism Since the Cultural Revolution." China
Quarterly 40 (Oct.-Nov. 1969):127-36.
    After the Cultural Revolution, nearly all the monasteries in China

ceased to function. But reliable sources indicated in 1969 that some temples in the rural areas were still open.

(16) _____. "Buddhism under the Communists." China Quarterly 6 (Apr.-June 1961):1-13.
    A survey of the control of Buddhism under the Communist government, discussing the socialist reform of the Buddhist clergy and the reinterpretation of Buddhist thought. Includes information regarding the preservation of Buddhist culture and China's participation in international Buddhist meetings.

(17) _____. Buddhism under Mao. Cambridge: Harvard University Press, 1972, 666 pp.
    Contains twelve chapters dealing with the treatment of Buddhist monks and nuns, reform of monastic life, control of temples, suppression of Buddhist opposition, and direction of Buddhism in support of domestic and foreign policy.

(18) _____. "The Reinterpretation of Chinese Buddhism." China Quarterly 22 (Apr.-June 1965):143-53.
    Deals with information concerning the reinterpretation of Buddhist doctrines in terms of Marxist materialism. According to Welch, the reinterpretation is a temporary expedient to be cautiously permitted and discarded as soon as possible.

(19) WRIGHT, ARTHUR F. "The Formation of Sui Ideology, 581-604." In Chinese Thought and Institutions (see 6.1[2]), pp. 71-104.
    A study of Emperor Wen-ti's (587-604) claim to be a legitimate founder of a new dynasty; it elucidates the fact that at a time when all three religious institutions were struggling for imperial favor, the emperor, himself a Buddhist, was compelled to choose elements from the three systems for an ideology that would appeal to the three constituents, while at the same time conveying the legitimacy of his imperial rule.

(20) _____. "Fu I and the Rejection of Buddhism." Journal of the History of Ideas 12 (1951):34-38.
    An account of the memorial to Emperor Kao-tsu (618-26) of the T'ang dynasty, by a Taoist named Fu I (554-639), who attacked Buddhism on nationalistic, intellectual and economic grounds.

(21) _____. "The Period of Independent Growth." In Buddhism in Chinese History. Stanford: Stanford University Press, 1959, pp. 65-85.
    Points out the fact that the growth of Buddhism as a religious institution was always under the control of the State and that the great suppression of Buddhism in 842-845 was largely because it became an economical and political threat to the State.

6.2   6.2 State control over Religious Institutions

(22) YU, DAVID C. "Buddhism in Communist China: Demise or Co-
Existence?" Journal of the American Academy of Religion 39 (March
1971):48-61.
    A survey of mainland newspaper articles concerning the Communist
attitudes toward religion and Buddhism, as well as the Buddhist leaders' views toward their own religion. It concludes with an evaluation
of the assessments of mainland Buddhism by scholars in the West.

(23) ZÜRCHER, ERIK. "Anti-clericalism and Buddhism Apologetic." In
The Buddhist Conquest of China. Vol. 1. Leiden: E.J. Brill, 1959,
pp. 254-87.
    A documentary analysis of the conflicts in ideology, society, eco-
nomics and ethics between Buddhism and Confucian bureaucracy, as reflected in the writings of the Confucians and the Buddhists in fourth-
and fifth-century China.

6.3 INFLUENCES OF CONFUCIAN IDEOLOGY AND INSTITUTIONS UPON SOCIAL,
     ECONOMIC, AND POLITICAL DEVELOPMENTS IN CHINA

(1) CH'U T'UNG-TSU. "Religion and Law." In Law and Society in
Traditional China. Paris: Mouton, 1965, pp. 207-25.
    The book deals with Chinese society as reflected by its law, while
the section referred to involves the relationship between justice and
the supernatural. The traditional Chinese law appears to admit the
intervention of the supernatural for the execution of justice.

(2) DOOLITTLE, JUSTUS. Social Life of the Chinese. Vol. 1. New York:
Harper, 1865, pp. 168-235. Reprint. Taipei: Ch'eng-wen Publishing
Co., 1970.
    Although published long ago, this work remains the most thorough
study of traditional local culture in the Foochow region. It is more
than that, however, as much of its contents refers to more universal
aspects of Chinese culture. Written by a missionary in an age when
few missionaries (or indeed Westerners of any profession) bothered to
conceal their contempt for the heathen and the Oriental, it is also
remarkably free from distorting biases, maintaining an attitude of
ethnographical objectivity. One of the best sources for study of the
traditional Chinese social--including religious--beliefs.

(3) LEVENSON, JOSEPH R. "Emphasis on General Validity: As an Attack
on Tradition"; "Communism." In Modern China and Its Confucian Past.
Berkeley: University of California Press, 1958, pp. 155-75; 176-91.
Reprint. Garden City, N.Y.: Doubleday, 1964.
    This analysis of the fate of Confucianism in modern China points
out the incompatibility of Christianity with the Chinese tradition and
shows the continuity of Confucianism with Communism (Maoism) through
the Maoist dialectic that both rejects and affirms Confucianism.

(4) NAKAMURA, HAJIME. "The Influence of Confucian Ethics on the Chinese Translations of Buddhist Sūtras." Sino-Indian Studies: Liebenthal Festschrift, edited by K. Roy, vol. 5, nos. 3-4 (1957):156-70.
An account of the adjustment of the translation of Buddhist sūtras to suit Confucian morality. For instance, terms such as "kiss" and "embrace" were deleted, and "husband supports wife" becomes "husband controls his wife."

(5) WEBER, MAX. The Religion of China (see 1.1[17]).
This is a portion of the famous work, Die Wirtschaftsethic der Weltreligion. The English title, Religion of China, should be understood in the broadest sense: it is, in fact, a sociological analysis of the politics, commerce, and value system of Confucian-oriented Chinese society. Weber's concepts of bureaucracy and rationality are applied to the study of Chinese society, which is contrasted to Western society of comparable eras. This comparison results in his well-known thesis that capitalism developed only in northern Europe. Although this book offers intellectual stimulation, many of its sources are outdated.

(6) YANG, C.K. "Operation of the Mandate of Heaven"; "Ethicopolitical Cult." In Religion in Chinese Society (see 1.1[20]), pp. 127-43; 144-79.
The author points out that many religious groups and cults in Chinese history taught and sanctified Confucian morality even though this might not have been their immediate purpose. There was a tacit collaboration between the Confucian state and the religious groups.

(7) YANG LIEN-SHENG. "The Concept of Pao as a Basis for Social Relations in China." In Chinese Thought and Institutions (see 6.1[2]), pp. 291-309.
An investigation of the Confucian concept of pao ("response" or "return") and its influence upon individuals, families, and government officials. Pao deals with the ethics of reciprocity. The author also points out the influence of the Buddhist concept of karma upon pao; however, the Buddhist karma is individualistic, whereas the Confucian pao sometimes involves the whole family.

6.4 INFLUENCES OF TAOIST IDEOLOGY UPON SOCIAL, ECONOMIC, AND POLITICAL DEVELOPMENTS IN CHINA
See also 2.17, Taoist Messianism

(1) CHAN HOK-LAM. "Liu Ping-chung (1216-1274), a Buddhist-Taoist Statesman at the Court of Khubilai Khan." T'oung Pao 53 (1967):98-146.
A biographical study of one of the chief advisers of the early Mongol emperors Ogodei and Khubilai Khan. Not much on religion as such, but interesting as showing the part Buddhist and Taoist studies played

in the life of a leading scholar-statesman of those times. Technical,
but not incomprehensible to students with some background in Chinese
history.

(2) MURAKAMI, YOSHIMI. "Affirmation of Desire in Taoism." Acta
Asiatica 27 (1974):57-74.
     A historical presentation of the attitude toward desire among the
Taoist philosophers and sectarians. It discusses "ho-ch'i" (harmony
between sexes) and the ideal of "spiritualization of desires," namely,
one responds to things with emotions but should not let the emotions
be attached to the self. As Murakami points out, this Taoist attitude
has also influenced the later neo-Confucianists. The desire for happiness (fu), wealth (lu), and longevity (shou) was promoted among the
Taoist sectarian groups.

(3) NEEDHAM, JOSEPH. "The Tao Chia (Taoists) and Taoism." In Science
and Civilisation in China (see 2.1.6[7]) 2:33-164.
     An investigation of the various movements and groups within Taoism
and their influences upon Chinese thought and institutions. Needham
finds mutuality between magic and science, mysticism and empiricism,
communism and democracy, within the complex system of Taoism.

(4) WEBER, MAX. "Taoism." In The Religion of China (see 1.1[17]),
pp. 173-225.
     A presentation of the magical, astrological, and alchemical aspects
of Chinese religion and their effects upon society and politics. Weber
viewed these aspects as "Taoism" in contrast to Confucianism which, for
him, is rationalistic. Like many other writers on Chinese religion,
Weber considered religious Taoism to be identical to the folk religion
of China. Whether or not these two are identical remains an open question at the present.

(5) YU, DAVID C. "Taoism: Influence on Higher Education." In
International Encyclopedia of Higher Education. Edited by Asa S.
Knowles. Vol. 8. New York: Jossey-Bass, 1977, pp. 3557-65.
     A historical survey of the influence of philosophical and religious
Taoism upon the Chinese state, political movements, literature, science,
and technology. It also touches upon the current archaeological dis-
coveries on mainland China. The study concludes a brief report of
Taoist studies undertaken in various centers in Europe, Asia, and the
U.S., identifying the Taoist scholars and their works. A useful article on the contributions of Taoism to Chinese civilization and the
current state of Taoist studies viewed from a global perspective.

6.5   TAOIST AND BUDDHIST CONFLICTS

See also 1.9.1 for the Controversy between Taoism and Buddhism

(1) KUBO, NORITADA. "Prolegomena on the Study of the Controversies between Buddhists and Taoists in the Yüan Period." Toyo Bunko, Memoirs of the Research Department 26 (1968):39-61.
   A detailed, critical examination of the major historical source for the subject, the Chih-yuan pien-wei lu, preceded by a brief summary of the controversies themselves. Concludes that the said source "in its present text, is not trustworthy as a basic source for clearing up the truth about the controversies in question, or, in other words, that we cannot grasp the truth of the affair on the sole authority of that single book." An important article for serious students.

(2) LINK, ARTHUR E. "Cheng-wu Lun: The Rectification of Unjustified Criticism." Oriens Extremus 9 (1961):136-65.
   Introduction and translation of text. The subject is the Buddho-Taoist controversy ca. 300 A.D. and the text in question is a refutation of a series of arguments by unnamed Taoist antagonists to the effect that "Buddhism was no other than a reflection of native Chinese Taoism, and that the Buddha was himself none other than Lao-tzu, or, if not Lao-tzu, one of Lao-tzu's disciples." Chinese text included.

(3) ZÜRCHER, ERIK. "The Conversion of Barbarians: The Early History of a Buddho-Taoist Conflict." In The Buddhist Conquest of China (see 6.2[23]), pp. 288-320.
   A study of the controversy between Taoism and Buddhism based upon the Taoist Hua-hu ching [Conversion of barbarians] and the Buddhist records. Taoists said that Lao-tzu went to the West where he converted the Buddha, while Buddhists in turn said that Lao-Tzu was a disciple of Buddha.

6.6   TAOIST RELIGION UNDER IMPERIAL FAVOR

(1) KALTENMARK, MAX. "The Taoist Religion." In Lao Tzu and Taoism (see 1.3[3]), pp. 109-13.
   Contains references to the imperial support of Taoism during the reign of Emperor Huan (147-67) of the Han dynasty and in the T'ang period (618-907).

(2) LI DUN-JEN, ed. "How K'ou Ch'ien-chih Became a Taoist Immortal." In The Essence of Chinese Civilization. Princeton: Van Nostrand, 1967, pp. 52-55.
   A brief account of the life of the Taoist magician K'ou Ch'ien-chih (d. 432), who won the favor of the emperor of Toba Wei in the fifth century and claimed to be the Celestial Master (T'ien-shih).

(3) WATSON, BURTON, trans. "Shih-chi 28: The Treatise on the Feng
and Shan Sacrifices." In Records of the Grand Historian of China
(Shih-chi of Ssu-ma Ch'ien, 145-86 B.C.). Vol. 2, The Age of Emperor
Wu. New York: Columbia University Press, 1961, pp. 13-69.
    An account of the Feng and Shan sacrifices performed by Emperor Wu-
ti (140-87 B.C.) of the Han dynasty. Although the Feng and Shan sacrifices to Heaven were traditionally associated with Confucianism these
rites performed by Emperor Wu-ti appear to be Taoist rituals offered
to the Great Unity (T'ai-i), a Taoist divinity. These sacrifices are
related to the following elements: Yellow Emperor, magicians, the
immortals, the island of P'eng-lai, longevity and dietary restrictions.

(4) WELCH, HOLMES. "The Taoist Church in Politics." In The Parting
of the Way (see 1.2.8[2]), pp. 151-58.
    Describes imperial support of Taoism beginning with the Northern Wei
dynasty (386-535) and the reigns of T'ang Hsüan-tsung (712-52) and Wu-
tsung (841-47). Sung emperors Chen-tsung (998-1022) and Hui-tsung
(1101-26) were enthusiastic Taoists, while the Mongol period (1260-
1368) and the reign of Shih-tsung (1522-1567) of the Ming period also
saw the ascension of Taoism.

(5) YU, DAVID. "Taoism: Influence on Higher Education (see 6.4[5]).

6.7   SECTARIAN REVOLTS

    See also 1.7 for the rebellious sects of T'ai-p'ing Tao and
T'ien-shih Tao in the second century A.D.

(1) EICHHORN, WERNER. "Description of the Rebellion of Sun En and
Earlier Taoist Rebellions." Mitteilungen, Deutsche Akademia der
Wissenschaften zu Berlin, Institut fur Orientforschung 2 (1954):325-52.
    The article discusses Han Taoism with special attention to Taoist-
inspired political upheavals. It then gives the historical sources
for the succeeding Chin period and concerns itself with the story of
Sun En's rebellion (399-402), "this rebellion which had begun with the
sectarian practices of one of the Taoist faithhealers and led up to
the first great pirate war in Chinese history." In sum, a paradigm
of many later rebellions which originated in religious inspiration and
ended up as political (or simply criminal) activity.

(2) GROOT, J.J.M. de. "The Eight Trigrams Sect and the Heaven and
Earth Sect." In Sectarianism and Religious Persecution in China (see
1.10.1[2]), pp. 335-47.
    A brief account of the rebellious activities of these two groups
in the eighteenth century. It should be noted that de Groot's sources
of information are government papers that reflect the point of view of
the state.

6. Social, Economic, and Political Developments

(3) LEAVENSON, JOSEPH R. "Confucianism and T'aip'ing 'Heaven.'"
Comparative Studies in Society and History 4 (1962):436-53.
   Several sections, discussing in turn 1) Chinese bureaucracy's long
imperviousness to social revolution--the influence of Confucianism,
2) the novelty of the T'aip'ing "Christian" assault on Confucianists
in power, 3) the crucial quality of the Confucian doctrine of imman-
ence, and 4) the directness of the T'aip'ing assault on Confucian doctrine (several subsections). This is a typical Levensonian essay, in
a brilliant, if sometimes difficult to follow, literary style that
may either please or irritate, depending upon the disposition of the
reader. The discussion is subjective, stimulating, and based mostly
on contemporary documents. Best read by more advanced students of
Chinese history and thought.

(4) LEVY, HOWARD S. "Yellow Turban Religion and Rebellion at the End
of Han." Journal of the American Oriental Society 76 (1956):214-27.
   A historical study which includes considerable detail on the beliefs
and practices of the early Taoist sects. Scholarly but not too technical for nonspecialists.

(5) MICHAUD, PAUL. "The Yellow Turbans." Monumenta Serica 17 (1958):
47-127.
   The author argues that the Yellow Turbans rebellion in 184 A.D. was
not the cause but the sign of the rapid fall of the Han dynasty. He
also points out that it is uncertain whether or not the Yellow Turbans
were Taoists. In disagreeing with Maspero, Michaud says that the sect
of the Five Bushels of Rice was not identical to the Yellow Turbans
sect: the former was strictly a Taoist movement. The essay ends with
a bibliography on the Yellow Turbans, in both Western and Chinese languages.

(6) MURAMATSU, YUJI. "Some Themes in Chinese Rebel Ideologies." In
The Confucian Persuasion. Edited by Arthur F. Wright. Stanford:
Stanford University Press, 1960, pp. 241-67.
   A discussion of the basic themes of rebel ideology among the major
sectarian groups. Many of the groups the author mentions are Buddhist
or Taoist or Buddho-Taoist.

(7) WAKEMAN, FREDERIC, Jr. "Rebellion and Revolution: The Study of
Popular Movements in Chinese History." The Journal of Asian Studies
36 (1977):201-37.
   A critical review of the recent English, French, Chinese, and
Japanese works on mass rebellions in Chinese history, particularly in
the periods of Yüan (1271-1368), Ming (1368-1644), and Ch'ing (1644-
1912). Although it is not concerned exclusively with sectarian rebellions, it definitely points out the inseparable relationship between
sectarianism and popular rebellious movements in Chinese history. The
author also states his own view about the Chinese millenarian movements,

which for him grew out of the sectarian tradition of White Lotus/Mai-treya/Venerable Mother cults. He also emphasizes the impossibility of separating the "secular" from the "religious" in the rebellious movements, due to the very nature of the Chinese perception of what is religion and what is politics. In the final analysis, it is the his-torical memories of these rebellions that have become an inspiration for the Chinese masses. As the author says: "Enshrined as a popular legacy, China's traditional rebellions may have acquired their greatest historical influences as mythical signposts toward a revolutionary social consciousness." The essay is accompanied by suggestions for further research and a ten-page bibliography.

(8) YANG, C.K. "Religion and Political Rebellion." In Religion in Chinese Society (see 1.1[20]), pp. 218-43.
    A summary of the major sectarian revolts against the state in Chinese history. The following groups are specially related to religious Tao-ism: the Yellow Turbans, the Ch'üan-chen sect, the Eight Trigrams, and the Hsien-t'ien sect.

6.8 SECRET SOCIETIES
    See also 1.10.2 for Secret Societies in the Twentieth Century

(1) CHAN HOK-LAM. "White Lotus-Maitreya Doctrine and Popular Uprisings in Ming and Ch'ing China." Sinologica 10 (1969):211-33.
    Focuses on the millenarianism of this popular Buddhist doctrine and its function in various uprisings of Ming and Ch'ing times. The author believes that this phenomenon represented a "value-oriented movement with the potential of modern revolutions"--a view that many historians nowadays likewise express about the T'aip'ing movement in mid-nineteenth century. A solid historical study, but comprehensible to nonspecialists.

(2) DEKORNE, JOHN C. "Fellowship of Goodness: T'ung Shan Shê." Ph.D. thesis, Kennedy School of Missions, Hartford Seminary Foundation, Grand Rapids, Mich., 1941, 109 pp.
    Describes in fair detail the organization, beliefs, and activities of a secret (although registered with the government) religious society during the 1920s. Data primarily obtained from the society's publica-tions, with the addition of data obtained from the author's personal contacts.

(3) GROOT, J.J.M. de. "The Sien-t'ien Sect and the Lung-hwa Sect." In Sectarianism and Religious Persecution in China (see 1.10.1[2]), pp. 176-241.
    An explanation of the organizations, beliefs and practices of these two Buddho-Taoist sects which prevailed in the eighteenth and nine-teenth centuries in south China.

(4) TOPLEY, MARJORIE, and HAYES, JAMES. "Notes on Some Vegetarian Halls in Hong Kong Belonging to the Sect of Hsien-t'ien Tao." Journal of the Hong Kong Branch, Royal Asiatic Society 8 (1968):135-48.
   A discussion of the nature and history of an important sect, the Hsien-t'ien Tao (Church of Prior Heaven), especially as it operates in Hong Kong today. (For an earlier study, see J.J.M. de Groot's "The Sien-t'ien Sect," in Sectarianism and Religious Persecution in China [1.10.1(2)], pp. 176-96.) Intelligent observations by trained social scientists.

(5) WAKEMAN, FREDERIC, Jr. "Rebellion and Reaction." In Strangers at the Gate: Social Disorder in South China, 1839-1861. Berkeley and Los Angeles: University of California Press, 1966, pp. 109-56.
   A historical presentation of the activities of secret societies which resulted in rebellious activities against the Manchu government. This study may serve as a microscopic view of popular religious revolts in Chinese history.

(6) WARD, JOHN S.M., and STIRLING, W.G. Hung Society, or the Society of Heaven and Earth. 3 vols. London: Baskerville Press, 1925-26, 524 pp. Reprint. New York: AMS Press, 1973.
   Extensive study of the major secret society of recent times, also known as the T'ien-ti Hui (Heaven and Earth Society), or the Triad Society. In reality it is a group of numerous societies. This work particularly compares the organization and ritual of Hung with that of European Freemasonry.

7. Practices

7.1 IMPERIAL WORSHIP OF HEAVEN

(1) SOOTHILL, WILLIAM E. "The Yueh-ling (Monthly Observations) of the Li-chi (Book of Rites)." In The Hall of Light (see 5.2[5]), pp. 16-51.
    A description of rituals observed by the emperor regarding dress, diet, personal behavior, and official conduct in each of the twelve months. The prescribed conduct of the emperor would bring forth seasonal occurences beneficial to the state.

(2) THOMPSON, LAURENCE G., ed. "The Imperial Worship"; "The Cult of Mount T'ai." In The Chinese Way in Religion (see 1.1[15]), pp. 130-38; 178-85.
    Chapter 17 is condensed from Joseph Edkins' Religion in China (1878) which describes the imperial worship of Heaven, Earth, Ancestors, and the gods of land and grain. The descriptions of rituals are graphic. Chapter 23 is excerpted from the editor's translation of chapter 1 of Edouard Chavannes's Le T'ai Shan: Essai de monographie d'un culte chinois (Paris, 1910). The cult of T'ai Shan has two levels: T'ai Shan as an agent of Heaven, and T'ai Shan as a pantheon. At a lower level, the cult of T'ai Shan belongs to religious Taoism.

7.2 CULT OF CONFUCIUS

(1) MOULE, G.E. "Notes on the Ting-chi, a Half-Yearly Sacrifice to Confucius." Journal of the North China Branch, Royal Asiatic Society 33 (1900-1901):120-56.
    Personal observations, followed by an account of the ceremonies in the Confucian temple as prescribed in a liturgical manual dating from 1868, which are in turn derived from official governmental compilations on institutions. Special attention to the musical score. An interesting and enlightening article.

(2) SHRYOCK, JOHN K. "Sacrifices to Confucius in the Yüan Period (1271-1368)." In The Origin and Development of the State Cult of Confucius (see 1.5[1]), pp. 168-80.
    A graphic description of sacrifices to Confucius at a temple during the Mongol period, when the cult became elaborate.

134

(3) THOMPSON, LAURENCE G. "The Confucian Temple and Its Rites." In
Chinese Religion (see 1.1[14]), pp. 72-74.
    A brief description of a Confucian temple and a quote from Shryock
(2) on the rituals of worship.

7.3 ANCESTOR WORSHIP

(1) AHERN, EMILY M. The Cult of the Dead in a Chinese Village.
Stanford: Stanford University Press, 1973, 296 pp. Illus.
    Field work for this anthropological study was undertaken in a north-
ern Taiwanese village during 1969-70. The author was focusing on ancestor worship and lineage organization, and the book represents the
most thorough, careful, and profound analysis yet to appear on the subject. The first part of the book is a typical anthropologist's description of the village and its people; the second part is the study of the
cult of the dead in that village. Perhaps the most important chapter
is the conclusion, in which the author attempts to assess the meaning
and relevance of the results from her community study in relation to
Chinese ancestor worship and lineage organization in general. The
most serious question that has been raised about this work is the
apparently somewhat singular characteristics of the particular community in which the study was made. One also wishes the author had not
focused herself so exclusively upon her special subject and had taken
the many other aspects of community religion into account.

(2) FREEDMAN, MAURICE, ed. "Ritual Aspects of Chinese Kinship and
Marriage." In Family and Kinship in Chinese Society. Stanford:
Stanford University Press, 1970, 163-87.
    The first part of this anthropological essay deals with ancestral
tablets and worship among contemporary Chinese in the Hong Kong New
Territories. A distinction is made between domestic ancestor worship
in terms of the four generations of ancestors, and local ancestral
halls in terms of prominent ancestors. Domestic ancestor worship involves the immediate ancestors, whereas the worship at the ancestral
hall involves distant ancestors. The second part refers to marriage
rituals in the premodern and Republic periods, viewed from the perspective of the bride. Emphasis is placed on the symbolic meaning of
the marriage rituals which demonstrate the bride's transition from a
member of her own household to a female member of her husband's family.

(3) GROOT, J.J.M. de. "Funeral Rites"; "The Grave." In The Religious
System of China (see 1.2.1[3]) 1:3-242; 2-3:341-1468.
    The section in the first volume gives a detailed description of
funeral rituals and burial rites, based primarily on the Confucian
classic, The Book of Rites, and the personal observations of the author.
The section in the second through the third volumes describes the construction of tombs, mourning rites, fasting, sacrifices, and geomancy

in pre-modern China, based upon classical and historical documents.
The author's Europe-centered personal judgments frequently detract
from his otherwise objective descriptions.

(4) NELSON, H.G.H. "Ancestor Worship and Burial Practices." In
Religion and Ritual in Chinese Society (see 1.1[19]), pp. 251-77.
    A study of the genealogy of the Lai family in the district of Sheung
Tsuen in Hong Kong's New Territories within the span of three centuries, involving the ascendancy of twelve generations of ancestors. The
primary data are the ancestral tablets, the gravestones, and informers
from the district. It is a detailed study of the "interaction between
ritual behavior and social reality." More specifically, it is a study
of the relation between social and economic factors of the descendant
families and how these factors have influenced the attitudes of these
families toward their ancestors. In the process of this study, the
author raises the question of whether ancestor worship is a religious
activity in China since it embraces so many aspects of Chinese secular
life.

(5) THOMPSON, LAURENCE G. "Funeral Rites in Taiwan"; "Ancestor Festivals." In The Chinese Way in Religion (see 1.1[14]), pp. 160-69;
155-59.
    The first section gives an account of the care of the deceased from
the washing of the corpse to the reburial of the bones eleven years
after the original burial. The second section contains an abbreviated
part of Francis Hsu's Under the Ancestors' Shadow (see 6.1[3]), in
which Hsu gave an eyewitness report of the ancestor festivals in
Western Town, Yunnan province.

(6) WALSHE, W.G. "Some Chinese Funeral Customs." Journal of the North
China Branch, Royal Asiatic Society 15 (1903-4):26-64.
    Focuses on customs of the prefectures of Ningpo and Shaohsing,
Chekiang province. A quite detailed outline, obviously based on the
author's personal observations and valuable for comparison with reports
from other localities.

(7) WILSON, B.D. "Burial Customs in Hong Kong." Journal of the Hong
Kong Branch, Royal Asiatic Society 1 (1960-61):115-23.
    Interesting observations of the current practices in Hong Kong, show-
ing the modifications of tradition that have been necessitated by rapid
modernization and urbanization.

(8) WOLF, ARTHUR P. "Chinese Kinship and Mourning Dress." In Family
and Kinship in Chinese Society (see 7.3[2]), pp. 189-207.
    A description of the different materials and colors of mourning
dress as worn today by the Chinese in Sanhsia in northern Taiwan. The
reason for these differences is the different distances between the
mourners and the deceased with respect to property rights. Thus the

sons of the deceased wear coarse hempen gowns, grandsons wear gowns
of flax, and great-grandsons wear muslin gowns dyed dark blue.   The
article also points out that whereas the white gown is a common mourning dress in China, it is in fact a neutral color and does not indicate
the actual relationships between the mourners and the deceased.   The
differences in dress materials and colors worn by female relatives are
also related to their rights of inheritance.

7.4   MARRIAGE

(1) AHERN, EMILY M.   "Affines and the Rituals of Kinship."   In Religion
and Ritual in Chinese Society (see 1.1[19]), pp. 279-307.
     A field study of Ch'i-nan, in the southwestern part of the Taipei
Basin, about the affinal relations between two families. The author's
thesis is that in this locality the wife's family is ritually superior
to the husband's family, irrespective of the previous economic and
social positions of the two families. Also, according to the author,
ideally speaking, the wife's family is expected to be socially and
economically superior to the husband's family. However, this paper is
only concerned with the ritual superiority of the wife-giving group.

(2) DORÉ, HENRI.   "Betrothal and Marriage."   In Researches into Chinese
Superstitions (see 2.1.6[1]).   Vol. 4, translated by M. Kennelly, pp.
29-39.
     A brief explanation of the importance of astrology in relation to
the birthdays of the betrothed and the wedding ceremonies.

(3) FENG HAN-YI, and SHRYOCK, J.K.   "Marriage Customs in the Vicinity
of I-Ch'ang."   Harvard Journal of Asiatic Studies 13 (1950):362-430.
     I-ch'ang is nearly 400 miles above Hankow on the north bank of the
Yangtze, where Feng did her field work in 1938. This is a rare account
of an actual, on-the-spot investigation of marriage customs on the mainland. The study goes into considerable detail. It is presented in an
interesting, nontechnical style.

(4) YANG, MARTIN C.   "Marriage."   In A Chinese Village.   New York:
Columbia University Press, 1945, pp. 103-22. Paperback reprint.
1965.
     Yang gives a graphic, in-depth description of traditional marriage
and wedding ceremonies in the village of Taifou, Shangtung province,
where he lived in his youth. The nuances of rituals with respect to
the families of the groom and the bride are fully discussed.

7.5 DIVINATION

(1) DORÉ, HENRI. "Fortune-telling, Divination and Omens." In
Researches into Chinese Superstitions (see 2.1.6[1]). Vol. 4, translated by M. Kennelly, pp. 321-80.
   A methodical explanation of different kinds of divinations, fortune-
telling, physiologomy, coin-throwing, astrology, lot-casting, throwing
of bamboo blocks, and dissecting written characters.

(2) NAKAYAMA, SHIGERU. "Characteristics of Chinese Astrology." Isis
57 (1966):442-54.
   "Chinese court astrology consists purely in the accumulation of
portents . . . and their empirical correlation with events in human
society which are relevant to the success of Imperial rule. . . .
Chinese astrology shares three essential features with that of ancient
Babylon: empirical collection of data, official character, secrecy."
Relates theoretical development to basic worldview. Points out that
"Chinese fate calculation is not astrology in any literal sense, but
an application of calendrical (i.e., time-numbering) elements to mundane personal affairs." Historical developments are then discussed,
in a section which is not fully comprehensible to one without a basic
knowledge of astronomy. Otherwise the contents of this interesting
article are not too technical for the layman.

7.6 TAOIST RITUALS

   See also 2.19.1 for the liturgical tradition as observed in Taiwan

(1) GOULLART, PETER. The Monastery of Jade Mountain (see 1.12.2[2]).
   In chapters 8-11 and 14, the author, a practicing Taoist who resided
in China for more than thirty years, describes the following rites as
witnessed by him: the Jade Emperor's birthday, exorcism, mass for the
ancestor, and the making of talismans by the priest-medium.

(2) GROOT, J.J.M. de. "The Priesthood of Animism." In The Religious
System of China (see 1.2.1[3]) 5:1187-1341.
   This is a discussion of the ritual of exorcism as described in the
literature of the Han (206 B.C.-220 A.D.) and post-Han periods. Ceremonies in connection with oracles are also described. The author's
characterization of Chinese religion as "animism" has prevented him
from appreciating Chinese religion from the viewpoints of anthropology,
psychology, and sociology.

(3) LIU TS'UN-YAN. "The Penetration of Taoism into the Ming Neo-
Confucianist Elite." T'oung Pao 57 (1971):31-102.
   In this detailed monograph, the author documents what he refers to
as "this long, tenacious, ever-growing and omnipresent Taoist social

and cultural background in the Ming dynasty." The work proceeds
through six sections, the first of which is on the "traditional and
official worship of the State," showing the amazing extent to which
this supposedly Confucian ritual was in fact permeated by Taoist practices and even performed by Taoist priests.   The second section discusses the universal practice of composing Taoist-style prayers, which
were called "blue-paper prayers" by the highest scholar-officials.
The third section notes how the attitude of "the amalgamation of the
Three Teachings" had by Ming times permitted Confucian scholars to
look with equanimity upon Taoist doctrines.   The fourth section shows
the thorough acceptance by emperors and officials of Taoist occultism
and sorcery.   The fifth section explains that the widespread acceptance
of practices conducive to longevity--"nourishment of life and the control of breath"--prove Taoist domination of the scholars in view of
the fact that there was no such technique in the tradition of the Confucian teachings.   The sixth section discusses two specialized terms
which were apparently quite familiar to Confucian scholars in the Ming
period, and which, being esoteric Taoist terms, indicate their familiar-
ity with such studies.   This is an important work, but it may be rather
too technical for students without considerable sinological background.

(4) MEYER, JEFFRY F.   "The Tao Ch'ang: Culmination of the Taoist Chiao:
Rite of Cosmic Renewal."   Typescript.   University of North Carolina at
Charlotte, 1973, 13 pp.
    An explanation of the ritual of cosmic renewal performed at a temple
in Taiwan and witnessed by the author in 1972.

(5) SASO, MICHAEL.   "Orthodoxy and Heterodoxy in Taoist Ritual."   In
Religion and Ritual in Chinese Society (see 1.1[19]), pp. 325-36.
    A description of the "orthodox" and "heterodox" Taoist priests in
northern Taiwan by a Western Taoist priest.   According to Saso, the
orthodox priests in Taiwan today are the Taoists of the Cheng-i sect,
whereas the priests of all other Taoist sects are "heterodox."   One
gets the impression that although all Taoist priests and priestesses
in Taiwan practice esoteric and magical rituals for pecuniary and meditational purposes, the rituals performed by the priests of the Cheng-i
sect are superior and more powerful because their rituals are based on
the canonical texts and their length of training is longer.

(6) SASO, MICHAEL R.   Taoism and the Rite of Cosmic Renewal.   Tacoma:
Washington State University Press, 1972, 120 pp.
    A scholarly investigation of the Taoist rite of chiao, or cosmic
renewal, based on personal observations in Taiwan.   The chronological
account of this three-day rite is meticulously described, with documentary support from the Taoist canon.   It is, in essence, a purification rite of macro-microcosm, in which all the important Taoist divinities are actually the external symbols of man's internal body.   Hence
the outer and inner spaces are in fact identical.   Among the Taoist

books discussed is the Origins of Religious Taoism (Tao-chiao yuan-liu),
a Taoist manual used by Taiwan priests as their professional guide.
Some flaws of the book are: 1) the identification of the yang and yin
principles as the principles of "good" and "evil," 2) the identification of religious Taoism with the "Chinese religion," and 3) the identification of Taiwan Taoism with the Taoism of China in general.

(7) SCHIPPER, KRISTOFER M.   "The Written Memorial in Taoist Ceremonies."
In Religion and Ritual in Chinese Society (see 1.1[19]), pp. 309-24.
     A meticulous description of the written memorial to the High Perfect
Beings of the Three Worlds at the three-day Taoist communal renewal
service conducted by the chief priest and his acolytes. The complete
memorial, written in literary style, is orally recited by an acolyte
three times during the service while the chief priest meditates. It
is intended to be an appeal to the highest divinities in Heaven from
the entire community for the purification of all families in it. These
recitations constitute the climax of the service. A scholarly description of a popular ritual by a European Taoist priest.

7.7   TAOIST ALCHEMY AND YOGA

     See 1.8.1 for Ts'an-t'ung ch'i. See 2.16 for Ko Hung. See 2.18
     for the Theoretical Basis of Chinese Alchemy. See 2.18[7] for
     Sun Ssu-mo

(1) CHANG CHUNG-YUAN.   "Process of Self-realization."   In Creativity
and Taoism. New York: Julian Press, 1966, pp. 123-68. Paperback reprint. New York: Harper & Row, 1970.
     Deals with the relationships between the physiological and psycho-
logical aspects of the adept in the context of breathing exercise.

(2) DEGLOPPER, DONALD R.   "Religion and Ritual in Lukang."   In
Religion and Ritual in Chinese Society (see 1.1[19]), pp. 43-69.
     A functional description of the value of the thirty-nine temples in
the town of Lukang, Taiwan, with a population of 28,000. According to
the author, the inhabitants support the annual festivals and rituals
performed at these temples primarily because these temples symbolize
the past history of the city, which a century ago was the largest city
in central Taiwan, even though it has a disproportionately large number
of temples today.

(3) ELIADE, MIRCEA.   "Chinese Alchemy"; Note I, "Chinese Alchemy";
Note J, "Magic Traditions and Alchemical Folklore."   In The Forge and
the Crucible: The Origins and Structure of Alchemy. Translated by
Stephen Corrin. New York: Harper & Row, 1971, pp. 109-26; 210-12;
212-14.
     A survey of the external and internal alchemy of China, with empha-
sis upon the correlation between the human body and the cosmos.

(4) GULIK, R.H. van. "Sexual Techniques and Longevity"; "Indian and Chinese Sexual Mysticism." In Sexual Life in Ancient China. Leiden: E.J. Brill, 1961, pp. 192-200; 339-59.

The first section discusses the view of a seventh-century Taoist physician, Sun Ssu-mo (581-682) on the technique of coitus reservatus and other instructions regarding sexuality and health. In the Appendix, the author argues that Indian Tantrism was influenced by the sexual ritual of the Taoist mystics of China. The ritual of coitus reservatus, says the author, was introduced to India from China via Assam.

(5) LIU TS'UN-YAN. "Taoist Self-Cultivation in Ming Thought." In Self and Society in Ming Thought (see 2.6.3[7]), pp. 291-330.

This section, dealing with the Taoist internal elixir school, explains twelve concepts, ranging from the golden pill to the dual cultivation of nature and life. It also traces the Taoist and Buddhist (Ch'an) influences upon neo-Confucian thought of the Ming period (1368-1644), particularly that of Wang Yang-ming (1472-1529). The author uses primary sources and has translated several passages from the Taoist canon hitherto unknown to English readers.

(6) LUK, CHARLES [Lu K'uan-yu]. The Secrets of Chinese Meditation. London: Rider, 1964, 240 pp.

Early chapters deal with Buddhist meditation, but chapters 5, 6, and 7 (pp. 163-214) deal with the meditational practice of Taoism. Chapter 5 is a partial translation of a 1914 edition of Yin Shin Tsu's Method of Meditation. Chapter 6 is a partial translation of Yin Shih Tsu's Experimental Meditation for the Promotion of Health, which shows the strong influence of Tantric Buddhism of Tibet. Chapter 7 includes a translation of an interesting meditational technique called microcosmic orbit. Whereas there is much affinity between Buddhist meditation and Taoist yoga, the latter is distinguished by its emphasis upon the concentration on the lower belly. Taoism uses esoteric terms referring to various bodily organs as having cosmic significance.

(7) _____. Taoist Yoga: Alchemy and Immortality. London: Rider & Co., 1970, 206 pp.

A translation of The Secrets of Cultivation of Essential Nature and Eternal Life (Hsin-ming fa-chueh ming-chih), by the Taoist master Chao Pi-ch'en, born in 1860. It is concerned with internal alchemy, i.e., breathing exercise for the attainment of the "immortal foetus." The glossary in the book is very useful for the understanding of the basic Taoist terminology. Hence we learn that Ching (sperm) is translated as "generative force" and ch'i (breath) is translated as "vitality." The book is heavily illustrated.

(8) SEIDEL, ANNA. "A Taoist Immortal of the Ming Dynasty: Chang San-feng." In Self and Society in Ming Thought (see 2.6.3[7]), pp. 483-531.

A study of the mythological Chang San-feng, an archetypal immortal

of the Ming and Ch'ing (1644-1911) periods. Here Immortal Chang is
studied in relation to the imperial court of Ming, to popular cults,
and to the Ch'üan-chen sect of Taoism. In essence, Immortal Chang
possesses magical power, is an expert in making the "gold pills," as
well as the bed-chamber techniques for longevity, and is the founder
of the T'ai-chi ch'uan, the popular Chinese physical exercise.

(9) THOMPSON, LAURENCE G. The Chinese Way in Religion (see 1.1[15]).
    An excerpt is included in this book from Chang Chung-yuan's article,
"An Introduction to Taoist Yoga," Review of Religion 20 (1956):131-48.
In addition to the Taoist cosmology, the excerpt deals with the Taoist
terminology and techniques of breathing exercise.

7.8 FOLK FESTIVALS AND RITUALS

(1) AIJMER, GORAN. Dragon Boat Festival in the Hunan and Hupeh Plains:
A Study in the Ceremonialism of the Transplantation of Rice. Stockholm:
Ethnographical Museum of Sweden, 1964, 135 pp.
    This study is based upon an essay from late Ming times by Yang
Ssu-ch'ang concerning the dragon-boat races in Wu-ling, Hunan. Aijmer
has utilized local gazetteers and other relevant materials to elucidate
the complex meanings of this major festival of the Chinese year. He
explains that it "told of the activities of dead ancestors in connection with the transplantation of rice." The unravelling of various
skeins of symbolism in the details of the ceremonials involved is a
striking lesson in the power of creative scholarship. Although a small
book, this is a monograph extraordinarily rich in enlightening insights.
Not difficult for nonspecialists to understand. Should be studied in
conjunction with the article by Chao Wei-pang, "The Dragon Boat Race in
Wu-ling" (6).

(2) BODDE, DERK, trans. Annual Customs and Festivals in Peking, as
Recorded in the Yen-ching Sui-Shih-Chi by Tun Li-ch'en. Peiping:
Henri Vetch, 1936, 147 pp. Reprint. Hong Kong: University of Hong
Kong, 1965. Illus.
    Excellent translation of an interesting Chinese work that describes
the round of the festival year as observed in one place in China, just
before the end of the nineteenth century. Highlights many aspects of
Chinese culture.

(3) BODDE, DERK. Festivals in Classical China. Princeton: Princeton
University Press; Hong Kong: Chinese University of Hong Kong, 1975,
439 pp.
    A study of twenty-one seasonal and state festivals based upon
Confucian and classical texts. Although these festivals were known
in the Han dynasty (206 B.C.-A.D. 220), most of them were originated
in the Shang and Chou dynasties. The author devotes half of the space

to the new year festivals, which include the Great Exorcism (ta-no)
performed at the new year eve. Although these festivals in later times
became a part of Chinese folk religion, during the Han period they
were state cults. This work is not a mere description of these festivals as they were performed in the Han period; it also deals with myths
and rituals of ancient China whose meanings had become obscure even
in the Han dynasty. Hence a major purpose of the book is the establish-
ment of hypotheses concerning the origins and meanings of these rituals.
In this regard, the author has applied his ingenious imagination based
on his knowledge of the ancient texts, as well as his study of works by
de Groot, Granet, Maspero, Karlgren and those of the Chinese and Japanese scholars. It has filled a great vacuum about knowledge of ancient
Chinese myths and rituals. It is intended for advanced students of
Chinese religion, ethnography, and anthropology.

(4) BREDON, JULIET, and MITROPHANOW, IGOR. The Moon Year: A Record
of Chinese Customs and Festivals. Shanghai: Kelly & Walsh, 1927,
514 pp. Reprint. New York: Paragon, 1966.
    An extensive description of the special features of each of the
twelve lunar months regarding festivals, gods, sacred places, customs,
and legends. The accounts are well informed, though with instances of
exaggeration. The work was based completely on Western sources written
in the 1920s.

(5) BURKHARDT, VALENTINE R. Chinese Creeds and Customs. 3 vols. Hong
Kong: South China Morning News, 1953-58. Illus.
    Originating as a newspaper feature column, the articles grew into
first one book, and eventually three. The material is, therefore,
presented in a series of brief vignettes written in popular style.
Their value stems from the personal acquaintance of the author with
his subject matter and his strong empathy with it. Particularly important is the material on the boat-people, whose culture has been
little noted by previous writers. Religious subjects occupy a good
deal of space in these volumes, affording us vivid glimpses of local
beliefs and practices. The attractiveness of this work is enhanced by
the many illustrations done by the author, some in watercolor.

(6) CHAO WEI-PANG, trans. "The Dragon Boat Race in Wu-ling, Hunan."
Folklore Studies 2 (1943):1-18.
    Annotated translation of an essay by the late Ming writer Yang
Ssu-ch'ang. The essay provides a detailed description of the well-
known ceremonial dragon boat races that were and are held during the
fifth lunar month, particularly in central and south China. This is
the basic source for the monography by Aijmer (1), which should be
studied after reading this translation.

(7) DAY, CLARENCE B. "Peasant Ceremonies." In Chinese Peasant Cults
(see 2.1.9[1]), pp. 15-36.

A detailed description of personal observations of the following
festivals: New Year, birthday of the Jade Emperor, mass for the dead,
and spring pilgrimage.

(8) Echo (Taipei), 1971-.
An English-language magazine published since 1971 in Taipei. This
is a high-quality, beautifully and copiously illustrated monthly which
contains a high percentage of articles on folk religion in Taiwan,
written in a popular style, by people who know what they are talking
about. It is perhaps the best way to introduce students to the subject, as it combines vivid color photographs, other types of illustrations, and exciting, brief articles.

(9) GRAHAM, DAVID C. "Chinese Lunar Festivals." In Folk Religion in
Southwest China (see 1.12.3[3]), pp. 144-55.
A brief description of the following festivals: New Year, spring,
Dragon Boat, All Souls' Day, autumn, and Tour to the Hills.

(10) GROOT, J.J.M. de. "The Priesthood of Animism." In The Religious
System of China (see 1.2.1[3]) 5:1187-1341.
See 7.6(2).

(11) HODOUS, LEWIS. Folkways in China. London: Probsthain, 1929,
248 pp. Illus.
A standard reference on the subject. The author spent many years
in China and his book reflects much of his personal experience as well
as his background in the literary sources. Descriptions are especially
those having reference to the Foochow region. The book covers major
festivals, important deities, and popular folklore. Popular style,
entertaining to nonspecialists; useful information for more advanced
students.

(12) HOU CHING-LANG. Monnaies d'offrande et la notion de trésorerie
dans la religion chinoise. Paris: College de France, Institut des
hautes études chinoises, 238 pp.
A study of the history of the use of artificial money (made of paper)
as a ritual object burned and offered to gods, ancestors, and ghosts
in Chinese society. This practice began near the end of the Six
Dynasties period (265-589). An explanation of two rituals for the
transference of money to the celestial and subterranean world and a
translation of two Taoist scriptures in connection with these rituals
are provided. It also discusses the intimate relationship between
celestial financial matters related to human birth and death and the
individual's lifespan in Chinese popular religion.

(13) LEUNG, A.K. "Peiping's Happy New Year." National Geographic
Magazine 70 (1936):749-92. Illus.
A typical National Geographic article, written in vivid, popular

style and containing excellent photographs. A lively panorama of the various activities of the festival season that will make it come alive for those who have never seen China.

(14) LO, DOROTHY, and COMBER, LEON. Chinese Festivals in Malaya. Singapore: Donald Moore, 1958, 66 pp. Illus.
     A small, popular book with eight short chapters on major festivals of the lunar calendar as they are observed by overseas Chinese. Photos and reproductions of paintings.

(15) SCHIPPER, KRISTOFER. "Divine Jester, Some Remarks on Gods of the Chinese Marionette Theater." Academia Sinica, Bulletin of the Institute of Ethnology 21 (1966):81-94.
     The author utilizes his field data in conjunction with purely Taoist material in the canon and in ritual texts he has collected and proceeds with a detailed analysis of the complex problem of the meaning of the three "jesters" who are the "gods" of the Taiwanese marionette troupes. One of his important intentions is "to demonstrate how much the so-called Chinese popular religion . . . and religious Taoism are the same." A somewhat technical study.

(16) WELCH, HOLMES. "Pictures of the Festival of Ch'ing Ming." In The Buddhist Revival in China. Cambridge: Harvard University Press, 1968, pp. 131-33.
     These are twenty-one pictures taken by Henri Cartier-Bresson at West Lake, Hangchow, in late March, 1949, of the festival of Ch'ing Ming (spring festival), which takes place 106 days after the winter solstice during the third lunar month. This festival transcends any religious affiliation.

(17) _____. "Rites for the Dead." In Practice of Chinese Buddhism. Cambridge: Harvard University Press, 1967, pp. 179-205.
     A description of the Buddhist rituals for the dead. They are: 1) anniversary rite ("the release of the burning mouths"), 2) rite performed on the fifteenth day of the seventh lunar month (festival of the hungry ghosts), 3) plenary mass (Shui-lu fa-hui), or service to save all souls of the dead on land and sea in a given district. Al-though these rituals were generally performed by Buddhist monks, they were conducted for Chinese families regardless of their religious preferences.

(18) WONG, C.S. A Cycle of Chinese Festivities. Singapore: Malaysia Publishing House, 1967, 204 pp. Illus. Bibl. Index.
     The festival year as observed by Chinese in Malaysia, from the per-sonal experience as well as the literary researches of the author. The first section has chapters on the calendar in Malaysian life and the zodiacal animals, the second section has seven chapters on the celebration of the New Year, and the third section has seven chapters

on other important festivals.   Popular style, but inclusion of Chinese
characters increases its usefulness to the more advanced student.

7.9 GYMNASTICS

(1) CHENG MAN-CH'ENG, and SMITH, ROBERT W. T'ai-chi. Rutland, Vt.:
Charles Tuttle, 1967, 112 pp.
    The book involves the collaboration of a Chinese master and his
American disciple. It introduces t'ai-chi as a means to a healthy
life, as a sport, and as a method of self-defense and presents the
thirty-seven essential postures of the exercise. More than 275 photographs, together with 122 foot-weighting diagrams are provided.

(2) DELZA, SOPHIA. Body and Mind in Harmony: T'ai Chi Ch'uan. New
York: Cornerstone Library, 1961, 184 pp. Paperback reprint. 1972,
192 pp.
    Written before the sudden interest in t'ai-chi chuan that began in
the early 1970s, this is an excellent summary of its philosophical
background, principles, and fundamentals of practice. The author
studied with a master in China and continued her practice in the United
States as a member of an organized group. The book is illustrated with
sketches of movements and positions.

(3) FENG GIA-FU, and KIRK, JEROME. T'ai-chi: A Way of Centering and
I'ching. London: Collier-Macmillan, 1970, 156 pp.
    A presentation in pictures of the sequence of t'ai-chi ch'uan, ac-
companied by a translation of the explanation of the twenty-four postures. The first half of the book is a translation of the names of
the sixty-four hexagrams, each with a six-line explanation.

(4) MAISEL, EDWARD. T'ai-chi for Health. Englewood Cliffs: Prentice-
Hall, 1963, 212 pp.
    A discussion of the contribution of t'ai-chi ch'uan to physical and
mental health, followed by a presentation of the t'ai-chi ch'uan in
one hundred and eight pictures of positions, with explanations.

8. Ideal Beings: Biography and Hagiography

8.1 IDEAL BEINGS

8.1.1 Legendary and Divine Sovereigns

(1) SOOTHILL, WILLIAM E. "Fu-hsi (First Sovereign)"; "Shen-nung (Divine Farmer)." In The Hall of Light (see 5.2[5]), pp. 70-71; 133-35.

Soothill describes Fu-hsi as the one who invented the Pa-kua (Eight Trigrams) and his son Shen-nung as the first builder of the Ming-t'ang (Hall of Light) and the first husbandman.

(2) WATSON, BURTON, trans. "Yellow Emperor." In Records of the Grand Historian of China (Shih-chi) (see 6.6[3]) 2:49-52.

A report on the ascension of the Yellow Emperor to Heaven.

(3) WERNER, EDWARD T.C. "Fu-hsi"; "Shen-nung"; "Nü-kua (Female Fertility Divinity)"; "Chu-jung (Fire Divinity)." In A Dictionary of Chinese Mythology. New York: Julian Press, 1961, pp. 196-98; 334-35; 419. (Orig. pub. Shanghai: Kelley & Walsh, 1932.)

A description of the Three Sovereigns and the relationships between Fu-hsi and Nü-kua.

8.1.2 The Western Queen of Heaven

(1) DORÉ, HENRI. "Hsi-wang-mu (Western Queen of Heaven)." In Researches into Chinese Superstitions (see 2.1.6[1]). Vol. 9, translated by D.J. Finn, pp. 31-34.

A sketch of the hagiography of the Western Queen of Heaven, who is generally associated with religious Taoism.

8.1.3 The Jade Emperor

See also 2.1.9 for the Origins of the Jade Emperor

(1) DORÉ, HENRI. "Jade Emperor (Yu-huang)." In Researches into Chinese Superstitions (see 2.1.6[1]). Vol. 9, translated by D.J. Finn, pp. 2-15.

The author believes that the worship of the Jade Emperor began with the reign of Chen-tsung (998-1023) of the Sung Dynasty.
This view, however, has since been repudiated.

(2) WALEY, ARTHUR, trans. Monkey (Hsi-yu chi) (see 4.3.3[3]),
pp. 53-62.
     A fictional depiction of the battle between the Jade Emperor
and Monkey Sun Wu-k'ung in this sixteenth-century novel.

(3) WIEGER, LEON. "The Jade Emperor." In A History of Religious
Beliefs and Philosophical Opinions in China (see 3.2.15[1]), pp.
603-9.
     Wieger took the erroneous view that the worship of the Jade
Emperor began with the reign of Emperor Chen-tsung. In fact,
the worship of this divinity started in the eighth or ninth
century A.D. (see 2.1.9[5]).

8.1.4 The Eight Immortals

(1) DORÉ, HENRI. "The Eight Immortals." In Researches into
Chinese Superstitions (see 2.1.6[1]). Vol. 9, translated by
D.J. Finn, pp. 35-68.
     A collection of literary sources on the hagiography of the
Eight Immortals, two of whom are historical figures.

(2) LING, PETER C. "Eight Immortals of the Taoist Religion."
Journal of the North China Branch, Royal Asiatic Society 49
(1918):53-75.
     Investigation of some literary sources. Section one traces
the rise and development of hsien-Taoism. Section two narrates
the lives of the Eight Immortals. Section three deals with the
group as a whole. A good discussion in semi-popular vein.

(3) YANG, RICHARD F.S. "A Study of the Origin of the Legend of
the Eight Immortals." Oriens Extremus 5 (1958):1-22.
     Notes that "the first type of literature in which the term
pa hsien is mentioned and in which the eight figures are treated
as an entity is the Yüan drama or tsa-chu. . . ." Yang discusses
the specific plays in which the term is used, then mentions the
subject's further appearances in certain Ming novels. The re-
mainder of the article discusses each of the eight hsien in
turn as they are found in Yüan plays. Scholarly, but not too
technical.

8.1.5 Kuan-yin (Avalokiteśvara)

(1) CH'EN, KENNETH K.S. "Avalokiteśvara." In Buddhism in China (see 1.9.1[1]), pp. 340-42.
A historical survey of the evolution of Avalokiteśvara in China, from the role of Bodhisattva to that of the giver of children.

(2) DORÉ, HENRI. "Kuan-yin." In Researches into Chinese Superstitions (see 2.1.6[1]). Vol. 6, translated by M. Kennelly, pp. 134-233.
A hagiographical account of the incarnation of Avalokiteśvara into the person of Princess Miao-shen, thus making the Buddhist divinity of Indian origin a Chinese personality. Kuan-yin has become an object of folk religion.

8.1.6 Kuan-ti

(1) DORÉ, HENRI. "Kuan-ti." In Researches into Chinese Superstitions (see 2.1.6[1]). Vol. 6, translated by M. Kennelly, pp. 71-88.
A description of the history of the Three Kingdoms period (220-80) and a hagiography of Lord Kuan (god of protection, fortune, martial virtue, and literature), including the history of the process of deification. Doré's designation of Kuan-ti as the god of war is incorrect.

8.1.7 Matsu

(1) THOMPSON, LAURENCE G., ed. "The Cult of Matsu." In The Chinese Way in Religion (see 1.1[15]), pp. 196-201.
A description of the evolution of the deity of the sea, Matsu, a popular goddess of the coast provinces of south China and Taiwan.

8.2 SAGES AND TEACHERS

8.2.1 Lao Tzu, Chuang Tzu, Lieh Tzu

(1) CHAN, WING-TSIT, trans. "Lao Tzu the Man." In The Way of Lao Tzu (see 2.7.1[1]), pp. 35-52.
A critical discussion of the historicity of the man Lao Tzu as recorded in the Historical Records by Ssu-ma Ch'ien. Chan says that the historicity of Lao Tzu is unquestionable.

8.   Ideal Beings: Biography and Hagiography

8.2   Sages and Teachers

(2) KALTENMARK, MAX. "Lao Tzu"; "Chuang Tzu." In Lao Tzu and Taoism (see 1.3[3]), pp. 5-18; 70-71.
     The author quotes two passages on Lao Tzu and one on Chuang Tzu from the Historical Records by Ssu-ma Ch'ien.

(3) WIEGER, LEON. A History of the Religious Beliefs and Philo-sophical Opinions in China (see 3.2.15[1]), pp. 145-46.
     Brief biographical sketches of Lao Tzu, Chuang Tzu, and Lieh Tzu.

8.2.2   Chang Tao-ling

(1) DORÉ, HENRI. "Chang Tao-ling." In Researches into Chinese Superstitions (see 2.1.6[1]). Vol. 9, translated by D.J. Finn, pp. 69-86.
     A collection of both legendary and historical sources on Chang Tao-ling, the first Celestial Master who lived in the second century A.D. The reader may find Doré's highly derogatory remarks on the Celestial Master amusing.

(2) WERNER, EDWARD T.C. "Chang Tao-ling." In A Dictionary of Chinese Mythology (see 8.1.1[3]), pp. 37-42.
     A description of the hagiography of Chang Tao-ling largely based on the Shen-hsien chuan [Biography of immortals]. The term "pope," referring to Chang and his successors, is incorrect.

8.2.3   Ko Hung

See 1.8.2

8.2.4   K'ou Ch'ien-chih

(1) LI DUN-JEN, ed. "K'ou Ch'ien-chih (d. 432)." In The Essence of Chinese Civilization (see 6.6[2]), pp. 52-55.
     A brief account of the biography of this fifth-century Taoist priest-magician who served Emperor Shih-tsu of the Northern Wei dynasty.

8.2.5   The Three Mao Brothers

(1) DORÉ, HENRI. "San Mao (The Three Mao Brothers)." In Researches into Chinese Superstitions (see 2.1.6[1]). Vol. 9, translated by D.J. Finn, pp. 216-18.
     A hagiographical account of the conversion of the three Mao

150

brothers, founders of the Mao Shan sect, from Confucianism to
religious Taoism.

(2) WERNER, EDWARD T.C.   "San Mao."   In A Dictionary of Chinese
Mythology (see 8.1.1[3]), pp. 403-4.
     A short account of the activities of the three Mao brothers
at Chu-ch'u Shan (Mao Shan) outside the city of Nanking.

8.2.6 Ch'iu Ch'ang-ch'un

See 1.9.1

8.2.7 Chang San-feng

(1) SEIDEL, ANNA.   "A Taoist Immortal of the Ming Dynasty:
Chang San-feng."   In Self and Society in Ming Thought (see
2.6.3[7]).
     See 7.7[8]).

8.3 CONFUCIAN SAGES

8.3.1 Culture Heroes of Confucianism: Kings Yao, Shun, and Yü

(1) "Shoo King" [Shu-ching].   In The Chinese Classics (see
1.2.7[4]) 3:1-151.
     An account of the virtuous rule of these three legendary
kings who ruled China in the Golden Era.   There was no heredi-
tary kingship until Yü founded the Hsia dynasty (2183-ca. 1752
B.C.).

(2) The Works of Mencius.   In The Chinese Classics (see 1.2.7[4]),
1-2:354-60.
     Mencius's interpretation of the succession of kingship from
Yao to Shun and from Shun to Yü on the basis of personal virtue
and administrative ability.

8.3.2 Confucius and Mencius

(1) "The Confucian Classics."   In The Chinese Classics (see
1.2.7[4]) 1:56-127.
     The first half of chapter 5, "The Prolegomena: Confucius
and His Disciples," is an account of the life of Confucius.
Since Legge relied heavily on the K'ung Tzu chia-yü [The school
sayings of Confucius], a work of the Han period (206 B.C.-220
A.D.), which attributes to Confucius things he would not have

done, much of what Legge considered to be historical is in fact legendary.

(2) CREEL, HERRLEE G. Confucius: The Man and the Myth. New York: John Day, 1949, 363 pp. Reprinted as Confucius and the Chinese Way (New York: Harper & Row, 1960).
   A critical presentation of the historical Confucius based on the evidence recorded in the pre-Han documents and sources compiled two centuries after the death of the Master (479 B.C.).

(3) CROW, CARL. Master Kung. New York and London: Halcyon House, 1937, 347 pp.
   A fairly lengthy work of popularization. Despite many errors apparent to the scholar, it is a good book for students, written in an easy style, giving the story in its essentials, filling in with plausible conjectures where the gaps must be filled in a work like this. Generally true to the pious tradition, it tells the reader what most Chinese would have believed was the life story of the Master. It should, of course, be supplemented by a critical study, most suitably that of Creel.

(4) DORÉ, HENRI. Researches into Chinese Superstitions (see 2.1.6[1]). Vol. 13, translated by D.J. Finn, 261 pp.
   The first four chapters of this volume deal with the "biography" of Confucius, essentially a legendary account, while the rest of the volume gives biographical sketches of 144 Confucian scholars whose spirit tablets are seen at a Confucian temple.

(5) FUNG YU-LAN. "Confucius and the Rise of Confucianism."
In A History of Chinese Philosophy (see 2.1.7[11]) 1:43-75.
   Fung quotes several passages from the Historical Records by Ssu-ma Ch'ien (145 B.C.) on the life of Confucius and says, rightly, that whatever is said about Confucius must be checked against the Analects.

(6) _____. "Life of Mencius." In A History of Chinese Philosophy (see 2.1.7[11]) 1:106-8.
   A brief biography of Mencius based on the Historical Records and The Book of Mencius.

(7) "The Life of Mencius." In The Chinese Classics (see 1.2.7[4]) 2:14-38.
   A description of the life of Mencius gleaned chiefly from The Book of Mencius.

(8) ROWLEY, H.H. Prophecy and Religion in Ancient China.
London: Athlone Press, 1956, 154 pp.
   A comparative study of the nature of prophecy between the

8.4   Mo Tzu, Founder of the Mohist School   8.4

eighth and seventh centuries B.C. prophets of Israel and
Confucius, Mencius, and Mo Tzu, by a British Old Testament
scholar. For the Chinese sources the author relied upon the
Analects, Works of Mencius, and the Mo Tzu. Based upon textual studies and the discipline of comparative religion, the
author has produced a dispassionate and balanced work on the
topic. Rowley credits the prophetic qualities of these three
Chinese sages, who are comparable to Hebrew prophets. These
Chinese sages believed that Heaven is personal; they were com-
mitted to special missions given to them by Heaven. Among
these three sages, Mo Tzu's mission was entirely religious;
however, in at least two areas these Chinese sages departed
from the company of the Hebrew prophets: 1) their attitude
toward Heaven is more of an appropriate reverence or propriety
rather than that of worship, and 2) they feel a sense of remote-
ness from Heaven. On the other hand, the Hebrew prophets worshipped their God and had intimate relationship with Him. By
admitting the prophetic qualities of these Chinese sages, Rowley
differs with those critics (e.g., Max Weber) who believe that
Heaven is impersonal and that there is no prophecy in Confucianism.

8.4 Mo Tzu, Founder of the Mohist School

(1) FUNG YU-LAN. "Mo Tzu." In A History of Chinese Philosophy (see
2.1.7[11]) 1:76-84.
   A tracing of the biography of Mo Tzu, the exponent of universal
love and the doctrine of Supreme Being during the Warring States period (403-221 B.C.). The information is valuable for an understanding
of the Mohist School as distinct from the Confucian School.

9. Mythology, Cosmology, Basic Symbols

9.1 MYTHOLOGY

(1) BEAUCLAIR, INEZ de. "The Place of the Sun Myth in the Evaluation of Chinese Mythology." Academia Sinica, Bulletin of the Institute of Ethnology 13 (1962):123-32.
 A discussion, a propos of an article by a Chinese scholar dealing with the sun myth in ancient China, of the various approaches that have been adopted by many scholars in the attempt to come to an understanding of Chinese mythology. The author passes these approaches and the arguments of their critics in review, affording a useful summary of the problem. Finally she deals with the question of the sun myth itself, again citing various interpretations to show the variety of approaches and problems. A good article, especially for emphasizing the importance of methodological matters in studies of archaic and ancient China. May be too technical for students without background.

(2) BODDE, DERK. "Myths of Ancient China." In Mythologies of the Ancient World. Edited by Samuel N. Kramer. Garden City, N.Y.: Doubleday, 1961, pp. 369-408.
 The author points out that the reason why pre-Han myths of China are fragmentary is because the Confucian writers or editors who recorded the ancient history of China have either deleted these myths or reduced them to sketchy forms. On the other hand, although Taoist literature abounds with accounts of ancient China, they are too fanciful to be viewed as myths. With these problems in mind, the author proceeds to describe the following: the creation myth of P'an-ku, Nü-kua's fashioning of the firmament, the separation of Heaven and Earth, sun myths, and flood myths.

(3) _____. "Some Chinese Tales of the Supernatural: Kan Pao and His Sou-shen Chi." Harvard Journal of Asiatic Studies 6 (1941-42):338-57.
 Study of the first work in which "ghost stories" are compiled (first half of fourth century A.D.), biography of the compiler, and brief note on the text, followed by translations of a few stories. Interesting and informative as to typical Chinese ideas of the time.

9. Mythology, Cosmology, Basic Symbols

(4) CAMPBELL, JOSEPH. "Chinese Mythologies." In The Mask of God:
Oriental Mythology. New York: Viking, 1970, pp. 371-460.
      This section relates Chinese mythologies to their "origins."
Campbell thinks that the earliest myths of the Chinese owe their origins to two regions: Mesopotamia and Northeast Asia. From Mesopotamia
the myth of the ten kings was derived, and from Northeast Asia the
Chinese brought with them myths of shamanism. It should be noted that
none of the Chinese authors on ancient China have subscribed to the
Mesopotamian origin of the Chinese myths. The latter part of this
chapter, dealing with the arrival of Buddhism and post-Buddhist China,
is not directly related to mythology.

(5) CHAN PING-LEUNG. "A New Interpretation of Two Ancient Chinese
Myths." The Tsing Hua Journal of Chinese Studies, n.s. 7 (August
1969):206-32.
      This article, written in Chinese with an English summary, posits
two views: 1) that mulberry trees are the cosmic trees in Chinese
mythology, and 2) that the ancestors of the Shang dynasty (ca. 1751-
1112 B.C.) are both marine and fire divinities. The second view is
based on the author's conviction that the "dark bird" (hsüan-niao)
is both a marine god and a sun god.

(6) CHANG KWANG-CHIH. "Classification of Shang and Chou Myths."
Academia Sinica, Bulletin of the Institute of Ethnology 14 (1962):
75-94 (English abridgement).
      The author was at the date of writing this article a promising young
scholar in Chinese archaeology, and he has since become a leading authority. The article first discusses the problem of sources for early
myths and then proceeds with a fourfold classification of principal
types: "nature myths, myths of the world of gods and its separation
from the world of man, myths of the natural calamities and human saviors,
and myths of ancestral heroes." The overlapping of these categories by
many myths is cited. In his concluding remarks the author discusses
the changes in the character of the mythology from Shang to Western Chou
and then to Eastern Chou and various reasons that have been advanced for
these changes. The article, while dealing with a technical subject, is
written in an easily understood style.

(7) CHRISTIE, ANTHONY. Chinese Mythology. London: Hamlyn, 1968,
141 pp. Illus.
      A comprehensive discussion of the principal myths of China: cos-
mogony, creation of man, separation of Heaven and Earth, cosmic restor-
ation, the inventors of food and the arts, and the founder of the empire. The author does not attempt to trace the origin of these myths
in Chinese history.

(8) DUBS, HOMER H. "An Ancient Chinese Mystery Cult." Harvard
Theological Review 35 (October 1942):221-40.

A historical probing of the cult of Hsi-wang mu (Mother Queen of
the West), at one time a female divinity of prehistoric China. There
are twenty-four quotes bearing on the historicity and evolution of this
cult from earliest sources to the History of the Former Han (206 B.C.-
9 A.D.). In the earliest time, this female deity was the bringer of
calamities, but by the time of the Former Han she had been transformed
into a benevolent goddess who promised health and immortality to her
followers. This tradition was eventually assimilated into religious
Taoism.

(9) EBERHARD, WOLFRAM. The Local Cultures of South and East China
(see 1.2.1[1]).
    A presentation of forty-five myths or mythical themes in the context
of historical evolution, as these myths became more elaborate in content and meaning. The book is not simply a collection of myths, but
a study of the functional meaning of myths in relation to agriculture,
economics, society and government. Eberhard holds the "diffusing and
evolutionary view" of myths in Chinese history.

(10) FERGUSON, JOHN C. "Chinese Mythology." In The Mythology of All
Races. Edited by John A. MacCulloch. Vol. 8. New York: Cooper
Square, 1964, pp. 5-203. (Orig. pub. 1928.)
    A descriptive presentation of the popular myths of China, including
discussions on alchemy, geomancy and astrology. The author does not
distinguish the later myths from ancient ones, nor does he relate them
to Chinese society.

(11) GIRARDOT, NORMAN J. "Myths and Meaning in the Tao Tê Ching:
Chapters 25 and 42." History of Religions 16 (1977):294-327.
    Girardot's continuing discussion on the mythological theme of Chaos
and its related myth of the cosmic egg (from which P'an-ku emerges) in
ancient China. His interpretation of the numerical meaning of one,
two, three (chapter 42) as containing mythological and paradisiacal
import is intriguing and persuasive. The first task of reconstructing
(or recovering) the mythological theme of the Tao-tê ching would seem
to involve a critical reexamination of the Confucian exegeses of that
classic--a formidable task for any scholar to undertake.

(12) _____. "The Problem of Creation Mythology in the Study of Chinese
Religion." History of Religions 15 (1976):289-318.
    A critique of the prevalent view among sinologists (Granet, Needham,
Creel, Mote) that ancient China did not have cosmogonic myths. According to the author, the comparatively late creation myth of P'an-ku
(third century A.D.) prefigures the archaic myth of Chaos (hun-tun)
recorded in the seventh chapter of the Chuang Tzu and alluded to in
many other ancient texts. The myth of Chaos and its later version of
the myth of P'an-ku may constitute a cosmogonic theme in ancient China,
according to Erkes, Chang Kwang-chih, Izutsu, and the author himself.

9. Mythology, Cosmology, Basic Symbols

This essay asks for a reappraisal of ancient Chinese records in which myths are adumbrated and envisions a cosmogonic theme in the pattern of the myth of Chaos.

(13) KARLGREN, BERNHARD. "Legends and Cults in Ancient China." (See 1.2.3[3]).
    A vast collection of materials on myths and legends of pre-Han China. Karlgren attributes the historicization of the Chinese myth to the rational efforts of the Confucians.

(14) MASPERO, HENRI. "Mythology of Modern China." In Asiatic Mythology. Edited by J. Hackin. New York: Thomas Y. Crowell, 1932, pp. 252-384. Illus.
    A lengthy discussion of the popular pantheon, together with much other information, particularly on folk beliefs. An authoritative discussion by an eminent scholar, although somewhat unsystematic.

(15) OU-I-TAI. "Chinese Mythology." In New Larousse Encyclopedia of Mythology. Edited by Felix Guiran. Translated by Richard Aldington and Delano Ames. London and New York: Prometheus Press, 1959, pp. 379-402. Illus. New ed., 1968.
    As befits an article in a one-volume encyclopedia, this is a brief, nontechnical survey of the subject. The author acknowledges his indebtedness to Doré and (especially) to Maspero for his "Mythology of Modern China" (14). Profusely illustrated with excellent plates. An article suitable for elementary orientation only.

(16) ROUSSELLE, ERWIN. "Dragon and Mare Figures of Primordial Chinese Mythology." In The Mystic Vision: Papers from the Eranos Yearbook. Princeton: Princeton University Press, 1965, pp. 271-92.
    "The force and clarity of the Chinese mind rest precisely on a living historical rapport between the days of the animal gods and the most recent wisdom, and this applies both to the culture as a whole and to the individual. The Chinese have never lost this knowledge of those forces which are the vehicles and movers of the world process." With this sort of "mystical" view of the Chinese, one can imagine the way in which this author develops the theme of his article, dragon and mare standing in the first instance for the first two diagrams of the I-ching, and then for all sorts of symbolisms in Chinese tradition. Very subjective essay, but intriguing nonetheless.

(17) SOYMIE, M. "China: The Struggle for Power." In Larousse World Mythology. Edited by Pierre Grimal. New York: Prometheus, 1965, pp. 271-92. Illus.
    An illuminating discussion of the ancient Chinese myths relative to creation and the state. Its thesis is that one must formulate several larger interpretive principles for the elucidation of the varied myths and legends of the different regions of China. These principles include

the relationship between chaos and creation and the corespondence of man with the cosmos. A good introduction to the study of the motifs of Chinese mythology.

(18) WERNER, EDWARD T.C. A Dictionary of Chinese Mythology (see 8.1.1[3]).
An alphabetically arranged handbook on myths, legends and divinities (including Buddhist myths and personalities), with Chinese words inserted in the appropriate places. Although this book offers no theoretical understanding about the nature of Chinese myths, it does give abundant information about them.

(19) WERNER, E.T.C. Myths and Legends of China. London: George G. Harrap & Co., 1922, 454 pp. Illus.
Despite the fact that Werner was a sociologist and prided himself on his serious approach, this work cannot be described as anything more than a mélange of popular Chinese beliefs. As such, however, it has its value. Easy-to-read style.

9.2 COSMOLOGY

(1) CHAN, WING-TSIT. "Cosmological Passages of The Chuang Tzu"; "The Taoism of Huai-nan Tzu"; "An Explanation of the Diagram of the Great Ultimate." In A Source Book in Chinese Philosophy (see 1.4.2[1]), pp. 202-7; 305-8; 460-64.
The first section contains excerpts on the cosmological meaning of Non-being and Tao as transformation and One. The second section deals with excerpts from the Huai-nan Tzu on the beginning of the cosmogony and the mutuality between macrocosm and microcosm. The third part contains a translation of the short metaphysical essay by the neo-Confucianist Chou Tun-yi (1017-73), which exerted great influence upon neo-Confucianism and Taoism. Introduction and commentary are provided.

(2) _____, trans. The Way of Lao Tzu (see 2.7.1[1]), pp. 97-100, 176-77.
Chapter 1 deals with the cosmological principles of Being (yu) and Non-being (wu), or the Named and the Nameless. Chapter 42 describes the cosmological sequence.

(3) De BARY, W. THEODORE; CHAN, WING-TSIT; and WATSON, BURTON, comps. "Cosmology of the Han Period." In Sources of Chinese Tradition (see 1.4.1[3]), pp. 207-20.
Includes passages from Huai-nan Tzu on the theory of ch'i (material force), two documents dealing with the ecliptical and equatorial theories of the universe, the Appendixes of the I-ching on the relations between the yin-yang principles and the hexagrams, and the Ch'un-ch'iu fan-lu on the theory of the Five Elements and their relationship with government.

(4) FUNG YU-LAN. "The Appendixes of the Book of Changes and the
Cosmology of the Huai-nan Tzu"; "Diagram of the Supreme Ultimate
Explained." In A History of Chinese Philosophy (see 2.1.7[11]) 1:
379-99; 2:435-42.
   The section in volume 1 is a discussion of the cosmology of the
I-ching in the context of the hexagram, the yin-yang theory, and the
Supreme Ultimate (T'ai-chi), as well as the cosmology of the Huai-nan
Tzu, with emphasis on Non-being as formlessness. The section in volume
2 is a translation of the short essay, with full explanation. Fung
believes that Chou Tun-yi's essay resembles an earlier Taoist essay
(T'ang dynasty). In substance, Chou's essay is more Taoist than Con-
fucian.

(5) I-ching [Book of changes]. Translated by Richard Wilhelm; English
translation by C.F. Barnes (see 1.2.7[3]).

(6) SHIH, J. "Ancient Chinese Cosmogony." Studia Missionalia 18
(1969):111-30.
   A widely ranging survey of the ancient literature (up to early Han
times) that attempts to derive therefrom a coherent concept of Chinese
cosmogonical views. The author asks two questions: 1) how they spoke
of the origin of things, and 2) when they spoke of it. To the first
question the author answers in sum, "that the early Chinese spoke of
the origin of the world in terms of either botanical or zoological
reproduction." From an examination of several passages dealing with
Taoist yoga, he answers the second question in a rather singular way:
"What used to be called the ancient Chinese cosmogony was not, properly
speaking, a cosmogony. It did not intend to give any scientific observations on the formation of the world. Nor did it venture to utter
any philosophical explanations about matter. It was rather a soteri-
ology. It conveyed a message of salvation." A stimulating, if rather
subjective, interpretation.

(7) WALEY, ARTHUR, trans. The Way and Its Power (see 1.2.8[1]), pp.
141-42; 195-96.
   Waley does not view these chapters as having to do with cosmology.
Chapter 1 reflects the debate between the Realists and the Taoists,
while chapter 42 teaches the importance of submission.

9.3 BASIC SYMBOLS

9.3.1 Sages ("Sheng")

    (1) FUNG, YU-LAN. Introduction to The Spirit of Chinese
    Philosophy (see 2.12[2]), pp. 1-9.
       Fung defines the Confucian sage as one who possesses "sage-
    liness within and kingliness without," a phrase derived from

chapter 33 of the Chuang Tzu. This suggests that the Confucian
sage is one who combines the sublime with the common, namely,
that he transcends and at the same time embraces the world.

9.3.2 Immortals ("Hsien") and Gods ("Shen")

(1) De BARY, W. THEODORE; CHAN, WING-TSIT; and WATSON, BURTON,
comps. "Ko Hung." In Sources of Chinese Tradition (see
1.4.1[3]), pp. 298-305.
     Translation of excerpts from the Pao-p'u Tzu [Philosopher
who embraces simplicity], which deals with topics such as physical immortality, alchemy, and the merit system. See especially
the Taoist doctrine of hsien (the immortal) or the chen-jen
(true man) as discussed by Ko Hung.

(2) DORÉ, HENRI. Researches into Chinese Superstitions (see
2.1.6[1]). Vols. 9-10, translated by D.J. Finn.
     Volume 9 deals primarily with the divinities of Taoism and
volume 10 with the divinities of Chinese folk religion. The
two volumes together may be said to present the basic symbols
of Chinese religion. Doré did not, however, make a distinction
between Taoist religion and folk religion in China.

(3) NEEDHAM, JOSEPH. Science and Civilisation in China (see
2.1.6[7]) 2:52-54.
     These pages contain a discussion of hsien (material immortal).

(4) SEIDEL, ANNA. "A Taoist Immortal of the Ming Dynasty: Chang
San-feng" (see 7.7[8]).

(5) WARE, JAMES R., trans. Alchemy, Medicine, Religion in China
of A.D. 320 (see 1.8.2[3]).
     Contains Ko Hung's Pao-p'u tzu, in which the notions of hsien
and chen-jen are discussed.

9.3.3 Bodhisattvas ("p'u-sa")

(1) DORÉ, HENRI. "Avalokiteśvara (The Looking-down Lord)."
In Researches into Chinese Superstitions (see 2.1.6[1]). Vol.
6, translated by M. Kennelly, pp. 196-233.
     Deals with Kuan-yin P'u-sa, the savior of the living. Al-
though Avalokiteśvara is an Indian Buddhist divinity, he has
become popular as the female divinity, Kuan-yin, in Chinese
folk religion functioning as the deliverer of living beings
from their present suffering.

(2) REICHELT, KARL L.   "The Origin and Development of Masses for the Dead."   In Truth and Tradition in Chinese Buddhism. Translated by Kathrina Van Wagenen Bugge.   Shanghai: Commercial Press, 1934, pp. 67-111.
    A discussion of Bodhisattva Kshitigarbha (Ti-tsang), the savior of the nether world.   Although Kshitigarbha is an old Indian Buddhist divinity, in China he is called Ti-tsang P'u-sa, a popular god of folk religion, who delivers the dead from suffering in hell.

10. Sacred Places

(1) AYSCOUGH, FLORENCE. "Shrines of History, Peak of the East--T'ai Shan." Journal of the North China Branch, Royal Asiatic Society 48 (1917):57-70.

An interestingly written discussion of T'ai Shan as a focus for religious cults throughout history. Draws heavily on the writings of other Western scholars, especially Chavannes, Le T'ai Chan: Essai de monographie d'un culte chinois (Paris, 1910).

(2) BAKER, DWIGHT C. T'ai Shan: An Account of the Sacred Eastern Peak of China. Shanghai: Commercial Press, 1925, 225 pp. Illus. Reprint. Taipei: Ch'eng Wen Publishing Co., 1971.

A sort of guidebook for the most famous sacred mountain of them all. The material is drawn from a variety of sources, particularly the T'ai-shan Chih, or local gazetteer, and earlier studies by Chavannes and Tschepe. There is a map of the pilgrim road up the peak.

(3) CH'EN, KENNETH K.S. "The Yün-kang Caves and the Lung-men Caves." In Buddhism in China (see 1.9.1[1]), pp. 165-73.

A description of the Buddhist rock sculptures in the caves of Yün-kang near Ta-t'ung, Shansi, and the caves of Lung-men near Lo-yang, Honan. The former were begun in the fifth century A.D. and the latter in the sixth century A.D., during the Northern Wei dynasty (386-534).

(4) DORÉ, HENRI. "Chang Tao-ling"; "Five Sacred Mountains." In Researches into Chinese Superstitions (see 2.1.6[1]). Vol. 9, translated by D.J. Finn, pp. 69-86; vol. 10, translated by D.J. Finn, pp. 153-67.

The section in volume 9 contains references to mountains associated with the first Celestial Master: T'ien-mu Shan (Mt. Heaven's Eyes), Hao-ming Shan (Mt. Crane Calling), and Lung-hu Shan. The section in volume 10 contains an explanation of the historical development of the five mountains: T'ai-shan of the East, Hua-shan of the West, Heng-shan of the South, Heng-shan of the North (the Chinese words for the two 'Heng-shans' differ), and Sung-shan of the Center. These five mountains traditionally symbolize the five points of the empire. T'ai-shan of the East is particularly related to the imperial court.

(5) GOULLART, PETER. The Monastery of Jade Mountain (see 1.12.2[2]).
   Contains valuable references to Taoist and Buddhist temples associated with sacred mountains personally visited by the author. The
places covered are: Monastery of the Jade Mountain and the Jade Spring
Monastery (Buddhist) in Hangchow, Monastery of the Lucky Star at the
Jade Emperor's Mountain (Hangchow), Monastery of the Heavenly Vault
at Soochow, and Palace of the Eight Immortals in Sian.

(6) GRAHAM, DAVID C. "Sacred Mountains." In Folk Religion in Southwest
China (see 1.12.3[3]), pp. 168-70.
   Refers to Mt. Omei and Mt. Ch'ing-ch'eng (Green Walls) in Szechuan,
the latter a Taoist sanctuary.

(7) LING SHUN-SHENG. "Kun-lun Chin and Hsi Wang-mu." Academia Sinica,
Bulletin of the Institute of Ethnology 22 (1966):253-55 (English summary).
   Succinct presentation of the author's new theories on the subject of
these two long-disputed terms. He believes the words kun lun "were
almost definitely the transliteration of the second and third syllables
of the word 'ziggurat,' a type of pyramidal structure of ancient
Mesopotamia." He also suggests that Hsi wang-mu is derived from the
Sumerian term for the God of the Moon, si-en-mu, a thesis which is
plausible because of the close connection between the two terms and
the fact that "the sacrificial palace or temple of Ur of Mesopotamia,
which was dedicated to the worship of the God of the Moon, was also
situated north of the ziggurat." It is interesting to see the unusual
case of a Chinese scholar doing what Westerners have done for so long:
trying to trace a Western origin for Chinese terms and cultural features.

(8) MORRISON, HEDDA, and EBERHARD, WOLFRAM. Hua Shan. Hong Kong:
Vetch & Lee, 1974, 135 pp.
   Mostly an album of photographs of this sacred mountain. Eberhard
has contributed a brief introduction and descriptions of the plates.
The photographic record and knowledgeable comments give a fascinating
insight into one corner of monastic Taoism. (The pictures were taken
in 1935.) The book is beautifully produced.

(9) MULLIKIN, MARY A., and HOTCHKIS, ANNA M. Nine Sacred Mountains of
China. Hong Kong: Vetch & Lee, 1973, 156 pp.
   The two authors, both artists, accomplished perhaps the unique feat
of visiting nine of the most sacred mountains in China during the years
1935-36. The book includes notes made during their pilgrimages and
many remarkable paintings and drawings they made on the spot. It makes
vivid the subject of sacred mountains and pilgrimages.

(10) PRATT, JAMES BISSETT. "Buddhist Temples in China." In The
Pilgrimage of Buddhism (see 5.2[1]), pp. 305-24.
   This chapter discusses Chinese Buddhist architecture and sculpture.

It gives a graphic description of a typical temple architecture and
art; it also shows regional differences in temple architecture. In
central and northern China the Buddhist temples reflect purely Buddhist
designs and art, whereas in west and south China they reflect Taoist
influence. Special remarks are made concerning the Taoist temple, Lao
Chuin Tung (Cave of Lao Tzu) and the famous Buddhist temples in the
Western Hills near Peking.

(11) PRIP-MOELLER, JOHANNES. Chinese Buddhist Monasteries (see
5.2[2]).
    A detailed firsthand study by a Danish architect of the architecture
of Buddhist monasteries. About 100 pages are devoted to the architecture of the monastery Hui chu Ssu (Wisdom-dwelling temple) in Pao Hua
Shan, Kiangsu.

(12) REICHELT, KARL L. "Pilgrimage." In Truth and Tradition in Chinese
Buddhism (see 9.3.3[2]), pp. 271-95.
    A brief sketch of the following Buddhist sacred places or mountains:
1) P'u-t'o Shan near Ningpo archipelago, associated with Bodhisattva
Kuan-yin, 2) Chiu-hua Shan in Anhwei, dedicated to Bodhisattva Ti-tsang,
3) Wu-t'ai Shan in Shansi, whose tutelary divinity is Bodhisattva Wen-
shu (Mañjusrī), 4) O-mei Shan of Szechuan, whose resident Bodhisattva
is P'u-hsien, 5) T'ien-mu Shan in Chekiang, 6) Ku Shan in Fukian, and
7) West Lake in Hangchow.

(13) THOMPSON, LAURENCE G., ed. "Confucius as a Patron Saint"; "The
Cult of Mount T'ai." In The Chinese Way in Religion (see 1.1[15]),
pp. 144-53; 178-85.
    Chapter 19 contains an account of a pilgrimage to the Confucian
temple at Ch'u-fu, the hometown of Confucius, as well as a description
of the architecture and the rituals of a Confucian temple. Chapter 23
is excerpted from the editor's translation of chapter 1 of Edouard
Chavannes's Le T'ai Chan: Essai de monographie d'un culte chinois
(Paris, 1910). Information on the Altar of Heaven (T'ien-tan) can
also be found in the book.

(14) WELCH, HOLMES. The Buddhist Revival in China (see 7.8[16]).
    Contains material on sacred places at West Lake, Hangchow.

(15) _____. "The Chang T'ien Shih and Taoism in China" (see 1.9.2[1]).
    The early part of this article discusses the history and geography
of Lung-hu Shan (Dragon-Tiger Mountain) and its relation to Taoism.

(16) _____. "Lay Pilgrimages." Practice of Chinese Buddhism (see
7.8[17]), pp. 370-75.
    Contains a description of pilgrimages to the sacred places at
T'ien-t'ai Shan in Chekiang, Heng Shan in Hunan, Wu-t'ai Shan in Shensi,
O-mei Shan in Szechuan, and Chin Shan in Kiangsu.

11.   Soteriological Experiences and Processes

11.1 CONFUCIANISM

(1) The Analects of Confucius. Translated by Arthur Waley (see 2.2[1]), book 2:4, p. 88; book 4:8, p. 103.
   Statements by Confucius showing his progress in spiritual growth and his relations with Heaven (T'ien).

(2) CHAN, WING-TSIT, trans. "Mencius"; "Chang Tsai"; "Wang Yang-ming's Own Confession." In A Source Book in Chinese Philosophy (see 1.4.2[1]), pp. 78-79; 515; 689.
   In the first section (7A:1-4), Mencius says that to exert one's mind (hsin) is to know one's nature and to know one's nature is to know Heaven. He also emphasizes the importance of waiting for one's destiny (Heaven's Mandate). The section on Chang Tsai contains a discussion on enlarging one's mind to enter into all things and on knowledge which goes beyond seeing and hearing. "Wang Yang-ming's Own Confession" describes Wang's experience of enlightenment while living in exile. From this experience he learned that innate knowledge is most important.

(3) CHAN, WING-TSIT. "Wang Yang-ming: A Biography" (see 2.6.3[4]).
   Page 65 describes Wang's enlightenment at the age of thirty-six, when he realized that all the principles of the world were in fact within his own mind.

(4) De BARY, W. THEODORE. "Neo-Confucian Cultivation and the Seventeenth Century 'Enlightenment.'" In The Unfolding of Neo-Confucianism (see 2.6.3[1]), pp. 141-216.
   This penetrating essay in one sense demonstrates that neo-Confucianism in both its school of Principle (Ch'eng-Chu) and its school of Mind (Lu-wang) should be viewed as possessing a religious dimension because of the emphasis upon meditative concentration aimed at transformation of life. But in the most general sense, this essay is a study of the nature of enlightenment in neo-Confucianism in its intellectual, moral, and aesthetic aspects and how this enlightenment experience as discussed by the Sung and Ming Confucianists has affected the "Enlightenment" movement in seventeenth- and eighteenth-century China. This latter "Enlightenment" refers to the intellectual movement in the Ch'ing period which emphasized "practical learning," i.e., textual, historical,

technological, and scientific studies in contrast to the metaphysical
learning of Sung Confucianism and the mystical learning of Ming Confucianism.   In a critical sense, this essay warns against a simplistic
characterization of Sung Confucianism as "school of Principle" and of
Ming Confucianism as "school of Mind."   The author has demonstrated
how both Ch'eng I and Chu Hsi emphasize mind as an ontological entity.
By the same token, the Ming Confucianists have not forgotten Principle
(li) as inherent structure.   According to De Bary, most of the modern
writers on neo-Confucianism have either distorted its nature by exag-
gerating its empirical and scientific aspects or have emphasized one
dimension at the expense of the multidimensionality of neo-Confucianism.
The writers with whom De Bary takes issue include Hu Shih, Levenson,
and Needham.   This essay is a useful guide for those who wish to know
the richness of the neo-Confucian tradition from the eleventh to the
eighteenth century, particularly in reference to its spirituality.

(5) The Doctrine of the Mean.   Translated by Wing-tsit Chan.   In A
Source Book in Chinese Philosophy (see 1.4.2[1]), pp. 95-114.
    This small Confucian classic discusses the Confucian way of spiri-
tual and intellectual transformation by explaining the meaning of tao,
human nature (hsing), sincerity (cheng), equililbrium (chung), and
harmony (ho).   The ontological and existential principle, sincerity,
is to be realized by doing one's daily chores.   As the translator
points out, this Confucian classic also appeals to Taoists and
Buddhists: it serves as a bridge between Taoism-Buddhism and Confucianism.

(6) The Doctrine of the Mean.   Translated by James Legge.   In The
Chinese Classics (see 1.2.7[4]) 1-2:415-16.
    Sincerity (ch'eng) enables one to realize his own nature and to be-
come a member of the Triad of Heaven, Earth, and Man.

(7) FUNG YU-LAN.   "Chou Tun-i"; "Ch'eng Hao's Theory of Spiritual
Cultivation"; "Ch'eng Yi's Theory of Spiritual Cultivation."   In A
History of Chinese Philosophy (see 2.1.7[1]) 2: 448-51; 520-27; 527-32.
    The first section is an explanation of Chou's notions of "absence
of desire" (wu-yu) and "absence of thought" (wu-ssu).   This spiritual
cultivation leads to comprehension (t'ung).   Pp. 520-27 are a discussion of Ch'eng Hao's doctrines of earnestness (ching) and composure
(ting), and the identity between the mind of Heaven and Earth and the
mind of the sage.   The third section is a discussion of Ch'eng Yi's
notions of investigations of things and extension of knowledge in order
to understand the principles.   But the principles of things and the
principles of mind are essentially identical, hence the understanding
of the world in the right sense is the discovery of one's mind.

(8) ____.   "A New System."   In The Spirit of Chinese Philosophy
(see 2.12.2[1]), pp. 202-20.

Fung develops a philosophical system on the basis of four formal concepts: li (principle), ch'i (matter), tao-t'i (evolution of tao), and Ta-ch'uan (Great Whole). When the sage understands all these four ideas, he reaches the highest state of being.

(9) The Great Learning. Translated by Wing-tsit Chan. In A Source Book of Chinese Philosophy (see 1.4.2[1]), pp. 84-94.
This short Confucian classic discusses the "eight steps" of spiritual progress: investigation of things, extension of knowledge, sincerity of will, rectification of the mind, cultivation of personal life, regulation of the family, national order, and world peace. The ten commentary chapters convey the intellectual and spiritual conditions of the "ideal being." The "eight steps" point to the ultimate state of human attainment in the Confucian tradition. Chu Hsi's comment on the first five chapters shows that the investigation of things in the moral sense may eventually lead to a "wide and far-reaching penetration" in the mode of enlightenment.

(10) The Great Learning. Translated by James Legge. In The Chinese Classics (see 1.2.7[4]) 1-2:354-81.
Chu Hsi's comment on the first five chapters of the Great Learning states that investigation of things eventually may enable the investigator to attain "a wide and far-reaching penetration" akin to enlightenment.

(11) TU WEI-MING. "Wang Yang-ming's Enlightenment." In Neo-Confucian Thought in Action (see 2.6.3[9]), pp. 95-146.
A persuasive analysis of Wang Yang-ming's banishment to Lung-ch'ang (1507-08), a desolate village in southwestern frontier of Ming China, where Wang experienced a unique enlightenment (1507). The author traces Wang's earlier Taoist and Buddhist experiments which might have affected this event. But Wang's own interpretation of it is definitely stated in Confucian terms. Wang's subsequent career as an active government administrator and military commander undoubtedly points to the fact that he wants this experience to be understood as a Confucian occurrence.

(12) YU, DAVID C. "Chu Hsi's Approach to Knowledge." Chinese Culture 10 (Dec. 1969):1-14.
Yu discusses the importance of self-cultivation as a prerequisite to knowing and points out that in the final sense the purpose of knowledge is to attain "thorough comprehension" (kuan-t'ung).

11.2 TAOIST RELIGION

(1) CHANG CHUNG-YUAN. Creativity and Taoism (see 7.7[1]).
The entire book deals with the experience of transformation or

enlightenment, with reference to the sayings of Lao Tzu, Chuang Tzu,
Zen (Ch'an) Buddhists, and leading neo-Confucianists. It also includes
a study of Chinese poetry and painting, manifesting the enlightenments
of the noted poets and painters in Chinese history.

(1a) _____. "An Introduction to Taoist Yoga." In The Chinese Way in
Religion (see 1.1[15]), pp. 63-76.
    Much of this article deals with the Taoist techniques of meditation
leading toward enlightenment.

(2) FUNG YU-LAN. "Chuang Tzu's Pure Experience"; "Hsiang Hsiu and Kuo
Hsiang on the 'Perfect Man.'" In A History of Chinese Philosophy (see
2.1.7[11]) 1:239-44; 2:231-36.
    The section in volume 1 deals with Chuang Tzu's notion of the en-
lightened person as the chen-jen (true man) who "sits in forgetting."
The section in volume 2 is an explanation of chen-jen by two neo-Taoists
as they glossed the Chuang Tzu. The perfect man is one who has equal-
ized all the opposites and lives in the state of their identification.

(3) GRAHAM, A.C., trans. "The Yellow Emperor." In The Book of Lieh
Tzu (see 2.7.3[2]), pp. 35-37.
    Lieh Tzu speaks of a nine-year spiritual progress until a state of
complete non-differentiation is reached.

(4) LIU TS'UN-YAN. "Taoist Self-Cultivation in Ming Thought" (see
7.7[5]).
    This section, dealing with the Taoist internal elixir school, ex-
plains twelve concepts, ranging from the golden pill to the dual cultivation of nature and life. It also traces the Taoist and Buddhist
(Ch'an) influences upon neo-Confucian thought of the Ming period (1368-
1644), particularly that of Wang Yang-ming (1472-1529). The author
uses primary sources and has translated several passages from the Taoist canon hitherto unknown to English readers.

(5) LUK, CHARLES [Lu K'uan-yu]. The Secrets of Chinese Meditation
(see 7.7[6]).

(6) _____. Taoist Yoga: Alchemy and Immortality (see 7.7[7]).
    Provides numerous references to the mystic experience arrived at
through Taoist yoga. Although this work is primarily on meditational
practice, it frequently gives philosophical explanations on why such
yogist techniques are required.

(7) No entry.

(8) WALEY, ARTHUR, trans. The Way and Its Power (see 1.2.8[1]), pp.
162-63.
    Lao Tzu says that to return to the root is the way to illumination
(enlightenment).

(9) WILHELM, RICHARD, trans. "Meditation Techniques." In The Secret of the Golden Flower (see 3.2.13[2]), pp. 55-64.
    A section of the translation of the Buddho-Taoist treatise T'ai-i chin-hua tsung-chi, which describes the meditational techniques that lead to enlightenment. These techniques involve the method of "backward flowing."

11.3 MAOISM

(1) GILKEY, LANGDON. "The Covenant with the Chinese." China Notes 15 (1977):1-6.
    The author, a noted Protestant theologian, in this article has undertaken to delineate the relationship between the religious dimension of Maoist Marxism and the Christian faith. He points out three aspects of Maoism that are religious in particular and with which a meaningful Christian dialectic may be made: 1) Maoism definitely has a transcendent, however implicit, which underpins the process of life. But this transcendence from the Christian perspective should be made explicit; otherwise the religious substance of a culture will be losing its creativity. 2) Maoism is certainly an exemplification of what liberation theology can mean through its transformation of the outmoded social institutions. But Christianity does not appear to be exhaustively social and political: it also admits human sin and fate. 3) Maoism has a remarkable sense of the mystery of history which implies an open future. But in Christian faith this openness is defined in terms of grace, which judges those who rule and those who rebel.

(2) LIFTON, ROBERT J. Revolutionary Immortality: Mao Tse-tung and the Chinese Cultural Revolution. New York: Random House, 1968, 178 pp.
    The author gives a sociopsychological interpretation of the meaning of the Cultural Revolution, considering it as the beginning of the "permanent Revolution." Mao intended to make the Revolution a transcendent reference, and by so doing, he has transcended his own imminent death. The Chinese youth, by identifying themselves with the Revolution, have become the revolutionary "immortals," thereby overcoming physical death.

(3) LIU SHAO-CH'I. How to Be a Good Communist. Peking: Foreign Languages Press, 1964, 95 pp.
    Liu's lectures were given in 1939. Although he has been discredited as an arch "revisionist," this work nevertheless has been known for its candid view that a good Communist must undertake continuous self-cultivation in the moral and ideological sense. (The Chinese title of this book is On the Self-Cultivation of a Communist Member.) The work is saturated with moral and ascetic commitment and is filled with quotations from classical Confucian sources, such as the notion that a Communist is "the first to worry and the last to enjoy himself."

(4) MAO TSE-TUNG. "Talks at the Yen-an Forum on Literature and Art."
In Selected Works of Mao Tse-tung (see 3.3[1]).

(5) STRENG, FREDERICK; LLOYD, CHARLES; and ALLEN, JAY. "Revolutionary
Immortality." In Ways of Being Religious. Englewood Cliffs, N.J.:
Prentice-Hall, 1973, pp. 461-67.
    This section consists of excerpts from Robert Lifton's book,
Boundaries: Psychological Man in Revolution (New York: Random House,
1969). Lifton says that the Chinese Cultural Revolution has to be
understood in terms of symbolism. It is a process of "death and rebirth" for the older generation, like Mao himself, as well as for the
Chinese youth. They overcome physical death by being reborn into the
immortal revolutionary process.

Author/Title Index

The Chinese Transformation
of Buddhism, 6.2(2); "Neo-
Taoism and the Prajñā
School," 2.15(3); "On Some
Factors Responsible for the
Anti-Buddhist Persecution
under the Pei-ch'ao," 6.2(4);
"Religious Changes in Communist China," 1.13(2)
Ch'en Kuo-fu, "Shang-yang Tzu,"
see under Davis, Tenney L.
Cheng Chung-ying, "Dialect of
Confucian Morality," 2.21.3
(2); "Religious Reality and
Religious Understanding,"
2.23(3); Tai Chen's Inquiry
into Goodness, 2.6.2(4)
Cheng Man-ch'eng, T'ai-chi,
7.9(1)
Cheng Te-kun, "Yin-yang Wu-hsing
and Han Art," 5.1(10)
Cheng Yeh, "A Brief Report on
the Excavation of Tomb No.
1," see under Chow Fong
Chesneaux, Jean, Popular Move-
ments and Secret Societies
in China, 1.10.2(3); Secret
Societies in China, 1.10.2(1)
Chin Kaiming, "Portraits of Wu
Ch'üan-chieh," see under
Tomita, Kojiro
Ching, Julia, To Acquire Wisdom,
2.6.3(6)
Chow Fong, "A Brief Report on
the Excavation of Han Tomb
No. 1," 5.1(11)
Chow Tse-tung, Wen-lin: Studies
in the Chinese Humanities,
4.2(4), 4.3.3(2), 4.4(1)
Christie, Anthony, Chinese
Mythology, 9.1(7)
Ch'u T'ung-tsu, Law and Society
in Traditional China, 6.3(1)
Chuan Tseng-kia, "Yuan Chi and
His Circle," 2.15(4)
Cohen, Alvin P., "A Bibliography
of Writings Contributing to
the Study of Chinese Folk
Religion," 1.1(4)
Comber, Leon, Chinese Festivals
in Malaya, see under Lo,

Dorothy; Chinese Magic and
Superstitions in Malaya,
2.1.7(6)
Comstock, Richard, Religion and Man,
1.1(1)
Creel, Herrlee G., The Birth of
China, 1.2.5(2), 1.2.6(1),
1.2.7(1), 3.1.7(2), 3.1.8(1);
Confucius: The Man and the
Myth, 8.3.2(2); Confucius and
the Chinese Way, 8.3.2.1(2);
Sinism: A Study of the Evolu-
tion of the Chinese World View,
2.1.2(2); "Sinism--A Clarifica-
tion," 1.4.1(2); "Was Confucius
Agnostic?" 2.2(2); What is
Taoism?, 2.7.1(4), 2.7.2(2)
Cressy, Earl, "Study in Indigenous
Religions," 1.12(1)
Crow, Carl, Master Kung, 8.3.2(3)

Dardess, John W., "The Transforma-
tion of Messianic Revolt,"
1.10.1(1)
David, A.R., "The Double Ninth
Festivals in Chinese Poetry,"
4.4(1)
Davis, Tenney L., "An Ancient
Chinese Treatise on Alchemy,"
see under Wu Lu-ch'iang; "Dualistic Cosmogony of Huai-nan-tzu,"
2.18(1); "Shang-yang Tzu,"
2.18(2)
Day, Clarence B., Chinese Peasant
Cults, 2.1.9(2), 7.8(7); "The
Cult of the Hearth," 2.1.9(3)
De Bary, William Theodore, A Guide
to Oriental Classics, 3.1.1(1);
"Neo-Confucian Cultivation,"
11.1(4); Self and Society in
Ming Thought, 2.6.3(6), 7.7(4);
Sources of Chinese Tradition,
1.4.1(3), 1.4.2(1), (5),
1.10.2(2), 2.2(3), 2.16(1),
2.19.3(1), 2.20(1), 3.1.12(1),
3.1.13(1), 9.2(3), 9.3.2(1);
The Unfolding of Neo-Confucian-
ism, 2.6.2(1), 2.6.3(7), 11.1(4)
Deglopper, Donald R., "Religion and
Ritual in Lukang," 7.7(2)
De Korne, John C., Fellowship of

in Lao Tzu and Chuang,
2.7.2(3); The Principle of
T'ien, 2.1.1(2)
Fingarette, Herbert, Confucius:
The Secular as Sacred,
2.1.6(2); "Human Community
as Holy Rite," 2.1.6(3)
Forke, A., The World-Conception
of the Chinese, 2.1.1(3)
Forte, Antonio, Political
Propaganda and Ideology in
China, 6.2(6)
Freedman, Maurice, Family and
Kinship in Chinese Society,
7.3(2), (8), "Geomancy,"
2.1.6(3); "Marcel Granet,"
2.1.10(1); "On the Socio-
logical Study of Chinese Re-
ligion," 1.1(6); "Ritual As-
pects of Chinese Kinship and
Marriage," 7.3(2)
Frick, J., "How Blood is Used in
Magic and Medicine," 2.1.7
(9); "Magic Remedies Used on
Sick Children," 2.1.7(10)
Fu, Charles Wei-hsün, "Confucian-
ism, Marxism-Leninism and
Mao," 1.11(1); "Creative
Hermenutics: Taoist Meta-
physics and Heidegger,"
2.7(1); "Morality or Beyond,"
2.6.1(3)
Fujino, Iwatomo, "On Chinese
Soul-Inviting and Firefly-
Catching Songs," 4.5(1)
Fukui, Kōjun, "A Study of Chou-i
Ts'an-t'ung-ch'i," 3.2.10(1)
Fung Yu-lan, A History of Chinese
Philosophy, 2.1.7(11),
2.5(4), 2.6.1(5), 2.12(1),
2.13(2), 2.15(6), 3.1.14(2),
8.3.2(5), (6), 8.4(1),
9.2(4), 11.1(7), 11.2(2); A
Short History of Chinese
Philosophy, 2.6.1(4),
2.11(1), 2.15(5); The Spirit
of Chinese Philosophy,
2.12(2), 2.15(7), 9.3.1(1),
11.1(8)

Gernet, Jacques, Daily Life in

China, 2.1.1(4)
Giles, Lionel, A Gallery of Chinese
Immortals, 2.9(1); Strange
Stories from a Chinese Studio,
4.1(4); Taoist Teachings from
Lieh Tzu, 2.7.3(1)
Gilkey, Langdon, "The Covenant with
the Chinese," 11.3(1)
Girardot, Norman J., "Myths and
Meaning in the Tao Tê Ching,"
9.1(11); "Part of the Way:
Four Studies on Taoism,"
1.1(7), 1.3(1); "The Problem
of Creation Mythology," 9.1(12)
Goullart, Peter, The Monastery of
Jade Mountain, 1.12.2(2),
7.6(1), 10(5)
Graham, A.C., The Book of Lieh Tzu,
2.7.3(2), 11.2(3); "Chuang Tzu's
Essay on Seeing Things as Equal,"
2.7.2(4)
Graham, David Crockett, Folk Religion
in Southwest China, 1.12.3(3),
1.12.4(1), 2.1.6(4), 7.8(9),
10(6); "Original Vows of Kitchen
God," 2.20(2); "Tree Gods in
Szechwan Province," 2.1.8(2)
Granet, Marcel, Chinese Civilization,
1.2.2(1), 1.2.3(1), 1.2.4(3);
Festivals and Songs of Ancient
China, 1.2.2(3); The Religion
of the Chinese People, 1.2.2(2),
1.2.5(3), 1.4.1(5), 1.7(1),
1.12.3(4), 2.1.10(1)
Grant, D., The Far East, 4.4(2)
Grimal, Pierre, Larousse World
Mythology, 9.1(17)
Groot, J.J.M. de, The Religious
System of China, 1.2.1(3),
1.2.4(4), 2.1.2(4), 2.1.3(2),
2.1.6(5), 2.1.7(12), 7.3(3),
7.6(2), 7.8(10); Sectarianism
and Religious Persecution in
China, 1.10.1(2), 6.2(7),
6.7(2), 6.8(3)
Grousset, René, Chinese Art and
Culture, 5.1(15)
Grube, Wilhelm, Die Metamorphosen
der Götter, 4.3.4(1)
Guiran, Felix, New Larousse
Encyclopedia of Mythology,

[Classic of filial piety],
1.4.2(2), 3.1.10(1)

Maspero, Henri, "Mythology of
Modern China," 9.1(14); Le
taoisme, 2.7.1(11), 2.18(5)

Mather, Richard, "The Conflict
of Buddhism," 6.2(10)

Mencius, 2.3(1)

Merton, Thomas, Way of Chuang
Tzu, 2.7.2(7)

Meyer, Jeffry F., "The Tao
Ch'ang," 7.6(4)

Michaud, Paul, "The Yellow
Turbans," 6.7(5)

Mitrophanow, Igor, The Moon Year,
see under Bredon, Juliet

Miyakawa, Hisayuki, "Legate Kao
P'ien and a Taoist Magician,"
1.7(3)

Moore, Charles A., The Status of
the Individual in East and
West, 2.23(1)

Morgan, Evan, Tao: The Great
Luminant, 3.2.7(1); "The
Taoist Superman," 3.2.7(2)

Morrison, Hedda, Hua Shan, 10(8)

Morsingh, Francis, "Elixir
Plants," see under Ho Peng-
yu

Moule, G.E., "Notes on the Ting-
chi," 7.2(1)

Mueller, Herbert, Die Metamorphosen der Götter, see under
Grube, Wilhelm

Mullikin, Mary A., Nine Sacred
Mountains of China, 10(9)

Munro, Donald J., The Concept
of Man in Contemporary
China, 2.22(4); The Concept
of Man in Early China,
2.2(9), 2.7.1(12)

Murakami, Yoshimi, "Affirmation
of Desire in Taoism," 6.4(2)

Muramatsu, Yuji, "Some Themes in
Chinese Rebel Ideologies,"
6.7(6)

Naess, A., Invitation to Chinese
Philosophy, 2.7.2(5)

Nakamura, Hajime, "The Influence
of Confucian Ethics on the

Chinese Translations of Buddhist
Sūtras," 6.3(4); Ways of Thinking of Eastern Peoples, 6.2(11)

Nakayama, Shigeru, "Characteristics
of Chinese Astrology," 7.5(2);
Chinese Science, 2.18(3)

Naquin, Susan, Millenarian Rebellion
in China, 1.10.1(3), 6.2(12)

Needham, Joseph, "Christian Hope and
Social Evolution," 1.13(6);
Science and Civilization in
China, 2.1.6(7), 2.6.2(6),
2.9(2), 2.11(3), 2.18(6),
3.2.1(3), 6.4(3), 9.3.2(3);
"Theories of Categories in
Early Medieval Chinese Alchemy,"
see under Ho Peng-yu

Nelson, H.G.H., "Ancestor Worship
and Burial Practices," 7.3(4)

Newell, William H., "Sociology of
Ritual in Early China," 2.1.6(4)

Ngo Van Xuyet, Divination, magic et
politique dans la Chine ancienne,
1.7(4)

Nivison, David S., Confucianism in
Action, 1.6(1)

Noss, John B., Man's Religions,
1.1(11)

Nott, Stanley Charles, Chinese Jade
Throughout the Ages, 5.1(23)

Ōbuchi, Ninji, "On Ku Ling-pao
ching," 3.2.1(4)

Osgood, Cornelius, Village Life in
Old China, 1.12.3(7)

Ou-I-Tai, "Chinese Mythology,"
9.1(15)

Overmyer, Daniel L., Folk Buddhist
Religion, 1.10.1(4), 6.2(13);
"A Preliminary Study of the
Tz'u-hui t'ang," 1.12.3(8)

Owen, G., "Animal Worship Among
the Chinese, 2.1.8(5)

Petty, D.A., Laymen's Foreign Missions Inquiry Fact-Finding
Reports, 1.12(1)

Plopper, Cliford H., Chinese Religion
Seen Through the Proverbs,
1.12.3(9)

Potter, Jack M., "Cantonese

Customs," 7.3(6)

Wang Chi-chen, Dream of the Red Chamber (574 pp.), 4.3.7(3); Dream of the Red Chamber 329 pp.), 4.3.7(4); Traditional Chinese Tales, 4.2(7)

Wang Shih-ch'ing, "Religious Organization in the History of a Taiwanese Town," 1.12.3(13)

Wang Sung-hsing, "Taiwanese Architecture and the Supernatural," 5.2(6)

Ward, John S.M., Hung Society, 6.8(6)

Ware, James R., Alchemy, Medicine, Religion in China, 1.8.2(3), 2.1.7(16), 2.7.4(1), 2.8(3), 2.9(3), 2.16(2), 2.18(8), 9.3.2(5); The Sayings of Chuang Chou, 2.7.2(9); The Sayings of Mencius, 3.1.5(5)

Waterbury, Florance, Bird Deities in China, 2.1.8(7); Early Chinese Symbols and Literature, 5.1(33)

Watson, Burton, Chuang-Tzu: Basic Writings, 2.7.2(10); The Complete Works of Chuang Tzu, 2.7.2(11); Hsün Tzu: Basic Writings, 2.4(4); Records of the Grand Historian of China, 6.6(3), 8.1.1(2); Sources of Chinese Tradition, see under De Bary, William Theodore

Weber, Max, The Religion of China, 1.1(17), 6.3(5), 6.4(4)

Wei, Francis C.M., The Spirit of Chinese Culture, 1.1(18)

Wei Hwei-lin, "Categories of Totemism in Ancient China," 1.2.4(7)

Wei Tat, An Exposition of I-Ching, 2.12(3)

Welch, Holmes H., "The Bellagio Conference on Taoist Studies," 2.1.7(17), 2.19.1(2), 3.2.1(4), 3.2.13(1);

"Buddhism Since the Cultural Revolution," 6.2(15); "Buddhism under the Communists," 6.2(16); Buddhism under Mao, 6.2(17); The Buddhist Revival in China, 7.8(16), 10(14); "The Chang T'ien-shih," 1.9.2(1), 10(15); The Parting of the Way, 1.2.8(2), 1.7(8), 1.8.2(4), 1.9(1), 2.1.9(8), 2.7.1(16), 2.10(3), 6.6(4); Practice of Chinese Buddhism, 7.8(17); "The Reinterpretation of Chinese Buddhism," 6.2(18)

Werner, Edward T.C., A Dictionary of Chinese Mythology, 8.1.1(3), 8.2.2(2), 8.2.5(2), 9.1(18); Myths and Legends of China, 9.1(19)

White, William Charles, Chinese Temple Frescoes, 5.1(34)

Wiant, Bliss, The Music of China, 5.3(5)

Wieger, Leon, A History of Religious Beliefs and Philosophical Opinions in China, 3.2.15(1), 8.1.3(3), 8.2.1(3)

Wilhelm, Hellmut, Changes: Eight Lectures on the I-ching, 3.1.6(1)

Wilhelm, Richard, Confucius and Confucianism, 2.2(12); I-ching [Book of changes], 1.2.7(3), 9.2(5); "On the Sources of Chinese Taoism," 1.2.4(8); The Secret of the Golden Flower, 3.2.13(2), 3.2.14(1), 11.2(9)

Williams, Mrs. E.T., "Some Popular Religious Literature," 4.3(3)

Wilson, B.D., "Burial Customs in Hong Kong," 7.3(7)

Wolf, Arthur P., "Chinese Kinship and Mourning Dress," 7.3(8); "Gods, Ghosts, and Ancestors," 2.1.2(5); Religion and Ritual in Chinese Society, 1.1(19), 1.12.3(1), (5), (11), (13), 2.1.2(3), (5), 2.1.7(15), 5.2(6), 7.3(4), 7.4(1), 7.6(5), (7), 7.7(2)

Wong, C.S., A Cycle of Chinese

Subject Index

-Hupeh, Religion in, 7.8(1)
-Kiangsu, Religion in, 10(11)
-Peking Region, Religion in,
7.8(12), (13)
-Peoples
--Pu, 4.5(2)
--Yüeh, 4.5(2)
-Philosophy, 1.2.4(6)
-Religion
--and Politics, 1.1(20). See
also Politics
--Anthropological Approaches,
1.2.2(1), 1.2.4(6), 2.5,
6.1(3), 7.3(1)
--Sociological Approaches,
1.1(17), (20), 1.2.2(1),
1.6(2), 2.1.4(4), 2.1.10(1),
4.1(2), 6.3(5)
-Shansi, Religion in, 10(3)
-Shantung, Religion in, 7.4(4)
-Szechuan, Religion in,
1.12.3(3), 2.1.6(4),
2.1.8(2), 10(6)
-Taiwan, Religion in, 1.9.2(1),
1.12.2(3), 1.12.3(2), (5),
(6), (8), (13), 2.1.2(3),
(5), 2.1.7(17), 2.1.9(7),
2.19.1(1), 5.1(13), 5.2(6),
7.3(1), (8), 7.4(1), 7.6(4),
(5), (6), 7.7(2), 7.8(8),
8.1.7(1)
-Tibet, 6.2(11), 7.7(6), 11.2(5)
-Worldview, 2.5(2), 2.11(3),
2.23
-Yunan, Religion in, 1.12.3(7),
6.1(3)
Chin P'ing Mei, 4.3(2), 4.3.5
Ch'ing, 2.6.2(1)
Ching, 2.6.1(2), 7.7(7), 11.1(7)
Ching-ch'i, 2.7.1(6)
Ching-shih t'ung-yen, 4.2(5)
Ch'ing-t'an, 2.15(3), (5)
Chin-ku ch'i-kuan, 4.2(3)
Chin-tan-ta-yao, 2.18(2)
Chiromancy, 2.1.7(1)
Chou, Duke of (d. 1094 B.C.),
1.2.6(1), 2.2(4)
Chou-li, 1.4.2(4), 3.1.9(1)
Chou Tun-yi (1017-1073),
2.6.1(4), 3.1.14, 9.2(1),
(4), 11.1(7)

Chou Wu-ti (5th century), 6.2(4)
Christianity, 2.1.8(7), 2.23(2),
6.3(3), 6.7(3)
-Relation to Maoist doctrine,
1.13(1), (3), (6), (8), 11.3(1)
Chu Hsi (1130-1200), 1.1(18),
2.1.3(1), 2.2(1), 2.6.2,
2.6.3(3), 2.21.3(1), 3.1.2(2),
3.1.3(1), 3.1.4(1), 11.1(4),
(9), (10), (12)
Chu-jung, 8.1.1(3)
Ch'u Tz'u, 1.2.1(4), 4.4(2), 4.5(1)
Chu Yüan-chang, 1.10.1(1)
Ch'üan-chen Chiao. See Taoism:
Ch'üan-chen Chiao
Chuang Tzu (ca. 399-295 B.C.),
1.2.8(2), 1.3, 2.7.2, 2.7.3(1),
2.15(7), 8.2.1, 11.2(1), (2)
Chuang Tzu, 2.7.1(4), 2.7.2(2),
(4), (8), (10), (11), 3.2.1(1),
3.2.3, 4.2(6), 9.1(12), 9.2(1),
9.3.1(1)
Ch'un-ch'iu, 1.2.7(5), 6.1(1)
Ch'un-ch'iu fan-lu, 1.4.2(1), 2.5,
3.1.12, 9.2(3)
Chung, 11.1(5)
Chung-ch'ang T'ung, 2.5(1)
Chung-Yung, 2.6.1(3)
Chung-yung [Doctrine of the mean],
1.4.2(4), 2.5, 2.12(2), 3.1.3,
3.1.9(1), 11.1(5), (6)
Chung Yung [Conduct of life],
1.1(15), 3.1.2(1)
Church of the Preservation of the
True Nature. See Ch'üan-chen
Chiao
Church of the Right Unity. See
Cheng-i Chiao
Classic of Filial Piety. See
Hsiao-ching
Clergy, 1.4.3(2), 4.3.7(2)
Collected Books of the Han and Wei
Dynasties. See Han Wei Ts'ung
Shu
Colors, 2.5(4), 7.3(8)
Commentary on the Meaning of the
Prophecy about Shen-huang in
the Great Cloud Sutra. See
Ta-yün Ching Shen-huang shou-
chi i-shu
Communism, 1.13(4), 2.22(1), 3.3,

Phoenix, 2.1.8(1), (4), (5)
Physiognomy, 2.1.7(1), 7.5(1)
P'i, 2.21.2(2)
Pigsy, 4.3.3(1), (7). See also
   Hsi-yu chi
Planchette. See Fu-chi
Po Chu-i (772-846), 4.4(1)
P'o-hsieh Hsing-pien, 2.10(1)
Po Hu T'ung, 1.4.1(9), 3.1.11
Poems of Mao Tse-tung, 2.22(2)
Poetry,, 1.2.1(4), 2.6.3(6),
   2.22(2), (3), 4.3.3(4), (5),
   (7), 4.4, 5.3(3), 11.2(1).
   See also Songs, Literature
Politics, 1.4.2(1), (5),
   1.12.1(2), 1.13(5), 2.12(1),
   3.1.12(1), 3.1.13(1),
   5.1(9), 5.3(4), 6.1, 6.2(2),
   (5), (6), (8), (21), 6.3(5),
   6.4, 6.7(1), 9.2(3). See
   also China: Religion: and
   Politics; State; Law
Portents, 1.4.1(3), 2.5, 7.5(2).
   See also Divination, Omens
Possession, 1.2.1(2). See also
   Exorcism
Pottery, 5.1(18)
Prajñā sūtra, 2.15(3)
Prajñāpāramitā, 2.15(11). See
   also Pen-wu
Precious Scrolls. See Pao-chuan
Primordial Heavenly Worthy,
   1.1(11)
Prince of Huai-nan. See Huai-
   nan Tzu
P'u-sa, 9.3.3. See also
   Buddhism: Bodhisattvas
P'u Sung-lin (17th century),
   4.1(4)
Purgatory. See Hell

Queen of Heaven. See Hsi-wang-
   mu (Western Queen of Heaven)
Questions and Answers on the Way
   of Pervading Unity. See I-
   Kuan Tao

Record of the Ten Islands. See
   Shin Chou Chi
Reverence. See Ching
Rituals, 1.12.3(9), 1.13(5),

2.1.2(3), 2.1.4, 2.1.7(16),
   2.1.9(2), 2.4(1), (4), (5),
   2.18(8), 3.1.7(1), 3.1.9(2),
   3.1.11(1), 3.2.1(7), 6.1(3),
   7.1(1), 7.2(3), 7.7(2), 7.8.
   See also Agricultural rites,
   Festivals, Sacrifice
River-lord, 2.7.2(5)
Romance of Three Kingdoms. See
   San-kuo chih yen-i

Sacred Animals and Plants, 2.1.8,
   2.18(9), 5.1(6), 9.1(5), (16)
Sacred Places. See Holy Places
Sacrifice, 1.2.5(1), 1.4.2(4), (5),
   2.1.4, 2.1.7(15), (4), 3.1.9(1),
   3.1.13(1), 5.1(22), 6.6(3),
   7.2(1), (2), 7.3(3), 9.1(6)
San-chiao, 2.6.1(7)
San-ch'ing, 1.1(11), 2.1.9(4),
   (8). See also Primordial
   Heavenly Worthy, Ling Pao
   Heavenly Worthy, Tao Tê
   Heavenly Worthy
San-huang ching, 3.2.1(8)
San-kuan, 2.1.9(4)
San-kuo chih yen-i, 4.3(2), 4.3.1
San Mao, 8.2.5
Sandy, 4.3.3(1), (7). See also
   Hsi-yu chi
The Scholars, 4.3(2)
The School Sayings of Confucius.
   See K'ung Tzu Chia Yü
Schools of Thought, 1.1(1)
Science, 2.1.6(7), 2.1.7(1), (17),
   2.6.2(6), 2.22(4), 6.4(3), (5),
   11.1(4). See also Medicine,
   Astronomy, Alchemy, Astrology,
   Sorcery
Scripture of the Heaven of Superior
   Purity. See Shang-ch'ing ching
Scripture of the Marvelous Jewel.
   See Ling-pao ching
The Scripture of Supreme Peace,
   1.1(12)
Scripture of the Yellow Court.
   See Huang-t'ing ching
Scriptures, 2.10
Sculpture, 5.1(26), 5.2(1), 10(10)
Sea-spirit, 2.7.2(5)
Seasons, 2.5(4), 7.1(1), 7.8(3)